S0-AGY-971

Mexico

4

National Planning Series

BERTRAM M. GROSS, GENERAL EDITOR

ROBERT JONES SHAFER has done research in Latin America for over two decades. Professor of History and Director of Latin American Studies at Syracuse University's Maxwell Graduate School of Citizenship and Public Affairs, he has often served the United States government, most recently as consultant to the Agency for International Development. Mr. Shafer is author of *The Economic Societies in the Spanish World,* co-author of *Contemporary Civilization* and *The Caribbean: Mexico Today,* and contributor to numerous professional publications. He has received both the Bolton Prize of the American Historical Association and the Silver Pen Award for his previous writings.

MEXICO

Mutual Adjustment Planning

ROBERT JONES
SHAFER

Preface by

BERTRAM M. GROSS

SYRACUSE UNIVERSITY PRESS

Library of Congress Catalog Card 65-25986

First Edition 1966

ACKNOWLEDGMENT

This and other volumes in the National Planning Series were initiated with the encouragement and support of Stephen K. Bailey, Dean of the Maxwell Graduate School of Citizenship and Public Affairs, Syracuse University, and of his predecessor, Harlan Cleveland. They have been made possible through a grant from the Ford Foundation for cross-cultural research by the Maxwell School. In the final editing of the manuscript valuable assistance was provided by Sherry Siracuse.

BERTRAM M. GROSS

Manufactured in the United States of America

Contents

TABLES

The Dynamics of Competitive Planning

Long admired as a tourist's paradise, Mexico also offers an admirable—although dangerous—case study in the guidance of national economic change by central government.[1] Mexico's artistic and cultural achievements, the spectacular terrain, the colorful flora and fauna, the Aztec ruins, the relics of the *conquistadores*—all these are rivaled by the fascinating processes through which Mexico is becoming a modern industrial society.

The Mexican case is dangerous for those who cherish certain political illusions. In the United States it has long been widely contended that democracy requires a competitive party system along the lines of the United States or British models. Yet right across the border Mexico's Institutional Revolutionary Party (PRI) has provided the world's outstanding example of a one-party monopoly that has not only strengthened democratic processes but has accelerated economic growth at the same time.

In other countries, the United States is sometimes viewed as a colossal "Yankee imperialist" dominating smaller nations, particularly those in Latin America. Yet in Mexico—the only Latin American country bordering on the United States—we find a country that has been conspicuously independent in both its foreign and domestic policies.

The Mexican case is also dangerous for those with illusions about

[1] "The guidance of national economic growth by central government" is what many people have in mind when they use the term "national economic planning." A full presentation of this concept of planning is provided in Bertram M. Gross, "National Planning: Findings and Fallacies," *Public Administration Review,* XXV (Dec. 1965), 263–73. "Planning" is often used, however, to refer more narrowly to various technical processes that contribute to the formulation of goals for change.

national economic policy. If one believes that nationalization always means inefficiency, he will be confused by the Mexican record in oil, electricity, and many other areas. If one in convinced that heavy government intervention is necessarily *bad* for business, he will be upset by the obvious fact that it has been *good* for Mexican businessmen, even welcomed by many of them. If one thinks that action against domination by foreign companies reduces foreign investment, he will nonetheless find that private foreign investment in Mexico has been growing.

Above all, the Mexican case is particularly dangerous for people with simplistic ideas on national planning. Those who equate the guidance of economic growth with the institutional symbolism of a central planning agency will be misled by the complexities of Mexican government. Those who categorize planning in terms of narrow techniques of macroeconomic calculation will be disappointed by the absence of an official series of technically-embellished national plans. Both will tend to see the sustained public discussions of plans and planning as "pious exhortations" and conclude that there is really no national economic planning in Mexico. Yet if they go further into the subject, they will find remarkable continuity in the Mexican government's management of economic affairs toward the attainment of openly stated objectives. If they are to understand how this has happened, drastic medicine may be needed to cure their intellectual "hardening of the categories."

Robert J. Shafer's study of Mexican planning may be described as a healthy tonic for all those interested in national planning, Latin American affairs, or modernization processes in general. Professor Shafer is the "new style" historian. He combines meticulous combing of documents and files with an intuitive interpretation of attitudes and trends. While using statistics, he carefully warns us against them. Recognizing the complexities of a multicausal world, he is always ready to suggest alternative perspectives toward the same phenomena. Although undertaken as a prelude to more comprehensive analyses now under way, his study already provides an invaluable guide to all who may be interested in learning from the Mexican case.

If anyone should suggest that the "Mexican way" provides a "model" to be followed by other countries interested in planned industrialization, Professor Shafer—if not the Mexicans themselves—would strenuously object. The Mexican experience is firmly rooted in the unique history and substance of the Mexican social system.

Nevertheless, Shafer's study points up certain aspects of national planning which have widespread international significance: (1) "plan oratory" and "plan agency" mortality, (2) the record of planned achievement, (3) the building of the "central guidance cluster," (4) the building of action institutions, (5) government-business symbiosis, and (6) the rationality of competitive planning. Let us take a brief look at each of these points.

"Plan Oratory" and "Plan Agency" Mortality

In 1933 Mexico's national political party ratified the country's first Six-Year Plan. Describing the Plan as "a banner unfurled rather than as a technical instrument" (p. 43), Shafer points out that it "was couched largely in the appropriate generalities of political communication" and "lacked the detailed quantitative and chronological goals (some were stated), the specific data on financing, and the attention to modes of execution expected in planning today" (p. 44). Miguel S. Wionczek, a Mexican economist, has called it "an economic plan in name only," has charged that the Second Six-Year Plan "remained even more a paper plan that the first one," and has branded both as "pious exhortations" that had very little practical effect.[2]

Although the "Second Six-Year Plan served as party platform in 1940" (p. 47), after the election "party interest in six-year plans seems to have evaporated" (p. 49). Writers like Mosk and Cline concluded that Mexican development was planless.[3] Apart from election campaigns, interest in formal and comprehensive planning does not seem to have revived until around 1962, when the government was seriously concerned about a temporary economic slowdown and when aid from the Alliance for Progress was made conditional upon submission of a general plan. The result was the "Plan of Immediate Action, 1962–64," quickly put together by an interministerial group. For a while, its contents were held secret. This probably contributed to the building-up of public interest in its details and to a consequent upsurge in public discussions of planning. By the presidential election of 1964, "the term 'plan' seemed to issue from every mouth—in hope or despair, congratulation or condemnation" (p. 59).

By now the tattered banner of planning has been redesigned, with local and visiting *technicos* insisting upon the inclusion of macroeconomic goals, private investment, and cross-sectoral national policies. A new six-year plan—surely to be accompanied by a new upsurge in political oratory and pious exhortations—is soon to be unfurled.

Under different circumstances, the political oratory surrounding

[2] "Incomplete Formal Planning: Mexico," in Everett E. Hagen, ed., *Planning Economic Development* (Homewood, Illinois: Irwin, 1963), pp. 150–52.

[3] See pp. 123–24 and p. 191 n38 (on Mosk), n40 (on Cline).

Mexican planning might have been regarded with less suspicion. But one of the central and most conspicuous facts about Mexican national planning has been the high infant mortality rate of any government agency designated as a "central planning organ."[4] Although national planning is a sacrosanct ideal in Mexico, any central planning organ is plunged into a deadly battle for survival the moment it is created. It immediately faces the threat of liquidation, merger, reorganization, or competition with a new agency set up for similar purposes. The trials and tribulations of officials serving in such agencies may be inferred from the following partial list of "births" and reorganizations:

1928 National Economic Council
1930 National Planning Commission
1933 Another National Economic Council
1935 Cárdenas Advisory Committee for Planning
1938 Planning Division in Ministry of Government
1941 Reform of National Economic Council
1942 Federal Commission of Economic Planning
Coordination and Development of Production
1944 Commission of National Economic Coordination
Federal Commission for Industrial Development
National Planning Commission for the Peace
1946 Ministry of National Assets
1948 National Investment Commission, Ministry of Finance
1949 Department of Economic Studies, National Bank
1953 Investment Committee, Ministry of Finance
1954 Investment Commission
1958 Ministry of National Patrimony
Planning Bureau, Ministry of Presidency
1962 Interministerial Planning Commission

This long list includes almost every permutation of organizational characteristics—full-time staff and part-time membership, single director and collegial body, intergovernmental representation and representation of external groups. Some have been inactive and have died unmourned. Some have been more active and been liquidated more quickly. Some have operated very visibly, others in quiet and mysterious

[4] The term "central planning organ" has been used by Perroux and Debeauvais in describing a "general trend to entrust the preparation of planning to a single central organ." François Perroux and Michel Debeauvais, *Administrative Aspects of Planning in Developing Countries,* prepared for the United Nations Meeting of Experts on Administrative Aspects of National Development Planning, Paris, June 1964 (mimeo).

ways. None has succeeded in becoming a permanent, institutionalized symbol—like CORDIPLAN in Venezuela, the Indian Planning Commission, or the French *Commissariat du Plan*—of the Government's sustained commitment to national planning for economic change.[5]

The Record of Planned Achievement

The facts on government structure and political exhortation are not the only information bearing upon economic change in Mexico. "As most Latin American republics stumble . . . ," Shafer reports, "Mexico seems to have found a way" (p. 1). Shafer's judgment is born out by other commentators. Thus, Raymond Vernon has compared Mexican growth rates with those of South America's Big Three—Argentina, Brazil, and Chile:[6]

Annual Growth Rates of Physical Output of Goods and Services (in per cent)

	1938–1954		*1950–1959*	
	Total	*Per Capita*	*Total*	*Per Capita*
Mexico	5.7	2.9	5.2	2.3
Argentina	3.2	1.1	1.7	Less than 0.1
Brazil	4.8	2.4	4.8	1.9
Chile	4.0	2.3	2.4	Less than 0.1

It must be recognized that there has been no effort to raise Mexican per capita income (still at lower absolute levels than in Argentina, Chile, or Venezuela) by reducing its rate of population growth, which is among the highest in the world. While never able to reach the size of Brazil, in another twenty years Mexico will certainly outstrip France, Italy, and the United Kingdom and become one of the ten most populous nations in the world.[7] From the Mexican viewpoint, the population explosion is a benign event that may lead to larger domestic markets and a greater role in world affairs.

If Mexican progress has not been the effect of planned action to achieve macroeconomic targets, it nevertheless cannot be disassociated from a long series of more specific goals toward which Mexican govern-

[5] For a valuable analysis of the growth of CORDIPLAN, see John Friedmann, *Venezuela: From Doctrine to Dialogue* (Syracuse: Syracuse University Press, 1965).

[6] *The Dilemma of Mexico's Development* (Cambridge: Harvard University Press, 1963), p. 4.

[7] Mexico is now the thirteenth most populous country in the world.

ments have been unequivocally committed over the past three decades.

Three of the most important achievement areas have been pointed out by Vernon:

> (1) The improvement of the education, health and general well-being of the ordinary citizen. . . . No government since the Revolution of 1910 has failed to assert its fealty to these objectives nor to contribute a little toward their achievement.
>
> (2) To provide the basic "industrial overhead" facilities, including transport, communication, power and water. . . . No administration has failed to make substantial contributions to the building of the nation's infrastructure.
>
> (3) To encourage import replacement as a matter of high priority. It has been taken as an article of faith that as soon as the domestic demand for a product was large enough to offer some hope of domestic production on a scale appropriate to the technology of the industry, every effort should be made to stimulate the necessary domestic investment and to eliminate imports.[8]

Three additional areas may be added:

> (4) Agricultural reform and growth. Land redistribution among the poorest farmers has been extensive. Although this meant a temporary decline in output during the mid-1920's, since then agricultural production—particularly in cotton and coffee—has risen spectacularly. Much of this was the result of vigorous government action in irrigation, rural education, agricultural extension services, and agricultural banking.[9]
>
> (5) Industrial expansion. Under government stimulus, industrial expansion "has been even more spectacular."[10] Modern industrial complexest now produce a vast variety of products from iron and steel, cement and tires to modern consumer durable goods.
>
> (6) Expansion of foreign investment. Wionczek has shown that from the period between 1941 and 1946 to the 1953–58 period external credit has risen from 7.1 per cent of Mexican public investment to 16.5 per cent.[11] Although this has meant increased

[8] *The Dilemma of Mexico's Development,* pp. 8–9.

[9] John P. Powelson, *Latin America: Today's Economic and Social Revolution* (New York: McGraw-Hill, 1964), p. 66.

[10] Benjamin Higgins, *Economic Development* (New York: Norton, 1959), p. 70.

[11] ""Incomplete Formal Planning: Mexico," p. 170.

debt service, it nevertheless represents considerable success on mobilizing resources abroad.

(7) Export expansion. Having made considerable progress in the replacement of imports, the government is placing ever-greater emphasis upon the promotion of Mexican exports. Toward this end, among other things, Mexican officials have played a major role in organizing the Latin American Free Trade Area. Indeed, its efforts in this direction have already led to charges that "they may be attempting to exploit the less-developed countries of Latin America."[12]

To back all this up, as Shafer has pointed out, there has been considerable success in developing market and distribution systems, obtaining and using managerial skills, and recruiting "into the modern sector of the economy from the big national pool of unemployed and underemployed" (pp. 29–30).

All these points add up to the inescapable conclusion that Mexico's rapid economic advances were largely the result of conscious and sustained promotion and coordination by central government. If this is not national planning for economic change, what is?

The Building of the "Central Guidance Cluster"

The guidance of a national economy is an immensely complex undertaking. It requires a broad array of skills related to the difficult tasks of general leadership, financial management, handling critical problems, and providing specialized and general staff services. It olso requires institutionalized symbols, public ceremonials, and informal—often totally invisible—arrangements. The comparative study of national planning institutions, accordingly, has increasingly led to conclusions along the following lines:

No single agency could ever handle all the many roles involved in the guidance of national economic change. They are too numerous, specialized, and different to be embodied in any single organization. Any effort to incorporate them all in a single organization would inevitably lead to such a large amount of subdivision as to convert the boundaries of the total organization into a formal façade. The subdivisions would become *de facto* separate

[12] *The Dilemma of Mexico's Development,* p. 148. This charge is answered, according to Vernon, by pointing to "the provision of the Association's treaty which seeks to protect the laggard countries from the dominance of the senior partners in the association."

> organizations. The central guidance of national economic change requires not merely some single agency with certain planning functions but a *complex and flexible network or system of central government institutions embedded in a broader system of relations with the society as a whole*. This is what is meant by "central guidance cluster."[13]

Whether through sheer intuition or the experience gained in military administration, President Lázaro Cárdenas shunted aside all proposals that he establish a single, central planning agency. Instead he set out realistically to build a flexible network of central guidance institutions. His example has been followed by his successors, Avila Camacho, Miguel Alemán, Ruíz Cortinez, López Mateos, and Díaz Ordaz. The result has been a central guidance cluster built largely around four powerful institutions: (1) the Presidency, (2) the Ministry of Finance, (3) the Bank of Mexico, and (4) Nacional Financiera.

If one examines the growth of these institutions, one finds an entirely different picture from that revealed by the "obituary list" of so-called "central planning organs." Here, too, there has been constant reorganization—but the reorganization, rather, that is inherent in vigorous, dynamic growth. Underlying these complex processes of reorganization and growth there has been a steady building-up of the institutional capacity to promote change and react constructively to changing, even unexpected, circumstances. There has been an impressive development of research capacities in the analysis of specific projects, broad sectors, intersectoral policies and macroeconomic trends and potentialities. Above all, there seems to have been a remarkable growth of *the institutionalized capacity to build other institutions*.

Against this background, it is easier to understand the role of the various "central planning organs." Many were undoubtedly set up to provide public symbols of dedication or rededication to economic planning in general or to minor adjustments in economic policy. Some were set up to provide a minor increment of services—usually on an *ad hoc* basis—to the Big Four in the central guidance cluster. Many were quickly "done in" or taken over by competitive units within the Big Four cluster. A few served as "sacrificial goats"—a form of ceremonial "bloodletting" even more important in modern government than public

[13] Bertram M. Gross, "The Managers of National Economic Change," in Roscoe C. Martin, ed., *Public Administration and Democracy: Essays in Honor of Paul H. Appleby* (Syracuse: Syracuse University Press, 1965), p. 114. This article also sets forth a detailed analysis of the various roles that may be played by the key individuals and groups in central guidance clusters.

sacrifices to the gods in the ancient rites of the Aztecs and the Hebrews. Others were too unimportant even to rate attention in a sacrificial ceremony.

A full analysis of Mexico's Big Four would undoubtedly add immensely to our knowledge of the building of national development institutions, particularly if attention were focused on their intricate interrelations. Even without such an analysis, however, a number of imporant points are rather clear.

First of all, the Presidency of Mexico is much broader than the Ministry of the Presidency and its planning and investment bureaus. The President is, above all, the chief of a remarkably powerful political party. "No one disputes the central and overriding power of the President of the Republic. He possesses an unquestioned authority throughout all the echelons of the elaborate hierarchical structure of the PRI—an authority much greater, for example, than that of the United States President over the apparatus of his party" (p. 6). The building of the national party was the single most important factor in counterbalancing the power of the local bosses *(caciques)* and welding Mexico into a genuine nation capable of purposeful action. At the same time, the President is more than the leader of a party organized into Farm, Labor, and Popular sectors. As chief executive, he also derives considerable strength from sustained extra-party contacts with two important interest groups not formally represented in the party: big business and the military.

Second, the Ministry of Finance—as in many countries throughout the world—is involved in much more than the passive handling of the traditional finance functions: budgeting, taxation, credit, and foreign exchange. It is an active, growth-oriented organization alive to the political realities, the economic refinements, and the technological aspects of domestic expansion and international negotiation. It is intimately associated at the working levels—as well as through interlocking directorates—with both the Bank of Mexico and Nacional Financiera.

Third, the Bank of Mexico is a rare entity. Admired by the world's central banking fraternity, it combines the competence and caution of a traditional central bank with a growth orientation alien to the central banking ethos of the Western industrial nations. As one observer has pointed out, "The central bank has become more and more the keystone of a banking system whose intended orientation is the financing of growth. . . . The system has maintained a continued tolerance for credit expansions (albeit a restrained expansion) and a considerable internal flexibility in apportioning funds. These have made the system viable in a rapidly changing Mexico committed to growth but short of voluntary savings and reluctant to expand public sector revenues rapidly. . . . The rate of inflation likely to accompany a politically tolerable rate of capital formation and economic growth has been reduced."[14]

Fourth, Nacional Financiera is probably the strongest, largest, most experienced, and most flexible institution of its type among all industrializing nations. Supported by government funds, it uses all possible devices of financing industrial development. It makes loans, buys securities, and guarantees foreign and domestic bank credit and investment. It promotes competing undertakings—private, public, and mixed. It fosters the private securities market. While unquestionably serving as an agent of political masters, it "has posted a profit record which would do credit to some of the best-managed of private enterprises."[15]

Finally, taken as a whole, the Big Four handle much more than the critical roles of general leadership and financial management. They provide technical research services—particularly through the staffs of the Bank of Mexico and Nacional Financiera. They provide such general staff services as communication and bargaining among key power centers, performance evaluation, and expediting. They are capable of responding rather quickly to any critical problem that demands central and concerted action—whether it be an inflationary upsurge, a foreign currency shortage, an unexpected collapse of a critical foreign market, or delicate politicoeconomic negotiations with other countries.

The Building of Action Institutions

A central guidance cluster would operate in an ivory tower if not "embedded in a broader system of relations with the society as a whole." A large set of intermediaries is needed not only to formulate specific goals but to get action. This is the essence of plan implementation.

Although a political party such as PRI has a role to play in this broader system of relations, much more is needed. Indeed, experience suggests that the major intermediaries in an industrializing society are the specialized, national agencies of the central government. In Mexico these have been numerous, increasingly more specialized and steadily growing in number and size. Successive waves of expansion have created not only fifteen ministeries and departments but "some four hundred

[14] David H. Shelton, "The Banking System," in Raymond Vernon, ed., *Public Policy and Private Enterprise in Mexico* (Cambridge: Harvard University Press, 1964), pp. 117, 184.

[15] Calvin P. Blair, *Nacional Financiera,* in Vernon, *ibid.,* p. 201.

decentralized organs of government *(organismos descentralizados)* and enterprises in which the government participates in one fashion or another *(empresas de participación estatal)*" (p. 11). This latter group includes organizations engaged in, among other things, (1) the production and distribution of goods or services for the market; (2) regional and local development; (3) credit, securities, and finance; (4) cultural development and scientific investigation; and (5) social assistance (p. 149, n. 30).

The complexity of this institutional labyrinth does immediate violence to those still suffering from outmoded concepts of public administration based upon simplistic concepts of "span of control" and "unity of command." These agencies defy depiction on an organizational chart. Their activities cannot all be reflected in the government's general budget. They connot be coordinated from some central spot. Indeed, one is apt to apply to Mexico the observation in *The Economist* contrasting "privately owned industries which are subject to stringent government control" with "publicly owned industries which are subject to no control whatsoever."[16]

But the rationale of developing these multitudinous agencies has been a compelling one. A new institutional infrastructure was needed. To build it in small pieces, however disconnected, seemed infinitely superior to the piling-up of a vast hierarchical bureaucracy in a small number of ministeries. It provided more upward career channels for people with ability and ambition. By placing scarce eggs in many baskets, there was more room for trial and error, more protection against failure. Promotion of new institutions took precedence over their coordination.

This kind of institution building has a pulse rate of its own. The more successful it is in getting things done, the more problems the new institutions create. This leads to increasing pressures to pull things together a little more tightly. As a result, efforts are inevitably made to subject the "quasi-independent" agencies to comprehensive budgeting and accounting controls—perhaps even to tighter regulations of the salaries and grades of personnel. But then the effort to get important things done leads once again to new spurts of decentralized institution building. Central promotion of decentralized institutions once again races ahead of central coordination.

It should not be thought that this institutional mushrooming is devoid of form and pattern. Careful examination might well show an

[16] February 3, 1962. The degree of perceived stringency, of course, depends upon one's expectations. In Mexico, as distinct from Britain (the subject of *The Economist's* comment), people tend to expect more control over private business and less control over government agencies.

interesting inner logic of expansion. For one thing, the development of "decentralized organs" in Mexico has served to build up local and regional initiative in many parts of the country without adding to the power of the old-style local *caciques*. It has probably helped create conditions under which more attention can now be given to the development of the agencies of state and local governments. Earlier emphasis on state and local governments, while more consistent with certain irrelevant principles of representative democracy, might well have slowed down the entire modernization process.

Government-Business Symbiosis

One of the most dangerous oversimplifications in current thinking about economic development is the idea that industrializing nations face some simple choice between probusiness and antibusiness policies, between private enterprise and public enterprise. This idea's most virulent form is the myth that private enterprise and market institutions can expand only if government responsibility and initiative are contracted.

The Mexican case is clearly one in which government intervention of all sorts has contributed to a remarkable growth in the size and influence of private business. This is not to say that the government-business relationship in Mexico has been blissful or simple. It has undergone many changes and suffered many crises. Many of these difficulties stem from the fact that the social environment in Mexico since the Revolution has been hostile to private business—a phenomenon widespread in preindustrial and industrializing societies. Indeed, one of the conditions of government promotion of private business has been a tacit agreement that the business of businessmen be business, not politics. This does not mean that businessmen are not allowed to complain about government intervention. One suspects that Mexican political leaders relish such complaints so long as they are not carried too far. If private business gave the impression of being ultrasatisfied, this would add fuel to the fires of the antibusiness sentiments cherished by old-fashioned Marxists and "Fidelistas" who have not yet heard of "Libermanism" in Russia and the still more newfanged experiments with profitmaking in Czechoslovakia and Hungary.

Another part of the tacit compact, Shafer suggests, is that political leaders recurrently reassure old-fashioned businessmen by describing the Mexican economy as unplanned (p. 2). This does not stand in the way of—and may indeed contribute to—increased sophistication in the guidance of national economic change. At the same time, "the widening of the public sector's role in Mexico was productive partly because the public sector did not often overreach. In general, the public sector's assumption of a new function only occasionally exceeded its capacity to exercise the function with some measure of responsibility. . . ."[17] Still more important, as Shafer points out, has been the sober reassurance that comes from rising business profits (p. 26).

At least a full generation ago, one of the first steps of the Mexican political leaders was to require most manufacturing and commercial companies to belong to one or another formal business association. As a result, the business community in Mexico is now highly organized. This phenomenon—itself promoted by government—means that private business is in a better position to resist government. It is also, let it be added, better equipped to consult and cooperate with government.

It is encouraging to note that Professor Shafer is extending his study of Mexican dynamics by initiating a study of institution building and innovation in Mexican business associations. He is concentrating on CONCANACO *(Confederación de Cámaras Nacionales de Comercio),* CONCAMIN *(Confederación de Cámaras Industriales de los Estados Unidos Mexicanos)* and the Employers' Confederation *(Confederación Patronal).* Basic emphasis is being placed on the development of their internal structures, their programs, the strategies and tactics formulated for both internal purposes and for trying to impress their values on the social environment, their efforts to improve productive technology and administrative methods, and their relations with the federal government. Preliminary results—not yet published—suggest that in the government-business symbiosis of Mexican institutions Shafer is finding a remarkable case study in the promotion of modern entrepreneurship. Similar case studies in other countries—Asia and Africa as well as Latin Americo—may be expected as a result of Shafer's own entrepreneurial leadership in this important field.[18]

The Logic of Competitive Planning

In this present review of Mexican society, Shafer reveals a variety of competitive processes going for beyond competition among businessmen. There is competition among interest groups, among the various

[17] Raymond Vernon, "Public Policy and Private Enterprise," in Raymond Vernon, ed., *Public Policy and Private Enterprise in Mexico* (Cambridge: Harvard University Press, 1964), p. 16.

[18] Shafer's study is under the auspices of the Inter-University Program on Institution Building, which is financed in part by the Ford Foundation and represents a joint effort by the University of Pittsburgh, Indiana University, Michigan State University, and Syracuse University.

wings of the Party, among the decentralized agencies of government, and among the major actors in the central guidance cluster itself. There is competition between government and business. All these forms of competition are an integral, if not growing, part of the Mexican system. At the same time there has been an undeniable growth of market competition.

Under these circumstances, national planning in Mexico may be partially described, with Peter J. D. Wiles, as "allocation through a regulated market,"[19] or, with Charles E. Lindblom, as "development planning through the market mechanism."[20] Yet such description, by focusing on one form of competition alone, would be a serious oversimplification. It would ignore nonmarket competition. In order to understand the realities of Mexican development, one must be willing to go one step further and recognize that *"national planning—while an alternative to unplanned market competition—is itself a form of structured competition."*[21] This, of course, is exactly what Shafer is talking about when, at both the beginning and the end of his study, he describes Mexican national planning as "mutual adjustment decision-making" (pp. 3, 127).

In using the term "mutual adjustment decision-making," Shafer brings within the realm of nationol planning discourse Lindblom's fascinating work in depicting the possibilities of coordinated action through "partisan mutual adjustment." In his *The Intelligence of Democracy,* Lindblom points out that "in many circumstances what appears to be a case of central coordination is, of course, a case of partisan mutual adjustment." For Lindblom a person is a "partisan decision maker" if "(a) he does not assume that there exists some knowledgeable criteria acceptable to him and all the other decision makers that is sufficient, if applied, to govern adjustment among them, and (b) he therefore does not move toward coordination by a cooperative and deliberate search for and/or application of such criteria or by an appeal for adjudication to those who do so search and apply." He identifies various forms of partisan mutual adjustment ranging from the simple adaptation to what others are doing to negotiation, bargain-

[19] *The Political Economy of Communism* (Cambridge: Harvard University Press), p. 18. More specifically, the Mexican case corresponds to Wiles' CM/RM model in which "the central authority decides investment projects, which are then operated according to the market, by decentralized management," p. xiii.

[20] "Economics and the Administration of National Economic Planning," *Public Administration Review,* XXV (Dec. 1965), 274–83.

[21] This proposition has been set forth more formally in my "National Planning: Findings and Fallacies," *Public Administration Review,* XXV (Dec. 1965), 263–73.

ing, reciprocity, and other forms of manipulation. He argues that through these very processes themselves common values, in some large part, originate. In rebuttal of those who may feel that these processes necessarily encourage disagreement, Lindblom offers a number of propositions concerning their role in promoting social agreement:

> (1) Many value conflicts that in central systems would constitute barriers to reaching agreed decisions do not constitute barriers in partisan mutual adjustment.
>
> (2) Participants in partisan mutual adjustment have stronger motives than do central coordinators to find an agreed decision or outcome.
>
> (3) The need for allies is an especially powerful motivation toward agreement in partisan mutual adjustment.
>
> (4) Agreement is also encouraged by the moderation imposed on demands in partisan mutual adjustment, by reason of the tasks and other responsibilities attached to making a demand.
>
> (5) Because, in partisan mutual adjustment, decisions or outcomes of adjustment are tentative and can easily be altered, participants will agree where otherwise they would not.
>
> (6) Participants find it to their advantage to make agreed concessions of specialized extra legal authority to each other, thus avoiding by prearrangement conflicts that would otherwise develop.
>
> (7) In partisan discussion, in contrast to cooperative discussion, is to be found an important potential for agreement.

In addition, Lindblom suggests that a multiplicity of decision-makers "mop up the adverse consequences of each other's inevitably imperfect decisions" and "compellingly call to others' attention aspects of the problem they cannot analyze."[22]

Lindblom's analysis, it might be noted, is based almost entirely upon illustrations of government and interest group operations above the Rio Grande. Moreover, no specific reference is made to the partisan mutual adjustment associated with the broad guidance of national

[22] (New York: Free Press, 1965), particularly Chap. 2, "The Participants and the Process," pp. 21–34, and Chap. 14, "Social Agreement," pp. 205–25. Lindblom's analysis of mutual adjustment is closely related to my presentation of polyarchy as an indispensable element in hierarchical structure (Chap. 15, "People-in-Organizations: Formal Aspects") and my analysis of "activation" as a mix of various forms of persuasion, pressure, and the promotion of self-activation (Chap. 29, "Rationality: Administrative Processes") in *The Managing of Organizations* (2 vols.; New York: Free Press, 1964).

economic change in the United States. Knowledge of decision-making in general is sure to be advanced if Lindblom and others follow Shafer's lead by applying this style of analysis to the experience of other countries and to national planning phenomena in particular.

Competitive planning in Mexico, it may be noted, began under what David E. Apter calls a "mobilization system" characterized by a mass party, an effort to organize the entire population, strong hierarchical authority, and a major role for military leaders. It then moved steadily toward a pluralistic "reconciliation system" in which specialization ond professionalization have contributed toward the emergence of democratic values and practices. Apter regards this transition as an illustration of the dynamic potentialities of mobilization systems, particularly to the extent that they encourage the emergence of scientific elites. Although he does not regard this tendency as inevitable, he does suggest that rapid modernization of preindustrial societies is impossible without mobilization systems. This is particularly true of Latin America, he suggests, where under government stimulus "the economist has displaced the lawyer as the key figure of modernity." In terms that relate to all preindustrial countries, not merely Latin America, he makes the following comment:

> We may view mobilization systems as the "best" political form for converting poor but modernized countries into steadily growing economies, since they will create their own "contradictions," to use the Marxist term, and as a result tend to move in the direction of a reconciliation system. If socialism and nationalism, or their modern combinations, are understood in this light, the mobilization system becomes a temporary form of politics, initiating activity, but subject to change because of its success."[23]

The Mexican case of economic growth under competitive national planning, with coordination through a large dose of partisan mutual adjustment, supports this viewpoint.

BERTRAM M. GROSS

Syracuse, New York
Winter 1966

[23] *The Politics of Modernization* (Chicago: University of Chicago Press, 1965), p. 449.

I

Will and Technique

As most Latin American republics stumble in search of paths to self-sustained economic growth and social development, Mexico seems to have found a way. For a quarter-century the growth rate has permitted some increase in levels of living, even in the face of a population increase among the highest in the world. If the Mexico of 1965 is not a perfectly flourishing garden, it is enormously more productive—of goods, services, and social hope—than the Mexico of 1915 or 1925 or 1935.

This achievement is the more interesting in that: (1) Mexico is one of the largest (760,000 square miles) and most populous (40 million) countries in Latin America, or, indeed, in the world; (2) it was done in the face of vast difficulties; (3) although the country has essentially a one-party system, the party has not built the apparatus of a police state and increasingly depends on the politics of conciliation and consensus; (4) although government intervention in the economy has been increasing, the private sector is much favored and has enjoyed large growth; and (5) there is much current concern with the question of whether growth can be sustained further without changes—and possibly increases—in economic and social planning by the government, and whether this can or should be attempted by increased direct government intervention in the economy or by the development of new relationships between government and private enterprise.

The second of these points deserves emphasis. The impressive Mexican achievement has emerged from a sea of troubles as deep forty years ago as those threatening so many emerging nations today. Mexico has had to contend with the destruction of civil war, a tradition of political turbulence, a difficult terrain, deficiencies in water supply, problems of regionalism, cultural pluralism, and class structure; and with the economic, cultural, and political pressures exerted by its neighbor, the United States. In Latin America, therefore, Mexico is an outstanding example of progress or development through will, organization, intelligence, and technique. For example, Argentina in 1940 possessed, as compared with Mexico, a number of natural, social, and historical advantages; but since then Mexico has moved forward rapidly, and Argentina essentially has wasted a generation—at least in many aspects of economic development.[1]

The Mexican will to develop has been fostered, organized, and manipulated by a remarkably effective political establishment. At the same time, the establishment has been active in its efforts to ensure that the aspirations aroused will be in some measure satisfied by economic growth and social development. The high rate of economic growth in Mexico did not simply happen, with a minimum of government intervention. Nor has the large amount of intervention been entirely haphazard, uncoordinated, and lacking in continuity. Thus the common assertion that the Mexican economy essentially is unplanned is misleading. The political establishment often says this, to reassure private enterprise; economic technicians in the Mexican government say this privately, because they believe that their talents are insufficiently employed in action programs; and the assertion—in the form of accusation—is made by leftist opponents of the establishment, and by humanists, out of impatience with the continued existence of poverty and immense social problems in the country, and out of failure either to perceive or to admit that the pace of development has been rather rapid and that it has been in large measure a creation of the government.

The Mexican economy also is described as unplanned by objective observers wedded to a relatively narrow definition of planning. For one thing, Mexico has not had comprehensive and centralized national planning concentrated in obviously labeled planning agencies on the model of the U.S.S.R., or on the model of the visibly institutionalized indicative planning of France. On the other hand, the government has a history of continuous use over a quarter-century of a web of institutions and policies and devices for the control and development of the economy. This has involved much action to achieve government objectives of many varieties, including some quantitative goals. There has been a great deal of national sectoral planning, especially in connection with infrastructure; a certain amount—not trifling—of regional planning; considerable effort to coordinate—in one way or another—development in manufacturing and in agriculture, and between these; a decade of activity in the coordination of public investment planning; and a more recent approach to the preparation of global national development plans, and to the coordination of public and private investment planning. In addition, in many ways intimately connected with economic planning has been the large amount of Mexican national planning for social development, especially in the fields of education and public health.

The Mexican system has been termed "incomplete formal planning."[2] This hints at the possibility that some areas are less planned than others, and at the additional possibility that "informal" (i.e., other than comprehensive and centralized) planning may exist. Although it is the point of view of this study that both of these possibilities are facts, we have adopted the position that this is less significant than the dispersal of planning and quasi-planning functions, and the system of "mutual adjustment" among government agencies, and between government and private enterprise, that this requires. This is especially noteworthy in that it is increasingly appreciated by students that mutual adjustment decision-making is a general characteristic of Mexican politics and government, and when it is increasingly necessary to concede the rationality of the Mexican politicoeconomic system (whatever all its critical components may be thought to be), especially in terms of self-sustained economic growth at a high level over a long period of time.[3]

One may be cautious about predicting the future of government planning in Mexico when it is observed that government and party figures sometimes describe the economy as essentially unplanned, but on other occasions talk spaciously about government plans and planning. It does not seem very audacious, however, to suggest that some expansion of government planning activity is likely in a country where so much discussion in the press and in scholarly publications connects concern about the possible necessity of new modes of action to sustain economic growth at least verbally with the terms *planeamiento* and *planificación*.

II

The Planning Environment in Mexico: Government and Society

Mexican planning theory, agencies, and implementation draw on international doctrine, but are rooted in the experience and judgment of a notably successful and pragmatic national leadership, and in a society vastly different even from those of other Latin American countries.

A. Politics and Government[1]

Mexican politics and government in recent decades have been highly effective. The transfer of power between administrations is accomplished regularly and peaceably. There is constant enlargement of the number of individuals and groups involved in national decision-making. The government bureaucracy handles adequately the increasingly complex tasks of state enterprise. And if the satisfaction of the commonalty is less than absolute, it is sufficiently widespread and intense to be almost unbearable to the opposition leadership.

1. *Political Power*

The Institutional Revolutionary Party (PRI) has been the overwhelmingly dominant organized political force in Mexico for many years.[2] The party enjoys a virtual monopoly of federal, state, and municipal office.[3] It wins elections with ease;[4] no significant threat to its dominance is apparent.[5] And, most remarkable, the PRI has not created a police state;[6] nor has long exercise of power led it far down that familiar path of exaggerated privilege which alienates party from people.[7]

The PRI has a large membership—possibly four million;[8] and few other voters can be said to "belong" to a party.[9] It is organized into Farm, Labor, and Popular "sectors," made up largely of functional interest associations. The party has had great success in organizing the rural population, in involving the peasant farmer indirectly in politics, and in satisfying some of his material needs. Thus party and government have enjoyed the allegiance or acquiescence of the huge rural populace, reducing problems of civil disorder, and minimizing the likelihood that rural dissatisfaction can be used as a base for opposition political growth.[10] The fact that critics believe that the peasant has misplaced his confidence is of little political interest. The relevance of this political triumph to the problems of leadership in many essentially agricultural countries is obvious. PRI domination of organized labor also has been so great as to infuriate critics, who have little success with assertions that the party is subservient to the entrepreneurial class.

Three important interest groups lack formal representation in the party: military, big business, and Church. Individual military officers are, however, active in party and government, and the officer corps firmly supports the system. The big business community has abundant —critics say excessive—access to the national decision-making apparatus. The Church is largely isolated from politics by law, party wish, and public sentiment.

The PRI maintains its position primarily by reason of popular support, founded on the evident achievements of the administrations it has installed; by generosity in welcoming new leaders into the fold; by attention to the needs of most of the country's many organized interest groups; by what has been called the "merciless publicity" given by government to the country's economic and social progress;[11] and, some would say, by reason of the political apathy and the low economic and social expectations of much of the population. In any event, these policies and conditions render relatively unimportant the use, usually nonviolent, if sometimes illegal, of government power in the interests of the party.[12]

The locus of decision-making within this system is not quite so clear as is the general political methodology. Both Mexican and foreign observers argue the importance of the visible apparatus of the PRI as compared with the elite of government, party, business, military, labor, and other groups.[13] Of course, similar dispute exists about political decision-making in other large and complex systems, including that of the United States. At the least, it seems clear that in Mexico and many other countries much decision-making occurs outside the visible apparatus of the party.

Whatever the identity and weight of the other critical elements in political decision-making in Mexico, no one disputes the central and overriding power of the President of the Republic. He possesses an unquestioned authority throughout all echelons of the elaborate hierarchical structure of the PRI—an authority much greater, for example, than that of a United States President over the apparatus of his party. This centralization of party decision-making in the presidency (for example, over nominations to Congress), coupled with the one-party system, makes the pressure against schismatics irresistible for all but the desperate.[14]

This does not mean, of course, that the President of the Republic does not respond to pressures and share his authority with others. On the one hand, the existence of party organs with some functions (however feeble, ceremonial, or merely hortatory) at the state, municipal, and ward levels, coupled with the PRI's close attention to public opinion and to the shibboleths of the Revolution (*read*: political/social/economic democracy) limits the freedom of action of all levels of party direction. Additionally, professional politicians in the PRI clearly are sensitive to the views of important interests not directly represented in the party, notably business groups and leaders. The responsiveness of PRI leadership to the interests of professional politicians and big business, as opposed to the obvious immediate, if not loudly articulated, interests of the party rank-and-file is in important measure made possible by the latter's poverty, poor education, and traditional diffidence or apathy toward the decision-making of the elites. Thus the President and the entire political establishment respond to the interests of both classes and masses in highly complex ways that have been little analyzed by scholars.

Ideology is too pretentious a term to apply to the cluster of beliefs and aims that link the party with the Mexican Revolution (1910–17) in the past, and with socioeconomic progress in the future. These beliefs developed over the years, out of Mexican experience, and have a pragmatic orientation. The party and the Revolution stand, among other things, for Mexican nationalism, integration of the Indian into the life of the country (which means racial and cultural equality as a theory, but "modernization" of the Indian community in practice), improvement of the material condition of everyman, and similar goals of what might be called a moderately socialist reformism, proceeding gradually.

There naturally are differences of viewpoint in a party so large and heterogeneous. There is a rough division between the dominant element of recent years, which favors increases of production and productivity, financed by enforced savings that press rather heavily on lower income groups, and emphasizes industrial expansion; and the left wing of the party, which would prefer emphasis on income redistribution in favor of the common man, and more concentration on the needs of farmer and laborer, and less on those of business and industry. It is not clear how serious this division in the PRI is. Some observers consider it so fundamental as to make the PRI almost a two-party or three-party "system," with some imminent likelihood of a formal division. Other observers consider that some well-publicized differences of opinion between party leaders are staged, or at least exaggerated, for the purpose of relieving political pressures and tensions through debate. Events during 1962–64 in connection with the presidential election of July, 1964—and many times earlier—suggest at least the partial validity of this interpretation.[15]

The fact is that for some years the party has nominated presidential candidates of rather neutral or centrist political coloration—certainly to most non-Mexican eyes—who have campaigned in such a way as to try to keep all party elements reasonably satisfied in this party of diversified interests, regional jealousies, and wide philosophical range. This sounds almost like the prescription for the candidate of one of the major parties in the United States, and indeed the requirements of conciliation in the two countries have displayed similarities for some years.[16]

The opposition to the PRI has been ineffective in the sense that it has not been able to win elections, or convince a significant portion of the populace that it has been deprived improperly of such victory.[17] In fact, the ineffectiveness of the opposition is so conspicuous as to constitute an occasional embarrassment. This is one reason for the fact that several opposition parties are subsidized by the government.

On the right, the most significant organized opposition is the Partido de Acción Nacional (PAN), a conservative party founded most notably on business distaste for "socialism" and on Catholic distaste for the anticlericalism of PRI. Other rightist groups are small and poorly organized. It is difficult to imagine the right significantly increasing its influence in Mexican politics in the near future.

The leftist opposition suffers from PRI's identification with the term "revolution," from the government's programs of economic and social assistance and its considerable success in economic development, from the great government and party advantages in the field of propaganda and communications, and—as the left opposition itself would emphasize—from the unremitting vigilance of the national security forces. In any event, the leftist opposition has had little success at the polls.[18] For a time in 1963 there was considerable expectation that the left might do better in the 1964 elections, primarily because ex-President Lázaro Cárdenas seemed to be adopting an antiestablishment view. Since Cárdenas ultimately supported the PRI candidate, much to the dismay of the left (within and without the party), one is led again to suppose that his aim was primarily to force modifications of PRI policy, possibly with the connivance of some other leadership elements of the party. In any event, PRI leadership is most sensitive to such suggestions when they involve apparent threats of formation of more effective opposition.

We have observed that the political process in Mexico has facilitated the growth of government intervention in the economy and some aspects of planning. Insofar as the party can be said to have an ideology, it favors broad action by the central government. This being true, such action is facilitated by the one-party system, maintained largely by peaceful methods, with a broad national system for obtaining consensus, and a high degree of centralization at the national level to promote implementation of policy. It is facilitated also by the wide representation of interest groups in the party, and by the considerable attention given to the needs and wishes of private enterprise, which is not directly represented in the party—both of which facilitate the commitment of the citizenry to government programs.[19]

On the other hand, the centralization of party decision-making has played a role in development of a system of quite autonomous operation by major government agencies. The system not only suits some of the political purposes of the president under current conditions, but suits the ambitions of the department heads to make records that will suggest their "availability" for the presidential nomination. To say the least, the system creates difficulties for integrated planning. And finally, the very eclecticism of the PRI, its hospitality to many views and interests, makes it reluctant to become tied to hard-and-fast integrated plans.

2. *Structure and Operation of Government*

Mexican governmental tradition, structure, and operation have both favored and hampered effective governmental management of the economy. Potentially favorable is the fact of a long tradition of use of the instruments of the state to control or administer society. In the Spanish colonial centuries, and in independent Mexico after 1822, broad state activity was justified in men's minds by theory; long usage; its presumed cultural propriety as part of the Hispanic "style"; the necessities of the Mexican international position; and by the circumstances of the social order, wherein relatively small elites considered it advantageous to themselves, proper for the lower orders, and in any event inescapable in view of the poor organization of the socioeconomic resources of the nation.

This does not mean, of course, that government always acted effectively. Nor does it mean that no objections to or suspicions of this tradition have existed. There always has been in Mexico a deep popular mistrust of government. But much of this has attached to the local boss, or regional military barracks, or to the taxgatherer, rather than to the distant federal government, from which in recent times many blessings flow, and in which justice is thought to lie, if only the peasant can get though the screen of underlings to the ultimate *patrón* in the presidential palace. In addition, the private business entrepreneur does not enjoy in the popular mind the esteem accorded him in some other capitalist countries. Business cannot, then, rally the populace against governmental activity. Furthermore, private business itself in Mexico is more (if less than absolutely) wedded to the necessity of governmental activity than it is north of the Rio Grande.[20]

Potential support for planning activities may be said to lie as much in the tradition of social as of strictly economic intervention. Certainly Mexico is heavily "administered" in both areas. In addition, both the strength and the weakness of centralization are fostered, depending on circumstances, by the tradition and practice of executive predominance over the other two branches of government, and by federal predominance over state and local government.

On the other hand, economic planning by the central government has been hampered by: (1) overcentralization of decision-making in the office of the president, without adequate machinery for study, and with possibly an occasionally excessive attention to political factors (though one would be hard put to measure this); (2) a need for more rapid improvement in the selection, training, and pay of civil servants; (3) the feebleness of the national legislature, which makes it incapable of functioning as a check on the executive; and (4) finally, as stated above, the relative autonomy of the government departments creates difficulties for global planning.[21]

The constitution may be said to favor planning, at least potentially, in that it states a social function theory of property, and specifically encourages government intervention in the economy. In addition, the constitution concedes the executive branch considerably more power in relation to the legislative and judicial than does the United States Constitution. More than this, executive predominance is even more a matter of custom than of constitutional dictum. In practice, no question arises of the legislative and judicial branches making effective use of the constitution to interfere with whatever economic planning the president undertakes. In fact, the operations of the legislative and judicial branches are of little practical interest in connection with planning. Finally, the president enjoys extraordinary prestige in Mexico, great advantages in the field of public communications, and a wonderful immunity from public campaign activity by potential successors to his office.[22]

Similarly, although Mexico is a federal republic, the federal government completely overshadows the other echelons. State and local governments receive so puny a portion of public revenues directly that they cannot approach the influence and activity of those levels in the United States. Additionally, the fact that most state and local officials are members of the PRI, and quite dependent on the national party organization, further reduces their ability to act independently of the federal government.[23]

It must be emphasized again, however, that although decision-making is highly centralized in the office of the president, both physical necessity and sound political practice urge the party into consultation of a wide variety of party, government, and private interests.[24] Consultation of the functionally specialized business and industrial organizations, which (as noted above) do not belong to the PRI, is provided by law. It is widely agreed that there is a tendency to increase the consulting role of groups outside the PRI.[25]

Consultation often involves *ad hoc* committees. The president does not meet the heads of the ministries as a cabinet for this or any other purpose. The consultation process tends to funnel through the Ministry of the Presidency (*Secretaría de la Presidencia*). Until 1958 this was a nonministerial post which the president used in part for coordination of government policies and programs; for the consultation of interest groups; and for the onerous task of managing PRI interests as they affected the government. As the government grew in complexity, it became evident that the following changes would be useful: (1) definition of the functions of the *Secretaría de la Presidencia*; (2) separation of the political from the other functions of the office, or provision of organization and staff that would permit such different functions to be carried on more acceptably in one office; and (3) provision of a proper staff for planning, consultation, and coordination, if those functions were to be retained. Some of this was attempted by a law of December, 1958, effective January 1, 1959, turning this office into a ministry, with the same name, and defining its functions as those of planning, coordination, and review.[26]

The presidency originates most legislation; and the congress does not enact measures of which the president disapproves. There is thus no longer reason in peacetime for the president to resort to legislation by decree, even though provision for such practice exists in law and tradition. In addition to his control over legislation, the president exercises wide power through issuance of the *reglamento* (detailing execution of the law). *Reglamentos* are published in the *Diario Oficial* (as are the laws), and are an executive interpretation of legislation, often issued shortly on the heels of the latter, and subject to no effective control by any agency of government. The effect of the occasional judicial interpretation of the constitutionality of legislation is minute. Finally, there is no question of congressional disapproval of presidential appointees.

The budget the president presents to the congress is accepted virtually without question. This is because nearly all congressmen are members of the PRI, and that party is so highly centralized in direction that nomination to congress is arranged in the Secretaría de la Presidencia, and also because executive control of all phases of government finance is traditional in Mexican government.

The Ministries (*Secretarías*) and Departments (*Departamentos*) of State number fifteen and three respectively, and differ in nomenclature rather than in rank or function.[27] These constitute the regular bureaucracy. In addition, there are some four hundred decentralized organs of government (*organismos descentralizados*) and enterprises in which the government participates in one fashion or another (*empresas de participación estatal*).[28] Most of these latter two types are engaged in economic activity, often in the field of development. Government activity in recent years has grown more rapidly in these two categories than in the ministries and departments of state. These agencies have budgets independent of the general budget of the government, although subject to various sorts of control, review, audit, and even coordination. They make large investments, and are heavy importers of producers' goods.[29] The proliferation of independent and quasi-governmental agencies has proceeded to the point where it is recognized that new methods of coordination, control, and planning are necessary.[30]

Two other aspects of government require a word. Local bosses or *caciques* retain considerable power. One reason for presidential support in 1961 of an agrarian reform bill was to cut the power of such individuals at the town and village level. Such *caciques* notoriously have interfered with the execution of official programs. The other matter relates to graft and inefficiency in government. That the Mexican civil service is not as efficient as the British seems certain, and is not surprising; still, it has improved greatly in recent decades; and its weaknesses have not been serious enough to constitute a critical menace to political power or to economic development. The amount of graft indulged in by Mexican officials is a favorite subject for denunciation, is difficult to measure, and probably threatens neither political stability nor economic development.[31]

3. *Government Policies*

Certain government policies, reflected in legislation, expenditure, and propaganda, importantly affect government economic development planning in Mexico. These policies constitute more or less inflexible commitments to activity. The policies fall into two classes: (1) those necessitated by adherence to shibboleths of the Revolution, such as nationalism, education, land reform, racial and cultural egalitarianism, and the social function theory of property; and (2) interpretations of the foregoing by the administration, such as emphasis on agriculture against industry, or on communal as against private rural land ownership, or adoption of tax and other policies that force accumulation of earnings in limited groups to facilitate investment in economic development.

Promotion and protection of domestic economic production is a policy furthered by all the devices available to the ingenuity of the state, and practically limited in Mexico only by the following factors: (1) consideration of the limitations of the physical and cultural environment; (2) prudence in international relations; and (3) an apparent disposition to leave a large area of economic activity—especially industrial, commercial, and service—to private enterprise.[32]

More specifically, some features of economic policy area: (1) fostering domestic production, both for consumption and for export; (2) maintaining an economic growth rate enough larger than population increase to permit some improvement in levels of income, even after siphoning off large amounts for investment; (3) nationalization of some forms of economic activity, either through expropriation (uncommon in recent years), total purchase, or acquisition (under various formulas) of controlling interest by nationals; (4) connected with the foregoing, an emphasis on Mexican control of nonrenewable natural resources; (5) continued expenditure for the communal (*ejidal*) farm system, partly for political reasons, while pouring support into private agriculture, whose record of productivity is superior to that of the communal operations; (6) heavy investment in infrastructure (transportation, communications, power, education); (7) large expenditures for irrigation; (8) efforts to control prices, partly for political and social reasons.[33] Government economic policy often is described as favorable to a "mixed" economy, or a combination of socialism and capitalism.[34]

The commitment to education is a sociopolitical as well as an economic matter. The outlays constitute a heavy and probably irreducible charge on revenues. There is reason to believe that this charge may become heavier, since there is dissatisfaction with educational progress, impeded as it is by other demands on revenues, and by the high rate of population increase.

Military policy is highly favorable to investment in economic development. In recent years military expenditures have averaged only about 10 per cent of the federal budget. In effect, Mexico has committed her protection against foreign attack to the United States, and has decided that the political and police need for military forces has drastically declined compared with pre-Revolution days. Mexico justifies the first of these two decisions on the ground that her chief contribution to the strength of the free world must lie in the promotion of economic and social strength at home; the record of recent decades justifies the second decision. Adoption and adherence to such a policy is a striking confirmation of the power and prescience of the PRI.

Mexico's general international policy may be described as: (1) independent or Mexican, especially when a question arises of subservience to the views of the United States; (2) proliberal, especially on what might be described as matters of conscience, or in opposition to dictatorship or tyranny; and (3) pro-United Nations and pro-Organization of American States, within the limits of Mexican reserves of attention to devote to such organizations when energies are so riveted on domestic affairs. International policy has had recent effects on economic development, when reluctance to move against Castro was interpreted by domestic and foreign investors as somehow connected with socialist domestic policies or aims.

4. *Government Fiscal Operations*

In recent years the government's fiscal position has been strong, the result of good economic growth, a near balance between government revenues and expenditures,[35] close control of credit and inflation, and a sound national balance-of-payments situation.[36] The high quality of Mexican fiscal operations has generally been conceded to be a chief reason for her good economic growth performance. As a consequence of the economic slowdown of 1961–62, the rate of growth of government expenditures was accelerated in 1963–64, and public borrowing was increased. This has given rise to fears of increased inflationary pressures, but the government is aware of the problem and apparently determined and able to limit price rises and to protect the international value of the peso.[37] The external public debt is mostly an obligation of the decentralized agencies and state participation enterprises, rather than a direct federal government debt. Furthermore, short-term external obligations are being reduced, with favorable effects on debt service charges.[38] In short, the will and the technique of the government in the fiscal realm remain at the impressive level they have maintained for many years.

The ordinary federal budget includes considerable sums for investment directly in productive facilities, and contributions to the investment of the independent agencies. In addition, and more importantly, it includes large sums for the socioeconomic infrastructure that is indispensable to the continuation of economic growth. It must be borne in mind, however, that much of the public investment for economic growth is handled by autonomous agencies with independent budgets based on their own revenues and on borrowing operations.[39] Ministry of the Treasury control of these autonomous agency budgets was increased for the fiscal year 1965.[40]

Federal revenues and expenditures have risen steadily for years, both in absolute and per capita terms. Expenditures (as originally budgeted) were 2.05 billion pesos in 1947, 9.67 billion in 1958, 13.8 billion for 1963,[41] 15.95 billion for 1964, and 17.85 billion for 1965. From 1950 to 1960 the federal budget increase per capita was from 105.8 pesos to 300;[42] in 1962 the budget provided for expenditures of approximately 332 pesos per capita, and in 1963 it was 363.[43] So, in the last few years, while the population has risen about 3.5 per cent annually, and prices have gone up some 5 per cent a year, the annual increases in the federal budget have been on the order of 10 per cent (12 per cent for 1963, and 15.6 per cent for 1964).[44]

In recent years high and increasing portions of the budget have been assigned to economic and social development, in the last decade always accounting for more than half the budget, and in most recent years hovering around three-quarters, as shown in the table:[45]

TABLE 1
EXPENDITURES FOR SOCIOECONOMIC DEVELOPMENT FROM FEDERAL BUDGET

Year	Million pesos for economic & social development in budget	Per cent of total budget
1952	2,156.2	53.8
1960	7,459.0	73.2
1961	8,018.0	72.0
1962	9,028.0	74.0
1963	10,201.0	74.0
1964	12,240.0	75.0

In per capita terms, such expenditures were 79.1 pesos in 1952, 219.2 in 1960, 244 in 1962, and 268 in 1963.[46] It has been well said of this distribution of expenditure that "thus there is relative congruence between political pronouncements of the PRI, campaign promises of presidential candidates, and the actual policy as measured by budgets."[47]

Mexico is not a high-tax country, although the percentage of national income going to government has been increasingly slowly for some years.[48] We thus encounter in Mexico the familiar situation of the developing or partially developed country in which the weight of the tax system is less than in many better developed countries. There have been some recent rather substantial changes, occasioned in part by the increased need for public expenditures due to the economic slowdown of the early 1960's. Tax changes legislated in 1961 speeded the growth of revenues,[49] partly by adding to the tax rolls; and changes that went into effect January 1, 1965, promised further modernization.

Mexican federal revenue sources are relatively varied as compared with the rest of Latin America, and especially notable for the relatively small, declining dependence on export-import duties, and for the increasing reliance on personal income and business and industrial levies.[50]

This indicates a transfer of "the weight of government revenues to the industrial system and the individuals it provides with higher incomes" —that is, to the "modernized" sector of society.[51] The proportion of federal revenues due to income taxes rose dramatically from 7.5 per cent in 1939, to 24 per cent in 1951, 30 per cent in 1961, and 34 per cent in 1962. Export-import levies accounted for only about 20 per cent of federal income in 1961 and 1962.[52] Tax evasion is widespread, but in recent years efforts to improve collections have had some success. Tax exemptions are made to certain types of enterprises, especially in their infancy.

The federal—as opposed to state and municipal—share of government revenues has been about 80 per cent for some years. The federal government apportions a modest part of its revenues to the states, on the basis of their needs rather than of their contributions to the fisc. The concentration of revenues at the national level is traditional in Mexico and all of Latin America, and is unlikely to change soon.[53]

Mexico has both public and private banks. The latter are supervised by the Ministry of Finance, the National Banking Commission, and the Bank of Mexico. A number (twenty in 1961) of national credit institutions, in which the government has a decisive influence, operate under government direction, but have separate legal personalities and capital. The Bank of Mexico is a central bank; its functions including those of mint, clearing house, credit rationing and channeling, and regulation of reserve requirements. The *Nacional Financiera* is a national development bank, supported in part by obligatory stock subscriptions by private financial institutions, in part by foreign loans. Its large investments since its creation in 1933 often—but by no means exclusively—have been in industrial fields not being served adequately by private capital.[54] Indeed, officials of the Mexican government assert that a good part of the investment activity of all government banks is undertaken only because private financial institutions are unable or unwilling to act. In the agricultural field, for example, the private institutions clearly are unwilling to make many investments that the government considers indispensable.[55]

In the years 1940–54 the government felt obliged to let the purchasing and exchange value of the peso decline considerably, though much less than occurred in many other Latin American countries, and possibly no more than obviously was required by the exigencies of international trade and the necessities of domestic capital accumulation. Since 1954 the value of the peso has been guarded carefully. The dollar-peso exchange rate was 4.52 in 1938, weakened to 6.88 by 1948, to 8.65 in 1949, went to 12.50 with the devaluation of 1954, and remains there today.[56] Careful fiscal management is reflected, also, in the fact that since 1954 annual price increases have averaged only about 5 per cent.[57] There is no way of knowing the relative importance in adoption of this policy of criticism of the effects of inflation on popular purchasing power and of the advice of technicians that economic development required tighter controls.[58]

Budgetary techniques have been judged quite good in Mexico.[59] There is said, however, to be a tendency for political decisions to weaken the operational effectiveness of the budget.[60] Comparison of this with similar phenomena in other countries is not available. It is common to say that most of the problem in Mexico lies in the fact that the making and execution of the budget are almost purely executive processes. This would seem, however, to require the dubious supposition that executive interference with the formalized budget process, in response to political considerations, necessarily is most importantly the result of some technical deficiency in the relations between the two branches of government, rather than something arising from the basic sociopolitical environment. Also, it has been asserted that budgetary planning as a means of getting continuity of program will be impossible in Mexico as long as the budget is subject to the personalistic relations between the president and his followers. It is said that no president will continue work begun by his predecessor (surely an exaggeration); as a result, it is charged that problems are attacked in "six-year spurts."[61] Finally, in recent years, and especially since January, 1959, efforts have been made to coordinate the public investment budgets of the ministries, departments of state, decentralized organs, and enterprises with state participation.[62]

B. SOCIAL CONDITIONS

1. *Population*

Population pressure, widely recognized as a force in stimulating economic planning,[63] has considerable effect in that regard in Mexico, where the population growth rate is among the highest in the world, at well over 3 per cent à year.[64] The population, now (1965) some forty million, increases more than one million a year, and may reach fifty million by 1970. This results from natural increase; there is little immigration. The birth rate of more than 40 per 1,000 is twice that of the United States.[65] The death rate declined from 33.3 per 1,000 in 1910 to 16.2 in 1950, and 12.5 in 1958.[66] This century will see Mexico more populous than such ancient powers as France, Italy, and the United Kingdom; but what the president of Mexico sees is the necessity of providing 350,000 new jobs annually.[67]

Mexico is becoming more urban. By the official definition that persons dwelling in places with fewer than 2,500 inhabitants are rural, the population was 65 per cent rural in 1940, 57 per cent in 1950, 55.4 per cent in 1958, and 49.3 per cent in 1963.[68] The trend is clear enough, despite dispute as to the value of the government's definition.[69] Also clear is the fact that the rural population remains so large as to constitute a massive problem in economic development and planning. The movement to the city is partly due to the attraction of better income opportunities; and it may be in part due to pressure on the land, as indicated by the fact that it occurs most heavily in central Mexico, where population density is greatest and agricultural methods poor,[70] and where job opportunities are greatest.

The growth of Mexico City is a phenomenon of such size as to deserve separate attention, since it creates great problems for government.[71] The city leaped from 1.5 million in 1940 to 2.2 million in 1950, and over 4.5 million today, making it possibly the sixth largest city in the world. And the metropolis holds an increasing percentage of the total national population: 7.3 per cent in 1940, 8.6 per cent in 1950, and 13 per cent in 1960.[72]

2. *Social Divisions and Income Levels*

Some quantitative and qualitative data exist on Mexican levels of living, income distribution, and class and cultural divisions. They are, however, intermittently illuminated and obscured by the differing techniques and attitudes of humanitarian passion, self-interest, and objective analysis. Most importantly, there is little doubt that social mobility has been increasing; but the rate of change is difficult to determine.

a. *Class and Cultural Divisions*. Definition of class or cultural division in Mexico is, for economic development purposes, primarily of interest for the light it sheds on the percentage of the population involved in, touched by, or attracted to the modern as opposed to the traditional society. This is a matter of practical import because cultural pluralism adds expense, physical and intellectual, to planning and development efforts. Light on this matter is shed in a variety of ways by data on rural-urban residence, literacy, per capita income, use of Indian languages, involvement in other ways in the Indian or the European cultural complexes (e.g., eating wheat bread, wearing shoes), and by occupational status. Although these may be only grossly suggestive, they do provide useful guides to socioeconomic development policy, and to supporting political activity. If it be said that in the psychological realm they provide only the basis for crude guesses as to human reactions and motivation,[73] it must be noted that Mexico's numerous talented political leaders—informed by the vast communications apparatus of the PRI—need little more for effective action. The most obvious dualisms in Mexico involve Indian and European culture, levels of income, achievement motivations, and training levels (with simple literacy the crudest measure).

Indianness is difficult to define, except in terms of language. Persons speaking only Indian languages declined by 35 per cent in 1940–50 (from 1.23 million to 795,069). So in 1950 less than 4 per cent of the population (five years and older) could speak no Spanish, and another 9 per cent spoke both Spanish and an Indian tongue. Thus the population monolingual in an Indian idiom is disappearing quite rapidly; but the bilingual population will long remain, partly because it is concentrated geographically.[74] To be sure, cultural pluralism is not just a matter of Indianness[75] but of ways of living and thinking.[76] Attachment to the village and to local components thereof (whatever their Indianness, if any) remains strong, and attachment to the nation and its goals still is weak or diffuse with many Mexicans.

Aside from the Indian question, some tentative efforts have been made to suggest class categories for Mexico. Cline founds his categories on occupational status, monthly income levels, and 300 pesos per month as "adequate." He suggests, tentatively, that of the economically active population in 1956: 5 per cent was "upper class" ("leisure" 1 per cent, "semi-leisure" 4 per cent), 30 per cent was "middle class" ("stable" 15 per cent, "marginal" 15 per cent), 20 per cent was "transitional," and 45 per cent was "popular."[77] Cline's categories support his general thesis that the Mexican politicogovernmental system has been greatly improving the social order, a conclusion bitterly disputed by some observers.[78] Some other efforts to suggest class categories in Mexico have put more stress than Cline does on such factors as training levels or achievement motivation.[79] It is common to suggest "class" divisions by occupational status,[80] although this is not very helpful. But the most serious controversy revolves around income levels and income distribution.

b. *Levels of Living and Income Distribution.* Income levels and distribution may not be the most important measures of difference between individuals and groups in Mexico, but many people affect to consider that they are.[81] In any event, the reduction of cultural dualism or pluralism in Mexico is related to the increase and distribution of national income. And it is a warm political issue. Income distribution, with the concomitant question of levels of living, arouses there—as elsewhere—on the one hand appeals to justice without reference to technical problems, and on the other hand dispute over consumer demand versus production facilities as the key to paradise.

A critical question with regard to levels of living is actual personal or household income, rather than statistical averages of per capita income on a national basis.[82] Similarly, comparisons with other countries are of only general interest.[83] Although considerable data are available on actual income distribution, they are for reported cash income. This can be quite misleading in a country with Mexico's socioeconomic arrangements.[84] It often has been pointed out that where so many live on the land, wage rates cannot be relied on as the sole measure of the welfare of the poor. The following are only some of the other factors that must be borne in mind. The cost of many of the essentials of existence, in the forms used by the poor, is quite low. Social security benefits, free medical assistance, and other welfare services are available to considerable numbers of low-income people. There are family and kinship systems of mutual assistance. There are some benevolent bosses (*patrones*) who give aid to their workers in addition to assistance provided by social security and workers' associations. Some income that is not reported is sent to families in Mexico by relatives in the United States. There are many moonlighters in Mexico, holding more than one job, some of whose earnings escape tabulation. Itinerant mechanics, peddlers, street performers, bootblacks, and others sometimes earn fairly good money without providing much information to statisticians. Many servants receive clothing, medical care, room and board, and other compensation in addition to wages. The bribery (*mordida*) system supplements the salaries of many police, judges, local politicians, bureaucrats, water-light-gas men, border officials, all kinds of inspectors, and even such minor personnel as eye-examiners in the drivers' license bureau.[85]

Cline and Ifigenia de Navarrete have provided us with recent statements on family income and its adequacy that differ sharply in detail and in interpretation. Cline shows for economically active individuals in 1956: some 13 per cent with incomes of over 1,000 pesos a month, 48 per cent with 300-1,000, 17.5 per cent with 200-300 (which Cline calls "transitional" between inadequate and adequate), and 21.5 per cent under 200.[86] Navarrete claims that 700 pesos a month per family is the minimum necessary for food, clothing, and diversion, and finds average family income to be 536 pesos in 1950 and 1,024 in 1957. The two authors agree that there are some inadequacies in their data. They obviously have done nothing to clarify the question of what a family "needs" in Mexico.[87] It may be noted that the new minimum wage set in the Federal District in 1964 apparently would provide about 537 pesos a month.[88] Finally, it may be observed that not even the experts of the Economic and Social Council of the Organization of American States find it possible to deal very firmly with the question of income distribution in Mexico.[89]

Also bitterly disputed in Mexico is the question of whether or not the popular classes are improving their position. Cline states that he has no doubt of this. Navarrete claims that the income of the poorest part of the population has declined in recent years. This—at least in much discussion of her work—has obscured her accompanying statement that the size of this "poorest" group is decreasing. Specifically, she claims that the benefits of economic development have in recent years been going only to that part of the population that gets an income equal to or greater than the average income, but that this group increased from 30 to 35 per cent of the total population in 1950–57. Some other careful observers assert quite strongly that a good many people have been improving their income positions in recent years—aside from the questions of whether they are getting their "proper" share, or whether everyone has improved his position, which no one believes.[90]

There are other observations to make about Mexican income distribution and living levels. Average incomes are higher in some parts of the country than in others, with the Federal District especially favored.[91] It is accepted that the cash income of huge numbers of rural dwellers is quite low, and that it may have declined (in real terms) during the boom years since 1940. It is agreed also that the rural population is declining steadily as a proportion of the total national population. It is agreed that the urban population as a whole enjoys a much higher average income than the rural, although we do not know exactly what family income is. It seems to be agreed—often by silence—that most of the population enjoys a reasonably adequate caloric intake, even if for many it is little more than barely adequate.[92] There certainly is much poverty in Mexico, with an "average" per capita income of some $400. Some observers prefer to emphasize that a huge population still is miserable (meaning poor), that squatters in their land-hunger seize property, that "hunger marchers" are afoot (though it is not always clear that they are hungry), and that much remains to be done. Some objective observers—for example, Scott and Cline—are fairly firm that casual observation over the years gives a rather clear indication of rising living levels. Possibly this testimony is not so contemptible as sometimes is pretended. Finally, to turn to another aspect of the question, there has been considerable recent discussion as to whether popular cash income is sufficient to support all the new industrial structure of the country.[93]

Could income have been channeled much more to the popular classes? The political answer is that it had its adovcates and they were overruled. But the political aspect of the matter is embarrassing to critics, and they prefer not to meet it directly. The economic answer is that it would have increased certain kinds of purchasing power, and might have immediately slowed investment, and no one could possibly be sure of the effects on economic development. To resort, as some critics do, to the non-answer that it would have been just, is only to say that justice for the popular classes today assuredly would guarantee justice for their posterity. No persuasive brief exists for this theory of economic development. Economic development without sacrifice—at least of immediate improvement—by somebody is a contradiction in terms, and its apportionment puts as much strain on economic technique and the political art as on the moral standards of developers.[94]

Large numbers of Mexican males of working age are unemployed or underemployed. One must remember, however, that the Mexican age profile bulges at the younger levels, so that there is a heavy percentage of males who would be considered of preworking age in economically better developed countries. According to one study, in 1950 possibly 12 per cent of Mexican workers were unremunerated, principally in agriculture.[95] There is no question, in any event, but that there is a large rural population that is underused economically. It also should be noted that considerable numbers of domestic servants and self-employed petty merchants and service workers are "employed" in the sense of receiving income—in money or otherwise—but do not appear in the statistics. Finally, it must be observed that while the Mexican government frequently emphasizes the necessity of providing more employment, and even lays this down as one of the purposes of economic development, it does not have the same problem of defending itself against levels of "unemployment" that exists in highly industrialized countries. Thus, the Mexican government can ignore the rural unemployed and underemployed when issuing statistics on unemployment, and speak of the "temporarily unemployed" in 1960 as 1.2 per cent of the economically active population.[96]

The economically active proportion of the population has grown modestly in recent years, from 29.8 per cent of total population in 1940, to 32.3 per cent in 1950, to 32.4 per cent in 1960. Thus, the number of the economically inactive sustained by each 1,000 active inhabitants declined from 2,543 in 1940, to 2,090 in 1950, to 2,081 in 1960. There seems to be considerable doubt as to the number of women in the economically active group. More than half of the economically active population is in agriculture and stockraising, though the percentage declined considerably between 1940 and 1960—from 65.4 per cent to 54.2 per cent of total actives.[97]

How many, and which, of the populace feel outraged or badly abused by historic and actual income distribution? The tentative answer to this question would seem to suggest answers to some of the earlier questions. There is no evidence of massive active dissatisfaction.[98] To the despair of the opposition, the Mexican population does not seem very demanding. The constant controversy (especially in Mexico City) over wages and other income may in part betoken a continued confidence in PRI and government. The restless may be thought of as still having some hope. The industrial labor group is favored in many ways (housing, medical care, education, social security), and many of them have recollections of a previous less satisfactory condition. The poor farmer has received many social and economic attentions that are difficult to measure in money. Above all, the popular class in both town and country constantly is wooed by party and government promises of a greener future. There are, as indicated, critics who call for reforms in income distribution, some on moral, some on technical, grounds.

As to government action, one may hazard that (1) any drastic effort toward redistribution in favor of wages for the popular classes is unlikely, but that (2) the government will give considerable well-publicized attention to the problem of improving popular living levels. The government and the PRI have for some years been displaying an increasing awareness of the expediency of fuller discussion of the charge of inequity, and this was notably evident during the presidential campaign of 1963/64.[99] It seems a fair assumption that such sensitivity to political strategy will continue to find expression, while policy-makers also continue to reject the claim that economic growth requires expansion of consumer purchasing power even at the expense of investment.[100] Although there is naturally some disagreement in the government on the matter,[101] for many years emphasis on investment has been a cornerstone of government economic policy. Nor is the government likely to adopt any other of the "technical" arguments of critical economists and sociologists.[102]

3. *Education*

The optimistic view of Mexican education emphasizes the great gains made in recent decades, the widespread faith in the value of schooling, and the commitment of the government to instruction.[103] Pessimists point out that much remains to be done, that many other requirements compete for limited resources, and that inadequate training still is a serious barrier to the improvement of productivity.[104] In addition to dispute over these points, there are differences over educational philosophy, with conservatives charging that socialism is taught in the schools, and leftists that nationalism is taught as an indispensable adjunct to capitalism and membership in the PRI.[105]

The schools are predominantly public, federal, secular. The basic structure is six years primary, five years secondary in either the university preparatory (*preparatoria*) or vocational (*secundaria*) paths, and higher schooling of varying periods.[106] Much of the secondary instruction would be considered college-level in the United States. The Ministry of Education directly controls many institutions, and supervises the state public schools.[107] Ministry of Education budgets have increased greatly since the Revolution, both absolutely and as a percentage (25 per cent in 1964) of the total federal budget.[108]

Primary school enrollment has been much expanded. In 1910 only 25.4 per cent of school-age children received instruction, 32.1 per cent in 1925, and 65.62 per cent in 1960.[109] Not only do some one-third of the eligible children still receive no schooling, but many others attend school so briefly that they reach maturity as functional illiterates. The current government claim of 65 per cent literacy for the national population therefore requires some interpretation. The situation is worst in rural areas, where schools seldom offer instruction beyond the fourth grade.[110] As for postprimary instruction, in 1961 the country enrolled 158,648 in *secundarias,* 77,207 in preparatory courses, and 135,785 in higher education (77,515 federal, 39,417 state, 18,853 private).[111] Of the 135,785 in higher education in 1961, about 55 per cent were in the Federal District.[112]

Education as a support for economic growth is assured in the sense that a wide dedication to some sort of instruction exists in Mexico. It also is assured to some extent by the spirit of experiment in the Mexican system, which searches for methods adapted to the needs of the country.[113] The concentration of graduates in the "commercial" programs is one measure of the success of this process.[114] Serious problems, recognized by Mexicans, nevertheless exist: (1) finances, involving pace of growth and choices between expenditures; (2) construction of facilities, including planning for population movement and increase; (3) teacher-training, the lead-time on which is quite different from that on school-construction; (4) ensuring enrollment and attendance, a social problem of some dimensions, intimately related to family income levels, hence to economic development;[115] (5) improvement of universities from the educational point of view, a matter that relates to students in politics, more financial support for students, procuring and properly using high-level faculty, and, possibly, persuading students to modify their attachment to university autonomy.[116]

The Planning Environment: Economy

Since 1940 the economic development accomplishments of Mexico have been the most notable in Latin America, in terms of growth rates, social and economic reinvestment, and of promise for continued development. Not only has good growth been sustained for more than two decades, but it clearly is internally based. There is, of course, continual debate in Mexico regarding the rate and direction of growth. Such dispute becomes especially bitter in those years (e.g., 1961) when growth is less than the recent Mexican average. A common criticism—in both good and bad years—is that profits are too high and wage and other lower-class income too low. This judgment rests both on moral grounds, and on the argument that low wages have caused a lag in demand for consumer goods and hence underuse of production facilities, wasted investment, and a brake on growth. Partisans of the income-distribution policy of the government emphasize, of course, that savings result in increased investment and productive capacity. Possibly the second most important general debate is that over the question of whether the mix of public and private economic activity has been wholesome. Argument expended in Mexico on the ethical, to say nothing of the metaphysical, aspects of these matters occasionally tends to obscure the crude material questions involved.

A. Government and the Economy

Since 1940 it has been common for careful observers to state that the Mexican government apparently is committed to wide direction and stimulation of, and intervention in, the economy, without an intent to destroy private enterprise.[1] Some students even declare, with pleasure or irritation, that the chief aim of the government has been the expansion of the private sector of the economy, even though deed and word intermittently hint at socialism. Not all interest groups in Mexico accept these judgments. On the one hand, leftists and humanists have for years denounced the "business orientation" of PRI and government, claiming that it is the central fact of economic decision-making, and that it represents an unholy and deliberately obscured alliance and a betrayal of the Revolution. On the other hand, the organized business community expresses fears that the aim of the government is socialism. The government, with patient agility, strives for consensus by soothing the left with land distribution to peasants and with nationalization of selected activities and Mexicanization of more, while calming the right with profits and an unremitting stream of reassurance.[2]

For at least twenty years it has been government policy to: (1) promote industrialization as the chief hope of the future; (2) leave much of the industrial and commercial activity of the country to private enterprise; (3) strive for agricultural self-sufficiency, promote production of export crops, and foster both communal and private farming; (4) promote national private and/or public ownership or control of subsurface resources and public utilities. Argument is incessant as to whether, and to what extent, and in what fashion, and at what pace, specific government actions support these aims. There is much detection of trends in few occurrences, and much imagination spent in reading ideological implications into the statements of notably pragmatic public officials.

Government intervention includes controls of all sorts, and direct ownership of some economic enterprises and participation in others. Controls and regulations affect all sectors of the economy, and include such familiar practices as management of money, credit, banking, and foreign exchange; tariffs for protection; import quotas; taxation for development as well as for revenue; price controls. Government fiscal management has been so good in Mexico as to constitute a major reason for the satisfactory growth of the economy.[3] There are extensive controls over labor. The subsurface resources of Mexico are reserved to the nation. And the entire system of control and regulation is increased by the discretionary power of executive departments to interpret and administer legislation. Although the intervention represented by the preceding partial list stimulates extended oratory, much of the debate centers on government ownership of economic enterprise, participation in and direction of investment, attitudes toward profits, and the over-all nature, extent, and tendency of the government's influence on the economy.[4]

Government ownership receives much attention from critics but is only one aspect of government participation in the economy. The railways, and petroleum production and distribution, have been state enterprises for a generation. The electric power industry is largely a state enterprise. The nationalization of a large group of private electric companies in 1960 did not fatally wound the sensibilities of private enterprise generally. For some years the public segment of the electric power industry had been growing more rapidly than the private, so the trend was well recognized; furthermore, the terms of sale were satisfactory to the companies. There is extensive government participation in communications, the production of fertilizers, aviation, and some in mining and other fields. The government role in finance is large. Nacional Financiera participates extensively in the ownership of industrial enterprise, including iron and steel. It is a moot question whether the long-term tendency of Nacional Financiera's operations will be to increase the government's share in ownership of economic enterprise,[5] and unclear how much of its ownership the state ever will relinquish.[6] With such extensive state ownership, it is not to be wondered that the pricing policies of government enterprise (e.g., petroleum products, electric energy) offer a fertile field for conflict on economic questions and on economic as opposed to social or political objectives.[7]

In 1959 the total public sector contribution to GNP was 9.5 per cent, considerably less than in some well-developed countries of Western Europe. Furthermore, much of the government activity has stimulated growth of the private sector. This is true not only in such fields as transportation and electric power, but clearly in investment, where government activity is large enough to be described as decisive.[8] The role of government can be made to seem greater by emphasizing state ownership of the largest individual enterprises in Mexico: (1) the 11 largest are 100 per cent state enterprises; (2) there is some government equity in 19 of the top 30 enterprises (the government owns 14 outright, has a majority interest in two, a minority interest in 3). One of the misleading aspects of this analysis is that it offers no information on the total private investment in the country.[9] In any event, it may be said that the private sector is large, that it is in many ways fostered and protected by government, and that there is no reason to predict state ownership of all the means of production in the foreseeable future.[10]

B. PRODUCTION

1. *General*

The growth of production in Mexico in recent decades has been impressive. In 1930 national production was little greater than in 1910, the year the Revolution began; but from 1930 to 1959 it almost quintupled, in real terms, from 14.73 billion pesos to 63.40 billion, while the population only doubled. There was thus in 1930–59 a per capita increase in production of more than 200 per cent in real terms. Also striking was the decline in the relative importance of agriculture, stock-raising, and mining, and the great growth in manufacturing and other activities. (See Table 2, below.) Whereas in 1910 agriculture and stock combined accounted for twice as much of the value of national production as manufactures, by 1961 the latter accounted for 25.6 per cent of GNP and agriculture and stock for 20.4 per cent. Put more generally, there was a gradual modification of the economy toward secondary activities, along with a tendency toward diversification of products. A clearly underdeveloped country in 1930, Mexico within three decades became a "developing" or "semiindustrialized" country.[11]

TABLE 2
GROSS NATIONAL PRODUCT BY ACTIVITIES, 1910, 1930, 1959[12]

Activities	(Millions of pesos at 1950 prices) 1910	1930	1959
Agriculture	2,308	1,800	8,193
Stockraising	919	1,004	2,514
Mining	955	1,337	1,270
Petroleum	13	247	1,488
Manufactures	1,653	1,776	13,062
Transportation	369	582	2,687
Other*	7,212	8,027	34,186
	13,429	14,773	63,400

* Forestry, fisheries, construction, electricity, commerce, finance, government.

Growth was most rapid at the beginning of the great spurt forward after 1940. Annual growth in real terms averaged 7.5 per cent in the 1940's, and between 5 and 6 per cent in the 1950's; and the government hopes to hold approximately the latter average in the 1960's. There have been, of course, considerable fluctuations in growth from year to year. A poor year always spurs the government to drastic measures to restore the momentum of the growth process, and incidentally faith in populace and interest groups in the establishment's ability and determination to continue the march toward plenty. The latest crisis occurred when the growth of 5.7 per cent in 1960 was succeeded by 3.1 per cent in 1961. With a population increase in the latter year of over 3 per cent, the economy stood still in terms of production on a per capita basis. There were many hysterical and splenetic predictions that growth was stalled permanently unless fundamental changes in economic policy were adopted. Many critics seemed genuinely unaware that often in the past the process of growth had temporarily slowed, only to recover. The government acted energetically, and apparently with considerable success. In any event, growth (in real terms) recovered in 1962 to about 5 per cent, to 6 per cent in 1963, and in 1964 a splendid 10 per cent (unmatched since 1954), with every sign of continuing boom in 1965.[13] Furthermore, some growth figures for the past have recently been revised upward by the Bank of Mexico. (See Appendix XII.)[14]

The relation of agricultural to industrial growth is, understandably, a delicate political question in Mexico. As I have written elsewhere,[15] this is

> an area in which everyone seems to fashion his own intellectual and emotional machete out of the statistics, picking the years and the factors that will hone the cutting edge to his need. If one wants to show the neglect of agricultural production, it is clever to state that in the twenty-two years, 1939–60, the value of agricultural production (at 1950 prices) increased 193% while that of manufactures soared 334%. The production figures will sustain this. The comparison, however, has a greater utility in political than in economic discussion. In the seven years, 1939–45, agriculture grew only 14%, while manufactures grew 68%, or nearly five times as fast. But in the next fifteen years, 1946–60, they grew at the same rate (138% for agriculture, 140% for manufactures). What happens is that if one figures from the relatively small absolute value of manufactures in 1939, and the large percentage increase in 1939–45, there emerges a "true" but misleading picture of what happened in the entire twenty-two years, 1939–60, whether one calculates percentage growth for the entire period or average percentage gains per year during the entire period.

Rapid and sustained economic growth in Mexico has been variously explained. The following factors may with some confidence be supposed to enter somehow into the explanation. First, the existence and expectation of public order and wide public consensus are at a high level. Ample evidence suggests that a serious deterioration of order or consensus might have grave effects on investment. Second, there are successful government controls over money and credit, prices, the foreign exchange value of the peso, and the country's international balance of payments. Third, there has been almost uninterrupted success in promoting the growth of commodity exports and of foreign tourism. Fourth, unsleeping attention has been paid to the maintenance of a high level of investment. Fifth, there has been considerable success in obtaining and effectively using managerial skills, both in public and in private activities. Sixth, recruitment into the modern sector of the economy from the big national pool of unemployed and underemployed persons of labor under conditions of compensation favorable to growth in terms of profitable operation has been accomplished. Seventh, the system seems to have been successful in offering incentives to performance at a reasonably high level. Eighth, markets and distribution systems have developed—with some planning—in approximately satisfactory rhythm with the growth of production capacity. The government has helped by providing protection from foreign competition. The development of the economy in so many lines simultaneously has provided individual and institutional income for an expanding demand for goods. The development of the national market has been subsidized through the construction of a state-owned transportation and communications system. Ninth, not only transportation, but other economic and social infrastructure essential to growth, have been built on a large scale by the state. Tenth, industrial integration would seem to have proceeded at a sensible place in terms of resources and demand.

This, of course, says nothing about why, or even how, these things occurred. How the PRI has managed to preserve order on a basis of consensus is something no one has adequately explained. Who knows why the Mexican popular classes are not more demanding? Granted that the pace of industrial integration has been sound, has this been the result of government action to secure this result, or did that action merely coincide with what was about to occur in any event as the result of decisions by private entrepreneurs?

2. *Agriculture*

Mexico is a big country, but agricultural land use encounters serious problems relating to mountain terrain[16] and insufficient or seasonal rainfall.[17] Natural obstacles are complicated by cultural shortcomings, including wide use of poor agricultural technology, concentration of farming folk in some of the least productive zones, and poor transportation. Production has, nevertheless, been greatly increased in recent years. This has been the result both of an increase in the cultivated area,[18] and of improved productivity.[19] Mexico now is nearly self-sufficient in agricultural commodities, and has a valuable export traffic. Unemployment and underemployment in agricultural areas is, however, far from solution. There was a recent crisis in growth, in that the value of agricultural production did not increase in per capita terms in 1960, declined in 1961, and barely grew in 1962.[20]

Mexico is the rare underdeveloped or developing country that has devoted large resources to agricultural growth while promoting industry rapidly. Also unusual in much of the western world is the large population on communal (*ejidal*) holdings. In 1930–59 *ejidal* land in cultivation increased from 1.9 million hectares to 8.8 million, while private property in cultivation declined from 12.7 million to 11.1 million hectares.[21] Lands distributed to peasants (not all in *ejidos*) from the Revolution to 1963 total some 53.5 million hectares (about 132 million acres).

Productivity on *ejidal* lands is lower than on private holdings.[22] This may be partly due to the low quality of some *ejidal* lands, but poor technology probably is the more important reason. The known productive shortcomings of the *ejidos* often must be overlooked because of their presumed social value, and because of the certain political potency of the tradition of agrarian reform.[23] To raise significantly the productivity of the *ejidal* segment of the agricultural population, which suffers from illiteracy, a lack of capital, and an antique productive culture, would require an investment that the government has been reluctant to make, in view of the fact that returns might be slow.[24] Private capital is not, of course, attracted to the *ejidos*.[25] Another important feature of agricultural development is the large investment in irrigation works, the economic justification for which sometimes is disputed.[26]

Possibly half the population still is directly dependent on agriculture,[27] including stockraising, but the industry probably does not account for more than 20 per cent of GNP.[28] The production of food crops has more than kept pace with the lively population growth.[29] This has contributed to an improvement of the diet of the average Mexican,[30] although one of the lowest increases in productivity in 1930–59 was realized on maize lands, much of which are poorly worked by small holders and *ejidatarios*.[31] Export agriculture has been nurtured carefully by the government, in terms of both increases in production and diversification of crops. These procedures have yielded benefits in both increased exports and in flattening the curve of fluctuation of agricultural exports.[32]

3. *Manufacturing and Energy Production*

Industrialization as the chief hope of the future is the oft-repeated doctrine of PRI and government. The numerous devices employed by government to encourage this growth are discussed elsewhere in this study. Suffice it to say here that these devices presumably have played some role in the great increase in the capitalization of industry,[33] and in the growth of production.

The value of manufactures increased 68 per cent in 1939–45, and another 140 per cent in 1946–60. The average annual increase of the value of manufactures was 5.8 per cent in 1945–59, 8.6 per cent in 1960, 3.5 per cent in 1961, 7 per cent in 1962, and 8.2 per cent in

1963. Growth rates tended to be higher than the average in petroleum, steel, electric energy, and sometimes in transportation. Expressed in other terms, the physical volume of manufactures doubled in 1931–45, and more than doubled again in 1946–59.[34] In 1939–61 manufacturing increased its share of national production by value from 15 per cent to 25.6 per cent.[35] Industrial employment increased 535 per cent in 1930–60, from 313,153 persons to 1.98 million, much faster than population increase.

The country is not far from self-sufficiency in a wide range of consumer goods. In recent years, industrial growth has been greater in producer than consumer goods. Recent changes in industrial production include lesser percentages devoted to food processing and to textile production, and increasing percentages in chemicals, steel, and machinery.[36] A large proportion of industry is concentrated in the Federal District and in a few other places in Mexico.[37] There has been a recent considerable percentage increase in Mexico's export of manufactures.

Many types of criticism are leveled at industrial growth in Mexico. The very idea of emphasis on it is viewed askance by some leftists and humanists who retain an antique affection for husbandry as somehow related to the wholesome society; who tend to view industry as the handmaid of conservatism, corruption, foreign influence, and science; and who contend that the doctrine as implemented has cruelly and unnecessarily pinched the huge farming population. Much of this, as we observed above, is based on careful selection of statistics. Of course, the government also makes its own choices and emphases.[38] Other criticisms include the charge that high tariff protection has resulted in unrealistic pricing and in underuse of production capacity, and failure to provide sufficient employment.[39]

Some discussions of manufacturing growth in Mexico neglect the linkages between manufacturing and other economic activity and social development. It has helped provide managers and technicians for other sectors. It has created demands for supplies and services of all sorts, contributing to the growth of commerce, construction, and services. It is oriented not only toward accountancy and statistics but also toward science and technology generally, and thus contributes to their improvement in the face of the tradition of concentration on the humanities in the Hispanic world.[40]

4. *Mining*

Known and suspected reserves of minerals in Mexico are quite large. The importance of mineral exports is still considerable, although the trend is downward. They were more than half of total exports at the beginning of the Revolution, fell to 35 per cent in 1950, and to 25.5 per cent of total exports in 1960 and 1961. Production simply has tended to stagnate. Mineral production, expressed in 1950 prices, was 955 million pesos in 1910, and 1,270 million a half-century later in 1959. In 1947–61 the value of mineral production increased a mere 13.5 per cent. Nor was this merely a matter of prices: in 1900–60 the physical volume of mineral production barely increased. As a consequence of these conditions, in a time when other production was soaring, the mining share of GNP fell from 6 per cent in 1940 to 2 per cent in 1963.

Mining has been in the doldrums for various reasons. Weakness of international demand for traditionally important copper, lead, and zinc has been part of it. Also important is government policy which inhibits investments in the privately owned mining industry: high taxes, fears of nationalization of "nonrenewable natural resources," and the law requiring Mexicanization (51 per cent Mexican ownership) of mining properties. Nor has the government chosen to channel public funds into mining as a whole. The question is open, however, whether much more investment in mining would have produced important results, since foreign and domestic market conditions were unfavorable to growth.

The government has tended to take action to assist in mineral growth where opportunities develop. It is government policy to stimulate domestic elaboration of minerals and to increase their export as manufactures, rather than as raw materials. When domestic demands have increased, production seems to have risen to meet them. The dependence of mining on exports has been declining: 70 per cent was exported in 1960. Domestic copper production has increased considerably in recent years. Iron ore production, to serve domestic industry, rose from 103,000 tons in 1942 to 313,000 in 1951 and to 1.09 million in 1962. There has been much recent growth in the production of nonmetallic minerals, both to serve domestic needs and to take advantage of new export opportunities. The rise in sulphur production is most important, both because of the magnitude of Mexican development and because of the importance of sulphuric acid in the new Mexican chemical industry. Sulphur production was a mere 2,000 tons in 1948, 492,000 in 1955, and 1.31 million in 1959, by which time Mexico was a significant contributor to world production, supplying the United States with 78 per cent of the latter's 851,000 tons of sulphur imports.[41]

5. *Other Goods and Services*

As the economy has been modernized, the commercial, financial, and service occupations naturally have grown to serve the new structure and the population enjoying increased income from its operations. Commercial activity accounts for about a fifth of national product, a situation often harped on by critics. Commerce in 1960 occupied 9 per cent (1.08 million) of the economically active, but accounted for 20.9 per cent of national product, which critics like to compare with agriculture's 54 per cent of the economically active and 20.4 per cent of the national product in the same year. It should be noted that commerce's share of national product was slightly less in 1960 than in the 1950's (and agriculture's share also declined slightly).[42] Workers in service occupations increased rapidly in 1950–60, from 877,000 to 1.5 million, or 58 per cent.[43] Although the construction industry accounted for only 3.5 per cent of national product in 1960 (and this was only a slightly higher percentage than in 1950),[44] it is often criticized on the grounds that too much activity is in private luxury residential building. Communications activity of all sorts has increased a great deal in recent years, with the growth of the literate population and the great increase of income among a large part of the population.[45] The highway, railway, and airline services of Mexico have been much expanded and improved in recent decades by heavy government investment and other action. This has been an indispensable basis for growth in all sectors of the economy. It also has promoted such things as the private haulage business, one factor in the recent decision to establish a domestic motor vehicle manufacturing industry, and was of critical importance in the promotion of tourism.[46] This last is a major industry, bringing 750,390 visitors to Mexico in 1959, compared with 238,508 in 1946.[47] The net return from tourism in 1961 was calculated at $386 million, making it the single most valuable earner of foreign exchange. Thus tourism is an important factor in giving Mexico a generally satisfactory balance of payments situation; in addition, this influx of foreigners has had effects on social attitudes in the country, some of them surely favorable to modernization.

6. *International Trade*

For the present study, possibly the following points are most important in connection with Mexico's foreign trade and international balance of payments situation.

(1) Merchandise exports and imports grew impressively in value after 1940, but slowed seriously in the late 1950's and early 1960's: from 1.62 billion pesos in 1940, to 22.95 billion in 1958, but only 24.95 billion in 1961, but a considerably better increase to 26.38 billion in 1962,[48] and a rise to 27.13 billion in 1963.[49] New highs were set in 1964. The slowdown for several years was due to weakness in the inter-

national market for most of Mexico's biggest exports in the period after 1940: cotton, coffee, copper, lead, and petroleum products. The slowdown in merchandise exports was a main cause of Mexican economic policy modification and discussion.[50]

(2) Contemporary Mexico commonly has a deficit in her merchandise exchange accounts,[51] but this is offset by other payments.

(3) There has been a recent notable diversification of merchandise exports, in response to the declining value of old exports, and in response to new opportunities. The older six top exports (the above five, plus zinc) accounted for 94.5 per cent of total value of merchandise exports in 1954, 76 per cent in 1955, and continued to decline to 45.8 per cent in 1960. At the same time the peso value of merchandise exports was increasing from 7.69 billion to 91.2 billion, indicating a large increase in the value of other export commodities than those of the old leader group.[52] There has been a large recent increase in manufactured exports,[53] signifying some improvement in demand due to the Latin American Free Trade Agreement (LAFTA), and productive capacity in excess of Mexican demand.[54] Much of this increase in manufactured exports involved simply refined products, but there has been a considerable percentage increase in exports of durable producers' goods.

(4) Mineral exports continue to account for a considerable portion of the value of exports (25.5 per cent in 1961), although their share has been more than halved since the Revolution. Minerals are thus much more important in exports than in GNP. Although mineral exports as a whole have been weak, there have been large increases in exports of nonmetallic minerals, where government activity spurred action to take advantage of new opportunities.

(5) Agricultural and stock products account for more than half of total commodity exports, and thus represent an important source of revenue for the promotion of economic growth generally.[55]

(6) There is a trend of increase in capital goods imports,[56] reflecting in part the growth of domestic production of consumer goods and in part the building of productive capacity.

(7) On the whole the balance-of-payments situation has been satisfactory, because of government care[57] and because of the great growth of three types of income originating largely in the United States: border transactions, *bracero* remittances,[58] and tourism. Government sensitivity to the balance of payments is well known. Critics describe it as "notorious," and assert that balance-of-payments problems are the only thing that ever impels the Mexican government to effective planning. Be this as it may, the government responds quickly to payments pressures by restricting imports, especially by public-sector importers, and by intensifying efforts to develop new export commodities.

C. Investment

1. *General*

Investment is a focal point of the Mexican government's economic strategy. Some observers hold that it is the field in which the nearest approach to national planning is achieved. For more than a decade the government has increasingly tried to increase the coordination—or planning—and control of public investment, and has more recently at least made preliminary moves to try to mesh more effectively public and private investment programs. The government declares—and probably means—that it would prefer to achieve better investment planning without increasing the public share of investment.

It may be noted of the recent history of investment in Mexico that: (1) post-Revolution investment has been mostly (about 90 per cent) domestic; (2) public investment since about 1940 has averaged some 40 per cent of total investment, but has been higher than that in 1962–64; (3) the government is sincere in its declared desire to leave much investment to the private sector; (4) government is not much impressed with the cries of critics for drastic action to correct the alleged excessive timidity or profit-hunger of domestic private capital; (5) the government is alive to the sensitivity of investors to real or fancied threats to political stability or private enterprise and to their ability to shift funds before the government can intervene effectively; (6) the government is chiefly concerned with the manipulation of improved profit-making opportunities in selected lines;[59] (7) there has been an expected decline of public investment in immediately productive high-yield projects, with a consequent increase in slowly maturing, capital-intensive enterprises;[60] (8) the levels and growth rates of investment have tended to be sufficient to support substantial per capita increases in production; (9) the decline in production growth in 1961, which was associated with serious slowdown in private investment, domestic and foreign, led to reassessment of the fiscal and other methods by which investment is induced and directed by the government;[61] (10) the decline also led to an increase in domestic public investment and in the use of foreign public credits.[62]

2. *Amount, Rate, Direction of Investment*

For some years after the Revolution of 1910–17 investment was low. There was some improvement from the mid-twenties, but the great investment growth came in the 1940's and thereafter.[63] The average annual investment growth in real terms in 1939–50 was 10.5 per cent;[64] in 1950–59 the increase averaged only 5.6 per cent annually.[65] Investment increased 13.5 per cent in 1960, but only 4.6 per cent in 1961, and 0.3 per cent in 1962.[66] Investment recovered, however, in 1963 with a growth of 11.3 per cent,[67] and continued high in 1964 and 1965. The slowdown in investment in 1961/62, coinciding with a slowdown in production growth, provoked a flurry of political controversy and of government corrective actions. The proportion of national product put into investment in 1939–50 was 12.8 per cent, with quite a favorable result during the war years because plant was used to capacity.[68] The percentage of product devoted to investment in 1950–59 rose substantially, to 14.8;[69] it was 14.6 per cent in 1959;[70] and 15.8 per cent in 1960.[71] The direction of investment has been heavily to industry, which accounted for 54 per cent of total domestic credits as of May, 1962, which was nearly three times that accounted for by agriculture and stock-raising combined, and nearly twice that for commerce.[72]

3. *Domestic and Foreign Shares of Investment*

For some years about nine-tenths of Mexican investment has been generated internally, although recently foreign investment has increased slightly. The drying-up of domestic and foreign private investment in 1960–62 led the government to intensify its efforts to obtain foreign public credits, and stimulated its interest in the Alliance for Progress, as a means of furthering that process, especially if long-term loans at little or no interest were to be forthcoming. The fright and flight of private capital were quickly dissipated in the face of the normally moderate policies of the government, and by 1964 there was a mild boom in United States private investment in Mexico.[73] Nearly all foreign investment now is direct investment, and in the last generation it has shifted drastically from transportation and mining, especially toward industry.[74]

In the 1939–50 period of rapid growth of production, foreign investment averaged 8 per cent annually of total investment; in 1950–59, when the production growth rate and total investment growth slowed, the foreign share of investment rose to 12 per cent.[75] Of total investment of 20.84 billion pesos in 1961, foreign loans accounted for 15 per cent. Net foreign investment was, however, considerably less due to amortization and interest payments on foreign loans.[76] The Mexican government since 1962 has worked hard, with some success, to increase the foreign share of investment,[77] and especially low-interest loans from international agencies.[78] In recent years the United States share of foreign credits to Mexico has been declining, partly as a result of Mexican efforts to reduce dependence on one source.[79]

4. *Public and Private Shares of Investment*

For many years the public share of total investment fluctuated moderately above and below 40 per cent,[80] and it is not clear whether the very recent increase in the public share will be long sustained, or at what level.[81] The public share of total investment was 40 per cent in 1939–50,[82] and somewhat lower in 1950–59, due in part to decreased government income as a percentage of national product.[83] Public investment rose to 42 per cent of 1960 total investment;[84] to 50.5 per cent in 1961;[85] and to nearly 55 per cent in 1962.[86]

Until recently, more than one-half of the public investment was from the federal fisc, which makes important investments in the independent and state participation agencies. The latter two types of institutions make investments from their own revenues and by internal or external financing. In 1950–59 the proportion of public investment contributed by the fisc as compared with that coming from the operations of the decentralized organs and state participation enterprises was higher than in 1939–50,[87] Government investment from the federal budget in 1950 was 61 per cent of total public investment, and even higher in 1951–53; but thereafter the *organismos* and *empresas* generally increased their share, so that in 1960–62 it was about 50 per cent of total public investment. The state enterprises handle most of this investment; the share of the decentralized organs is minor.[88]

The direction of private investment has been heavily to industry and to commerce, with much less to agriculture and livestock, and almost nothing to mining; and of course large fields are either preempted by the state or unattractive to private investors (e.g., electricity, railways, petroleum production and distribution, and some of the petrochemical industry).[89] Private investment is geographically quite concentrated near the largest cities, as might be expected from its interests.[90]

Since public investment is directed especially to economic and social infrastructure, which improves productivity and access to materials and markets, its effects are in many respects highly beneficial to private enterprise, as the government constantly insists.[91] For example, in 1939–59 public investment in transportation and communications increased eighteen times, from 143.2 million pesos in 1939 to 2,790.3 million in 1959, and a total during those years of 21,757.5 million pesos.[92]

IV

History of Mexican Planning

The men of the Revolution repudiated the economic philosophy of the Díaz régime, but neither group was acquainted with planning in the modern sense. The early post-Revolutionary administrations were preoccupied with matters of public order and political discipline, indispensable preconditions for economic development. Cárdenas popularized the idea of national socioeconomic development under broadening government auspices and publicized the notion of planning. During and after the Second World War, with the great push for industrialization in Mexico, there was much development of sectoral and regional planning, accompanied by growth of the institutions and skills they required. Recent years have seen a movement toward broader national planning, spurred by the asserted need for better coordination of the multiplying facets of public socioeconomic development, and of integrating them with the activities of private enterprise. Apparently there will be increasing integration, but it is not clear what the mix of conciliation and cooperation and coercion between public agencies and private enterprise will be.

A. To 1933

The Porfiriato (1876–1911) made a contribution to later planning in the sense that the reaction to it helped define Mexican attitudes toward economic development after its fall. The régime of Porfirio Díaz held to an interpretation of *laissez faire* that encouraged growth of the hacienda system, at the expense of the general rural populace; and a narrow industrial, mineral, and commercial expansion, for the benefit of the entrepreneur and his governmental allies, and without regard for the laborer. Elites in other Latin American countries in the same years held to similar principles. This rigorously channeled development policy of Porfirian Mexico was supported by a brutal system of preserving public order and popular quiescence, and by inducements to foreign capital that quickly resulted in the alienation of much of the resource base of the country. If the aims of the Porfirian elites included even theoretical and remote concern for the ultimate welfare of the commonalty, it was so nebulous as to defy description—and no one is left who is willing to try.[1]

The Revolution of 1910–17 drastically reduced the power of the old propertied class, and of its ally the Church. It produced some largely egalitarian shibboleths that for years had small practical effect in the economy, but in the long run had the effect both of inducing and of supporting economic development and, finally, planning. The Revolution also produced the Constitution of 1917, which provided potential support to planning, by asserting the new egalitarianism, emphasizing nationalism, promoting social and economic as well as political justice, enunciating a social function theory of property, and encouraging state intervention in the economy.[2]

Although the Revolution destroyed the old order, it remained to construct a new. The governments after 1917 had to contend with the traditional praetorianism, now strengthened by the presence of battalions of Revolutionary officers, hungrier for personal rewards than for general reform. The political and economic effort required to preserve public order strained the energies of the new and inexperienced leaders and the feeble administrative apparatus of the government. They had to contend also with serious problems of foreign relations, growing out of Revolutionary damage to persons and property, and arising from fears of danger to foreign investment from the new philosophy. In addition, the Church question in the 1920's continued to assume political forms that the government felt obliged to contest, at great expense in attention and treasure. Finally, the presidents conspicuously lacked in all of these endeavors a reliable political instrument for the mobilization of support. It took years to build the national party.

Economic development after 1917 was slow. Mexico had sustained severe damage during years of civil war. Public funds were meager, and inescapably drawn heavily to police and political functions. Internal capital resources were sparse and poorly organized, and persons with substantial amounts tended to be dubious of the new regime, and to hoard, often abroad. Credit abroad was poor. As a result, as shown above, the growth of national product declined drastically in 1910–21 to 0.7 per cent annually, compared with 2.9 per cent yearly in 1895–1910; and in 1922–29 it rose only to an average of 1.7 per cent a year.

Although the government in the 1920's and early 1930's slowly developed policies and institutions for intervention in the economy, government economic activity was feeble.[3] Some land was expropriated and distributed to communities (*ejidos*), with useful social and political results, but without much affecting production. The continuing social and political effects of the *ejidal* program were to be important as a basis for other government action. Other efforts that helped lay the basis for economic development occurred in the fields of sanitation, education, road-building, irrigation, and the organization of labor and improvement of its working conditions.

The creation in 1929 of a national party, the PNR (*Partido Nacional Revolucionario*), was an event with important implications for future government activities in economic development. In the beginning the PNR was primarily an alliance of regional military chiefs, with Calles as Highest Chief. It was at least indicative of a break with the Porfirian tradition that now to the influence of the business community upon the country's *jefes* were added the voices of the newly organized (however imperfectly) peasants and industrial workers, and of the unorganized but now freely vocalizing intellectuals. Under Calles' leadership (to 1934) the PNR provided an improved machinery for mobilization of support for the government. This new institution also was available for the expression and integration of views critical of Calles' policies, and the new directions of government action under Cárdenas were largely based on the restructuring of views within the party before he took office. Thus Calles passed on to Cárdenas the clear beginnings of a system by which the dominant voices of Mexico were herded within the party, and accepted (often reluctantly) a process of policy modification within the structure rather than by efforts at more or less violent fragmentation of the major components in the power alliance. This was to be the key political achievement of the Revolutionary generation from the point of view of managing the economic development of take-off into self-sustained economic growth.

The national party became so important to the development and execution of government economic policies that some students find that it is the "policy of the PNR since 1929 which shows the clearest continuity to the economic and social development of Mexico."[4] In this view, when examined "at the operational level, the interventionist pattern in Mexico appears to be of a purely pragmatic, experimental, and patchwork character."[5] This judgment has merit as applied to the early history of the party, but as the government increased in size, functions, and effectiveness, it tended to provide increasingly clear indications of coherent intent in economic development.[6]

There were created in these years a few public institutions whose functions included some directly relating to economic development. The Bank of Mexico was reestablished in 1925, and until 1932 functioned both as a central bank and as an ordinary commercial bank (a function it lost in 1932). Although the monetary policies of the government were not a success, this was due in part to international conditions over which it had no control. The National Agricultural and Stock Bank was created in 1926, but its resources were small.[7] In 1933 the government established the National Bank for Urban and Public Works Mortgages. Some public investment in works of general interest began with the creation in 1925 of the National Commission of Irrigation and the Road Commission.[8]

There was, however, no planning by present standards.[9] Among other reasons, the organization and staffing of the government, especially as they related to information collection and analysis, were ill-suited to economic planning. On the other hand, the achievement of substantial public order, and the creation of some national economic institutions which had at least modest programming functions, was creating an atmosphere more favorable to government planning. This is suggested by President Calles' message to the congress, September 1, 1928, that

> now is the time to form a program that is based on calculation, on statistics, on the lessons of experience; we should study what we can accomplish, given the possibilities of our resources and circumstances.[10]

In 1928 the government created a National Economic Council (*Consejo Nacional Económico*), which was given a broad mandate to study and to consult with the government. Apparently it accomplished nothing.[11] Then in 1930 a National Planning Law was passed. Without mentioning the council of 1928, it provided for a consulting body, the National Planning Commission. The commission was to be established in the Ministry of Communications and Public Works, but to cooperate with other departments in preparing studies and a "National Plan for Mexico," aimed at "coordinating and regulating the orderly and harmonious development of the nation." Commission membership included a technical representative from each of the Departments of State, and over twenty other representatives, including some for professional, scholarly, and business organizations. There also was provision for a Program Commission, in the Ministry of Communications, to execute all the studies, plans, and programs specified in the law; in addition, it had wide authority itself to study. The law included a suggestion that the country be zoned by "predominant features"; another suggestion that a National Civic Encyclopedia be formed, with a wide variety of information; and mentioned a number of subjects as of especial importance for study and planning, including ports, transportation, and the hydrography of the Valley of Mexico.[12] This was at least a yearning for order.

Although this law apparently had no significant material effect, it is interesting that it existed only three years before the first Six-Year Plan of the national party was produced. The two documents resemble each other in their generality, their lack of cohesion, and their conception of a plan as a banner unfurled rather than as a technical instrument. Indicative of this is the statement of the Law of 1930 that the National Plan of Mexico must be thought of as

> a graphic, dynamic, vivid document, which while flexible and adaptable to different conditions, and subject to variations in accordance with any new necessities which may arise, and kept up-to-date in accordance with the changes that may be made, shall, at the same time, be a basic guide and general outline controlling the logical and progressive growth of the country.

A law of 1933 provided for a National Economic Council of 107 members, which was to cooperate with the delegates of Local Councils to coordinate the economic action of the federal government with that of the states. Apparently, the council never functioned. It was reorganized in 1941, and dissolved in June, 1942.[13]

B. FIRST SIX-YEAR PLAN AND CÁRDENAS, 1933–40[14]

The Cárdenas administration proclaimed the idea of integrated national development under government direction, and began the mobilization of the indispensable political support for it. While its Six-Year Plan may have promoted the *idea* of integrated development rather more than its achievement, it certainly made a potent contribution to the mobilization of support for such development. Similarly, if the administration popularized the idea of a Plan, rather than establishing a system of planning in the present sense, this was an achievement in itself; and the former led on toward the latter.

1. *First Six-Year Plan*

There was dissension among the leadership of the PNR in 1933 as the time for the presidential nominating convention approached. This resulted from a combination of the effects of the world depression with what seemed to some the conservatism, corruption, and lack of reforming fervor of the Calles group. To meet the grumblings of the liberal wing of the party, Calles agreed to composition of a Six-Year Plan promising implementation of the policies they advocated. The Plan, and the candidacy of Lázaro Cárdenas for president for the term 1934–40, were approved, after some debate between right and left party factions, at the PNR convention of December, 1933.[15]

The Plan was couched largely in the appropriate generalities of political communication and enunciation of policy. The expressed hopes of the framers were abundant and diverse, but they included the summary that the "main aspects of the Plan" were: economic nationalism as self-defense, social justice sought by agrarian reform, child mentality protected by education, protection for organized labor, and sound financial practices.[16] The framers' list describes the objectives of the Plan well enough, except for the omission of reference to the Plan's concern for increased and diversified production, and the omission suggests the weakness of the Plan in this regard.

Lower levels of generalization supplemented the higher: government action to aid agriculture became dissipation of latifundia, promotion of crops, erection of irrigation works, and combat against the middleman. Lower echelon generalizations in places descended to such specifics as lists of roads and railways to be built during the life of the Plan. But the Plan conspicuously did not discuss matters in quantitative terms, of production, construction, training of technicians, financing, or other factors. It did state that the Plan was to be executed in six annual stages, "each of which will be carefully calculated and planned by the Federal Executive, with the Party's cooperation." It also provided for the formulation by "all communities" of "programs based on this . . . Plan"; and for PNR study of such local plans, and of state plans, with the party to "make every year a computation of the public works which the various communities commit themselves to undertake." This last must be taken not simply as the common attachment of political parties to the distribution of favors, but as indicative of the absence of strong instruments for such activity in the government.[17]

The Plan lacked the detailed quantitative and chronological goals (some were stated), the specific data on financing, and the attention to modes of execution expected in planning today. Thus, it could not be expected that it would contain any other integrative element than that imparted by the framers' wish to state demands for economic development and justice in the Mexican social environment.[18] Ninety-five per cent of the text was taken up with sections (such as agriculture, labor, public health, education) that could have been prepared and published separately with no damage to the Plan's problematical value as a technical instrument. So fragmented, however, the Plan would have lost not only its label but much of its political impact. This would have damaged its usefulness in helping establish the sociopolitical preconditions for self-sustained economic development, to use a terminology not then in existence.

The PNR noted in 1937 in these scornful terms contemporary doubts as to whether its document deserved to be called a plan:

> Whether or not this Plan is properly such according to the type fixed by plans for controlled economies in other countries, or whether it is merely a party platform, is an idle although frequent discussion.[19]

As the government selected and executed projects from year to year, in speech and publication it linked its actions to the Plan. In Cárdenas' annual message to the nation on January 1, 1936, he reported in some detail on some aspects of government action in 1935, relating it generally to the Plan. In stating his program for 1936, he used even more general terms.[20] The PNR energetically celebrated social and economic developments as implementation of the Plan.[21]

Some critics thought a special body was required for supervision of the Plan.[22] Cárdenas did not agree, and such planning as occurred was handled much as in later administrations.[23] This meant that there was some partial, or sector, but no integrated, or national, planning.[24] Cárdenas did in 1935 create an advisory committee for planning, made up of heads of agencies and the government banks; but this was replaced in 1938 by a planning division in the Ministry of Government, which worked with the party in drafting the Second Six-Year Plan.[25]

2. *Other Developments*

Mexicans often say that Cárdenas "reaffirmed the Revolution." Although there was much party, government, and private discussion of "socialism" and "socialization" in those exciting years, the reaffirmed Revolution continued to develop and implement doctrine in ways little pleasing to international ideologues.[26] Much of the reaffirmation involved extension of state intervention in the economy. The most striking actions were: nationalization of petroleum and many of the railways; distribution of more land to *ejidos* in six years than in the preceding seventeen, and some increase of aid to the communities; expansion of public works construction; and reorganization of the party (renamed

PRM) on a "functional" basis, with agrarian, labor, military, and popular sectors. The government also created some institutions that became important to its intervention in the economy, including the following which still exist: the National Bank of Ejidal Credit; Nacional Financiera, the development bank; the National Bank of Foreign Trade; the Federal Electricity Commission; and Pemex.[27]

Various statistical or economic study agencies were founded in the government or expanded their operations as government intervention increased. These included the General Bureau of Statistics (*Dirección General de Estadística*) of the Ministry of the Economy;[28] the Department of Economic Studies (*Departamento de Estudios Económicos*) of the same ministry; and others in ministries, in the Bank of Mexico, and in Nacional Financiera.[29] In addition, it may be noted that a small amount of municipal planning was done in Mexico in the 1930's.[30]

Study and publication in the field of economics somewhat improved in Mexico in the 1930's, although it is not clear that the PNR considered this essential.[31] Shortly after 1930 the University of Mexico began training professional economists, with the "stated objective . . . to train leaders in economic science for governmental policy positions."[32] In 1934 the *Fondo de Cultura Económica* was established; in succeeding years this publishing house put out many native and foreign works in economics and public administration. Two important journals began publication in this period: *El Trimestre Económico* (1934) and *Revista de Economía* (1937).

There is no doubt that the immediate material effects of the Cárdenas policies were in some respects unhappy. They helped created a balance-of-payments problem, frightened foreign capital, led to deficit financing, caused inflation, and were not helpful to that agricultural production in which most of the population was engaged. While national product increased some 21 per cent during 1934–40, only about 5 per cent of the increase was due to agriculture. On the other hand, manufacturing production accounted for nearly one-third of the growth during those six years, and commerce grew quite briskly.[33] Of course, only a small part of the population labored in these latter fields, and the benefits went in any event to entrepreneurs rather than to laborers. Finally, it may be noted that although Mexico was cut off from foreign investment, the mobilization of internal investment permitted double the investment in 1940 of that occurring in 1935. But this increase was much less than the investment growth to come in the next administration.[34] In any event, it seems possible to assert that Cárdenas made at least as much contribution to industrial as to agricultural growth, in both the short and the long run.[35] Cárdenas also helped promote the formation of business associations and helped tie them to government decision-making.[36]

Whatever the criticism of the immediate effects of Cárdenas' economic policies, or the carping at his lack of interest in administration, or the real weight of corruption in those years, the fact remains that the national economy sprang from the material and spiritual accomplishments of his administration into a period of rapid and self-sustained growth. Although the succeeding administration had the advantage of wartime demand for Mexican products, the same leap could not have been made from the institutions and public temper of 1933.[37] A part of the change in both institutions and public temper relates to confidence in the ability of Mexico to achieve growth; a part relates to the notion that growth could be attained with internal resources, ownership, and management; and a part relates to enthusiasm for the notion that government action, including at least a modicum of planning, was a serviceable instrument for the increase of the national product and for its more equitable distribution. Cárdenas, in sum, performed that service of widening demand for change, which antique philosophers recognized as a prelude to change itself, and which a recent literature celebrates as operative in connection with the economies of underdeveloped countries as well as in relation to modifications in class structures and changing fashions in the content of higher education.

C. PLANNING SINCE CÁRDENAS

Developments after Cárdenas stepped down in 1940 included: (1) an immediate leap forward in economic growth (especially in industry), for reasons and with effects still debated;[38] (2) the emphases of government and party seemed to shift from social to economic criteria, and although no one can be sure of the long-range effects of this upon social development, it stirred up many humanistic and other critics; (3) the party's enthusiasm for a collectivist society dwindled; (4) private enterprise grew apace, though directed and channeled by the growing apparatus of state intervention; (5) although a Second Six-Year Plan served as party platform in 1940, it had no successors; (6) several national coordinating or planning bodies were set up during World War II, but they were consultative organs, and generally ineffective; (7) partial or sectoral economic planning grew rapidly, with impressive (if not entirely undebatable) results;[39] (8) it became increasingly evident, especially after the war, that there was a need for integrated investment planning and for more coordination of the control, operations, and general planning of the growing government; (9) there was a huge increase in the absolute number, and considerable increase in the percentage, of the population committed to or yearning for "modernization." These last, largely indifferent to the ideologies of right and left, tended to swell support for the party's pragmatic approach to development.

1. *New Emphasis on Industry*

There is no question but that a swing to industry occurred after Cárdenas; the problems involve cause and effect. Although the why of the matter seems inescapably plural, the literature teems with fragile specimens of monistic interpretation. Most of these are founded either on a devil-theory of history, insulated humanistic value systems, or socialist doctrine; and some polemicists manage to blend the three.[40] No effort will be made to analyze the intellectual and glandular elements involved in simple assignment of the changed emphasis of government to "betrayal of the Revolution," a "swing to the right," "subservience to business," or a "new materialism" replacing something undefined and unquantified but vaguely resembling a farmer close to heaven in the good earth and far from the wicked city. One admires some of these people, but nostalgia is a frail social weapon, even if wielded by Thomas Jefferson, Mahatma Gandhi, or Lázaro Cárdenas.

Since for some critics the mystique of the Revolution demands obliteration of selfish interests, possibly we must begin by agreeing that, alas, they play a role in Mexican as in other human affairs. With that disposed of, we may offer the following, possibly more illuminating, reasons for the policy shift: (1) the apparent productive shortcomings of the *ejidos*; (2) the evident values (social and economic) of industrialization; (3) wartime opportunities and problems; and (4) the bases laid by the Cárdenas administration in promoting government intervention, the building of socioeconomic infrastructure, the considerable industrial growth, the partial achievement of many of the sociopolitical aims of the agrarian reform, and the improved mobilization of support in the PRM.[41]

The effects of the changed policy emphasis were not as fundamental as those flowing from the decisions of 1933 and thereafter, which, as we have indicated, constituted the real "policy revolution."[42] As soon as we agree that the policy change with regard to industry was a new "emphasis,"[43] we state that it did not represent a break with the Cárdenas policies. We have seen, indeed, that Cárdenas did numerous things to aid industry, and that during his years manufacturing grew more rapidly than agriculture. The new emphasis thus becomes a matter of degree, and many competent observers have been struck by the amount of aid Mexico continued to give agriculture even while pushing industrialization. The new administration did greatly slow the headlong pace of *ejidal* expansion, for reasons that are so persuasive economically that critics are well advised to attack the change on other grounds. The great rise of production in non-*ejidal* units did not accrue directly to small farmers, and the indirect and long-term benefits to the nation were not only difficult for some to see but admittedly small comfort in the short run. It often is said that there was more "corruption," but no one really offers very useful specification on a national scale, or explains why it occurred if it did, or what measures might effectively have curbed it. Finally, on the question whether it was a "betrayal of the Revolution": it is the possession of the Mexican people, and they must quarrel over its interpretation themselves.

2. *Second Six-Year Plan*

In 1939 a committee of the PRM prepared a plan for 1941–46, with assistance from the Ministry of Government's new planning division. The party's National Assembly approved the plan in November. The second plan was much like the first. The study committee that drafted the Plan declared:

> Inasmuch as it is not a case of a detailed and rigid program enunciating all . . . of the activities to be undertaken, which would be undesirable, but of a true general guide. . . . The annual programs of execution must . . . give details.

In more than a hundred printed pages the Plan dealt with most subjects in general terms. The chapter on industry simply stated broad aims, without figures. The spirit of the document was that the party favored an improved life—material and spiritual—for all. At the end came two pages on "Planning and Coordination," which recommended cooperation between federal government and states, but not too rigidly; and coordination between agencies of the federal government (without specifying how). The "planning" section also stated that the government must carry out the Plan, with the aid of the party; thus a National Supreme Council should be established, with representatives of all segments of the country (economic, social, political, and military). Annually, this body would present to the President of the Republic a proposed Program of Execution of the Six-Year Plan.[44] After the electoral effort of 1939–40, party interest in six-year plans seems to have evaporated.[45]

Avila Camacho often is charged with having subscribed to the "collectivist" or "socialistic" aims of the second plan during the campaign, only to repudiate them during his administration.[46] Whatever validity or utility there may be in this charge, the ambiguity of the document permitted many interpretations. The Plan's preamble alone offers comfort to various points of view. It subscribes to democracy, but reserves the right of state intervention for the national good. Although it "recognizes the present reality of the battle of the classes," it states that justice may be won gradually. It declares that if private initiative respects the rights of labor, it need fear nothing in the Plan; and if it respects the laws and the aspirations of the people, it will get the aid it deserves due to "its condition as a powerful factor in the economy" that is needed for "national progress." And it asserts that "the Six-Year Plan is characterized by its humanist sense," and that it is wedded to "the revolutionary idea of progress." Finally, almost anything can be read into the statement that "to plan the activities of the State" is not "a mere requisite of the modern technique of government" but a "revolutionary right" for achieving public objectives.[47]

So general and ambiguous a document only made it the simpler for Avila Camacho to conduct his administration without feeling inhibited by a document prepared before he took office. In any event, the nature of Mexican politics and government were such that the president could scarcely be tied to the letter of what was essentially a campaign document.[48] And the country lacked the tools for national planning.[49]

3. *Partial Planning*

Most planning in Mexico to the present has been partial or noncomprehensive (usually sector or regional). Some of this, as we have observed, occurred in Cárdenas' time, but it was much expanded thereafter. Some of the expanded sector activity dealt with sizable projects over considerable periods of time. Some of it was in ministries, much of it in the nonministerial agencies of the government. Some planning was done by offices not labeled for that function, some by specifically designated planning staffs, and some was done or served by research or statistical groups. In addition to planning in such fields as electrification, transportation, irrigation, and petroleum (to say nothing of such social planning as that in education), there was some regional planning, and a more modest growth of state, municipal, and Federal District planning. As the operating and investment budgets of the government increased, the amount, variety, and competence of this work greatly increased, too.[50] Also, there was a large interest in planning techniques and theory, especially after the war. This was assisted by publication of foreign literature in translation in Mexico, by increasing personal relations with foreign planners and theorists, and by technical assistance in planning and allied subjects provided by international agencies.[51] The improved sector planning provided a base for efforts at integrated national planning.

4. *Wartime National Planning Bodies*

During the years of wartime industrial boom, several economic study, coordination, and planning commissions were set up in Mexico. Essentially, they were consultative bodies,[52] and neither planned or executed plans of any consequence. Some of this activity grew out of the emergency situations created by the war.

A law of April, 1941, reformed the National Economic Council that had been created in 1933. The new National Council of the Economy of the United Mexican States (*Consejo Nacional de Economía de los Estados Unidos Mexicanos*), an advisory body to the Ministry of the Economy,[53] was to study various economic matters, including the function of Local Economic Councils.[54] It was composed of twenty members, and proved unwieldy.[55] A law of June 1942 displaced this body with a Federal Commission of Economic Planning (*Comisión Federal de Planificación Económica*). This smaller, seven-man body was headed by the Minister of the Economy.[56] A representative from each of four other organizations participated in discussions as technical advisers, without vote.[57] The Federal Commission was to study economic problems created by the war, formulate plans for economic mobilization that might be required by inter-American cooperation, and study economic problems likely to arise at the end of the war. It also was to study, from the point of view of national integration, the program of the Mixed Councils of the Regional Economies (*Consejos Mixtos de Economía Regional*). It began publication of a periodical titled *Economic Planning*.[58] The Federal Commission was ended by a decree of May, 1943.[59]

A law of October, 1942, created a decentralized organ called Coordination and Development of Production (*Coordinación y Fomento de la Producción*), headed by a coordinator named by the president. Other members were to be appointed by the coordinator. All served without pay. Functions included: initiation of new industrial and agricultural activities; determination that new industries were suited to maximum satisfaction of national needs; aid to mining and transportation. It was to be supplied with data by the General Bureau of Statistics in the Ministry of the Economy, and other agencies. A decree of February, 1944, ended this body on the grounds that by that time its functions were being performed by the *Comisión de Coordinación Económica Nacional.*[60]

A law of June, 1944, created a three-member decentralized organ called the Federal Commission for Industrial Development (*Comisión Federal de Fomento Industrial*). Its object was the planning, financing, organization, and establishment of industry indispensable for the "rational industrialization of the country," and which private interests would not establish. It was to stimulate and only temporarily supplement private investment. It was abolished in 1953,[61] having accomplished little.[62] Some other emergency planning agencies were established during the war.[63]

A decree of February 15, 1944, created a National Planning Commission for the Peace (*Comisión Nacional de Planeación para la Paz*). Its forty-two members included many important government officials. Its only report contains a very general section on economic problems. This Commission was dissolved in December, 1944.[64]

5. *Efforts to Coordinate Planning, 1946–58*

During the administrations of Miguel Alemán (1946–52) and Ruíz Cortines (1952–58) the rapid economic growth of the country continued, although at a slackening and more uneven pace in the latter administration. Public investment continued high, and was increasingly handled through the autonomous agencies of the government, rather than by the regular departments.[65]

There was considerable expansion of partial or sectoral planning during these administrations. For one thing, the large and growing government public works effort made this necessary.[66] More and better-trained technicians became available for planning activity.[67] Government economic investigation and planning offices were expanded and improved.[68] Statistical data were upgraded somewhat.[69] An increased proportion of the population became aware of planning and its importance to the country.[70] And, in addition to partial planning, the government turned its attention to the coordination of plans—to national planning.

The government was aware of the need for coordination of investment programs and plans of the government and quasi-governmental agencies, before the International Bank recommended such a step in 1953.[71] Most of the government's efforts at coordination in 1946–58 related to public investments, although some other activity occurred.[72] Apparently, the first important indication of intent to supply this need was in a law of December 31, 1947, for the control of the sprawling agencies of the government.[73] The law gave the Ministry of Finance authority to supervise all three categories of agencies for the purpose of systematizing their fiscal methods, including supervision of their operating and investment budgets.

A presidential decree in January, 1948 (*Diario Oficial,* Jan. 31),[74] created a National Investment Commission (*Comisión Nacional de Inversiones*), as a dependency of the Ministry of Finance, to deal with the agencies mentioned in the law of December 31, 1947. This body made "exhaustive studies" of the finances of these agencies, so that they could make recommendations on the use of their resources.[75] But when the Finance Ministry tried to establish tight control of the agencies, some of them resisted, even carrying it into the courts. So the commission was "reduced to studying the less important agencies." The commission worked hard for ten months in 1948, then tapered off in 1949, until it was abolished in December, 1949.[76] A circular of the Ministry of Finance, published December 27, 1949, informed all agencies that the functions of the suppressed commission now would reside in a designated agency of that Ministry.[77]

Apparently before the creation in January, 1948, of the National Investment Commission in the Ministry of Finance, the Bank of Mexico had undertaken a sizable effort at centralized public investment planning.[78] It is not known what relation, if any, was expected to obtain between the bank's efforts and those of the National Investment Commission. The study by the bank's Department of Economic Studies was to be used as the basis for a loan of $250 million from the International Bank. The plan was to provide an investment schedule for all federal agencies for the administration of Miguel Alemán. The plan was not completed until August, 1948; and in any event only a fraction of the proposed loan was obtained. The plan was not put into operation, but was turned over to the Technical Economic Commission of the Ministry of National Assets (*Bienes Nacionales*; now *Patrimonio Nacional*) to see what use might be made of it.

The bank's plan did not resemble the party's six-year plans. It included a time schedule; priority classifications, with justifications; for each project there were statements on its object, its importance to the development of Mexico, the urgency of its being undertaken, work under construction, and work contracted for; total expenses year by year on each project; the sources of funds; the extent to which projects would be self-liquidating; an estimate of the repercussions of the programs on the national income, on tax income, and on the international balance of payments.[79] This would appear to have been an improvement over previous national investment planning.[80]

In 1952 Nacional Financiera's research office undertook a study of national income, public and private investments, and allied questions. The Undersecretary of Finance, Rafael Mancera Ortiz, declared in 1953 that this Nacional Financiera study was "the first serious attempt in Mexico to project into the next six years the pattern of a desirable line of economic development for the entire country, by sectors."[81] The objectives considered in this investment program were to: (1) raise the standard of living; (2) attain a higher rate of economic growth; (3) achieve a more coordinated development of the economy; (4) gain a greater growth of production; (5) attain a certain price stability; (6) finance the investment program without a budget deficit; (7) persuade local private capital to participate in the investment program; and (8) channel financial resources through those sectors of the economy which needed them most, or apply those resources to the solution of the more pressing problems of the economy.

In 1953 the government began to take actions that before long promised a real system of investment planning. Presumably this action was "caused" by all the developments we have mentioned: national economic problems, government fiscal difficulties, the confusion of government investment policy as it was increasingly fragmented among agencies, and the accumulation of pressures for integration and planning from a growing corps of personnel with technical knowledge in economics. It has been asserted, however, that this action was at least precipitated by the Nacional Financiera "program of development" in 1952.[82]

In any event, a presidential order of June 9, 1953, obliged the Ministries of State, the Department of the Federal District, the decentralized organs, and the state participation enterprises to send to the Finance Ministry investment programs for 1953–58, to include designation of the projects to be executed each year, to be accompanied by financing schedules, with specification of origin of funds, the amounts provided by the government budget, bond sales, foreign loans, and from the agency's own funds. With the aid of this data, the Ministries of Finance and the Economy were to present for the president's consideration a coordinated program of investment in the public sector. With a view to complying with this order, on July 20, 1953, the Minister of Finance created an Investment Committee (*Comité de Inversiones*). It functioned about a year, and then was replaced, probably because its activities had stirred up resentment within the government departments and the autonomous agencies.[83]

On September 7, 1954, a presidential order created an Investment Commission (*Comisión de Inversiones*) as a dependency of the presidency itself, presumably in the hope of reducing friction and exerting greater pressure upon government agencies to cooperate.

The commission began work that month, with a director, subdirector, programming chief, ten analysts, and some technical help. It studied the investment projects of public agencies, coordinated such programs of investment, ranked them, made recommendations to the President of Mexico for an annual program of investment, incorporated whatever changes the latter ordered, and saw that the approved annual programs were put into effect by the government agencies involved. This last, or execution, phase of the commission's work was done in collaboration with the Ministries of Finance and National Property, through their control of funds and of contracts or supply orders for public works.

The work of the Investment Commission during its lifetime (1954–58) was a step toward integrated national planning, although it did not in fact plan, but coordinated the investment plans of other agencies. The latter did the planning studies, developed the principles of development, and set the goals on which the investment programs were based. On the other hand, the Investment Commission did set up criteria for determining investment priorities on a national basis, and did exert influence on the activity of the agencies by reason of partial control of their investment plans and expenditures. The commission was, at least, a more potent integrative force in the economic planning field than had existed heretofore.[84]

6. *Since 1958*

A number of developments since 1958 have affected attitudes toward planning in Mexico. The leftist opposition to PRI leadership, within and without the party, has been stimulated by events in Cuba, and by *fidelista* propaganda. The force of this opposition as a threat to the PRI, or to the present leadership of the party, was enhanced by the involvement of Lázaro Cárdenas. He expressed sympathy for the Cuban revolution, demanded more aid for the common man in Mexico, denounced private business as lacking social conscience, and participated in 1962/63 in formation of a new peasant organization to compete with that of the PRI. The force of these activities was considerably blunted when, in 1964, Cárdenas—to the consternation of some liberals and leftists—finally supported the PRI candidate for the presidency in the July election.

These opposition pressures were, presumably, important factors in the decision of López Mateos to push land "reform" (i.e., distribution) at a furious pace, despite the dubious economic utility of this program. It also must have contributed to his vigorous implementation of the policy of "Mexicanization" of certain economic activities—notably electric power and mining—in which foreign investment was heavy. It has helped keep the government committed to a policy of nonintervention with regard to Castro's régime in Cuba, despite (or because of) United States pressure for multilateral intervention through the OAS. It led, also, to the delightful public statement by López Mateos that he was "of the far left within the Constitution," a politicism that apparently pleased neither right nor left but probably struck just the right note with middle-of-the-road PRI leaders.

These policies induced, in turn, a wave of pessimism in private business circles, and a serious flight of capital abroad. Foreign private investment capital became similarly skittish. The slowdown in investment contributed in 1961 to a major decline in the growth of production, which barely kept up with population increase. The political as well as economic consequences of this well-publicized decline in production growth drove the government in 1962 to a considerable increase in public investment, and this in turn helped to keep bubbling the fears of business that the economy gradually was being socialized. (It was difficult to claim that it was being socialized rapidly.)

By a law of December 30, 1958, the López Mateos administration at least asserted its intention of carrying much further the efforts of Ruíz Cortines to centralize control of government investment, public property, governmental organization and procedures, natural resources, and planning for economic development.[85] The law rearranged the ministries and departments of state, and prescribed a new system of planning for economic development. The office of the presidential secretary, which had for years managed much of such coordination of development plans as occurred, was converted into a ministry and given the planning function in law.[86] A new Ministry of National Patrimony received powers related to planning. The Finance Ministry lost to these two ministries some of its power to authorize activities and contracts. Subsequent presidential and ministerial orders reflected efforts to implement this law and to adjust it to the realities of Mexican government and politics.[87]

This appeared to be a stride toward integrated national planning. Creation of a national planning staff in the new Ministry of the Presidency seemed a plausible institutional culmination of the events of the preceding decade—of the tentative efforts at centralized planning, and especially the work of the Investment Commission; of the pressures by technicians for integrated planning; of the need to control the sprawling government establishment; of the apparent necessity of better management of the growth of an increasingly complex economy; of the need for economic growth in a political environment in which leaders spouted statistics almost as copiously as patriotism. It also was suggested by the continuing appreciation of the necessity of depending more on foreign public investment, a recourse that would require more centralized planning, as a means of providing the data required for justification of loan applications. These activities early in the López Mateos administration impressed the Committee of Nine of the OAS as showing

> a clear conception of the importance residing in planning as an instrument to accelerate a balanced development and to ensure that its benefits may effectively reach all social sectors.[88]

In May, 1959, the Minister of the Presidency announced creation of three bureaus (*direcciones*): Planning, Investments, Inspection and Control. The new ministry proceeded to try to perform the function of the Investment Commission of 1954–58, and to prepare Mexico's first national economic development plans. This brought it into conflict with other government agencies, which not only felt their interests and power threatened, but considered themselves (with reason) better qualified to perform these functions. The president tended to support the older institutions, so that the Ministry of the Presidency did not develop all the large planning powers apparently assigned it in the law of December, 1958. Instead, much of the planning study and function remained in the Ministry of Finance, the Bank of Mexico, and Nacional Financiera.

The government in 1961 completed several planning studies on economic development for the 1960's. One of these was a "Projection of the Global Growth Averages of the Mexican Economy in 1965 and 1970"; another was "Sectoral Projections of the Growth of the Mexican Economy"; and there were several related studies, including projections of external demand and of industrial investment.[89] Most of the work on these studies was accomplished in the older agencies of the government, not in the Ministry of the Presidency.

In later 1961 and early 1962 the government of Mexico was seriously concerned about the economic slowdown. One result of this concern was a presidential order on March 1, 1962, creating an Interministerial Planning Commission, which in effect reinforced the dominant position in the planning process of the Ministry of Finance and its allied institutions, the Bank of Mexico and Nacional Financiera, at the expense of the Ministry of the Presidency. Another result of this concern was a decision to prepare a Plan of Immediate Action for 1962–64.[90] One of the uses of such a plan would be the acceleration of lending under the Alliance for Progress by meeting the planning requirements of that agreement. By April, 1962, the Minister of Finance was informing the press that the long-range national plan would be finished soon. President

López Mateos, in his annual message of September 1, 1962, was able to discuss the content of the Plan for 1962–64.

The Immediate Action Plan was drawn up by a small group under the aegis of the Interministerial Planning Commission. The "Projection of the Global Growth Averages," mentioned above, was the base for the Plan.[91] The Plan was sent by the Minister of Finance, as Mexican representative to the Inter-American Economic and Social Council, with a letter dated September 12, 1962, to the Secretary General of the OAS. In the letter the Minister of Finance described the document as containing

> the plan of public and private investments and the corresponding financial plan, with which the Government of Mexico has proposed to accelerate national economic development and to continue improving the social condition of the country, under the terms of the Charter of Punta del Este.[92]

In accordance with the procedures of the Charter, an Ad Hoc Committee of the Committee of Nine of the OAS's Inter-American Economic and Social Council was appointed to examine the Plan of Immediate Action for 1962–64. The Ad Hoc Committee on the Mexican Plan began its work in Washington on October 2, 1962. It visited Mexico in January, 1963. In April, 1963, two of its members again visited Mexico. World Bank personnel evaluated the Plan, too, visiting Mexico in that connection in 1963 and 1964. Liaison between personnel of the Ad Hoc Committee and World Bank personnel prevented excessive overlap of function. In August, 1964, a 263-page commentary on the Plan of Immediate Action for 1962–64 was presented to the Mexican government.[93]

In the meantime, a planning committee of the Mexican Federal Senate drew up a project of a federal planning law, which was presented to the Senate, with an elaborate introductory analysis, in September 1963. The committee noted that although there was considerable national legislation on planning, recent practices showed serious defects in this area. It called for establishment of a National Planning Commission, as a consultative and technical body, to work out the means of meeting the basic political and social objectives set by the federal executive. Since "planning should be democratic," it called for Sectoral Commissions, with wide representation from peasant, labor, and other interest groups. The committee asserted its rejection of the notion that budgeting and planning should be merged. In a "mixed economy," it was asserted, private enterprise could not be coerced, but it was observed that the government had many means of persuasion. An interesting suggestion was that there should be wide publicity on planning—something that has not existed in Mexico, as we observe elsewhere—as a way of getting "the greatest possible cooperation of the diverse components of the population and the maximum coordination in the public administration." The current faith in the idea of planning, as well as continued attachment to the Mexican tradition of dispersed, or competitive, or mutual adjustment planning may be seen in the committee's call for the creation of planning bureaus, as appropriate, in the ministries and departments of state and in the decentralized organs and the enterprises with state participation. The projected law was given its first reading in the senate and published in the *Diario de los Debates* of that body for October 24, 1963.[94] No data are available on the later fate of the projected law. It is presumed to be dead.

After López Mateos' message of September 1, 1962, the Plan of Immediate Action for 1962–64 became a matter for political discussion, somewhat hampered by the fact that little of its content was made public at first. Some additional information was released in January, 1963, when the OAS study group went to Mexico to discuss the Plan. By this time it was apparent that government economic development planning would be a popular topic in the presidential campaign leading to the election of July, 1964. The term "plan" seemed to issue from every mouth—in hope or despair, congratulation or condemnation. Mexican publications swarmed with the development plans of state governors, federal bureaucrats, party officials, and the President of the Republic. The PRI set up Popular Committees on Programming (*Juntas Populares de Programación*) to permit large numbers of party members to help plan party policy and platform and the economic program of the next administration.[95] The party leaders thus retain the attachment to the idea of "planning"—at least for political purposes—which they have demonstrated in one form or another in every presidential campaign since 1934.

But all this concern with the terms *planeación* and *planificación* only slowly changes the Mexican government's philosophy or habit of operation. Sectoral planning continues in the agencies where it has been done for years, and it is not clear how much it may ultimately be affected by creation of the Ministry of the Presidency and other recently adopted devices. Public sector investment planning continues much as under the Investment Commission, with the Ministry of the Presidency taking up the latter's function, subject—as was the Commission—to advice, consent, and pressure applied by other government agencies and private interests. In 1965 the government continues to grapple with the difficult problems of coordinating planning between federal agencies, and with state and municipal government, and with private enterprise. Thus, the changes since 1958 leave basically unchanged: (1) the government's determination to retain the market economy; (2) the dedication of PRI and government to the methods of persuasion and compromise in increasing pressures for better integration of public and private planning; and (3) the considerable dispersion of planning and planning studies among public agencies, a system that seems to some foreign observers to be describable as "competitive" or "mutual adjustment" planning.

V

The Framework of Planning

Mexican planning doctrine—within and without government agencies—assumes continuation of the market economy. The world literature on the subject is widely and increasingly known, discussed, and even used, in Mexican planning studies and operations. Training and research in economics and in public administration as they support planning studies and operations probably should be considered no more than adequate, but improving. There are many—and apparently will be more—government planning offices, and staffs that produce studies in support of planning. Coordination of the activities of these offices, and of the government establishment generally, is a growing problem and important to the formulation and implementation of development plans. There has been considerable coordination for many years by the Ministry of Finance, the Bank of Mexico, and Nacional Financiera. The formulation and implementation of development plans are affected by conflicts of goals and value systems in Mexico, especially as they assertedly relate to the Revolution. The government's implementation strategy and tactics largely involve relations between organized interest groups, and most importantly within the PRI and between the latter (and the government) and business associations.

A. Planning Doctrine

Mexican awareness of foreign plans and planning doctrine has grown rapidly in recent years, paralleling the general upward spiral of man's fascination with planning, and coinciding with improvements in Mexican education and communications, and with a broadening concern for national economic development and administration under new conditions of relative success and stability. Awareness of foreign operations and ideas has come from observation of the performance of other states,[1] and from study of foreign theoretical literature. These processes have taken place both in Mexico and abroad. Mexican education in economics and allied subjects has expanded, foreign works increasingly are translated into Spanish and published in Mexico,[2] and numerous Mexicans travel and study abroad.[3] Also, this awareness of foreign planning works and ideas notably has come since World War II from Mexican connections with foreign states and international organizations: the United Nations, and especially its Economic Commission for Latin America (CEPAL to Latin Americans), and the International Bank for Reconstruction and Development; the Organization of American States; and the United States, through various loan and aid programs, but especially in recent years through the Alliance for Progress.[4]

Only a few of the effects of United Nations action upon Mexico can be mentioned here. Mexican officials have been influenced by the loan policies of the International Bank, and by the latter's published and unpublished studies of Mexico and other Latin American countries. The work of CEPAL has directly and indirectly done much to influence planning in Mexico. The annual Economic Survey of Latin America promoted attention to improved statistics and economic growth rates and to development policies; it tended to stimulate economic nationalism. CEPAL also served as a forum for Raúl Prebisch, whose theories of Latin American economic development included expanded attention to planning and have had considerable currency in Mexico.[5]

In connection with planning, programming, and allied subjects, CEPAL has published manuals and other materials,[6] since 1952 has conducted seminars and courses of instruction,[7] and in 1962 set up the Latin American Institute of Economic and Social Planning, which became very active in training, research, and promotional activities of all sorts.[8] Mexico in early 1963 sent a delegation to the Geneva United Nations conference on the application of science and technology to underdeveloped regions.[9] In September-October, 1964, the Fifth International Congress on Planning was held in Mexico City, with representatives from sixty countries.[10] Community and regional development programs are among others being conducted today in Mexico by the United Nations that must be supposed to have some influence on planning doctrine and operations.[11]

The Organization of American States (OAS)—largely through its secretariat, the Pan-American Union, and the Inter-American Economic and Social Council (IA-ECOSOC)—has for years promoted interest in economic and social planning. National planning doctrine and activities have been widely disseminated through publications and meetings.

Considerable effort has been put into the study and promotion of urban and regional planning.[12] The Pan-American Union's Division of Housing and Planning has for some time published a periodical, *Vivienda y Planeamiento*.[13] In 1956, at the Inter-American Economic and Social Council's First Inter-American Technical Meeting on Housing and Planning at Bogotá, there were Mexicans in attendance.[14] In 1961, after some years of discussion, the OAS established an Inter-American Program in Urban and Regional Planning, as part of the OAS Technical Cooperation Program.[15]

The Alliance for Progress has greatly stimulated OAS planning activity, and shifted the focus of Latin American planning interest from the UN and CEPAL toward the OAS and its IA-ECOSOC.[16] The Charter of the Alliance, adopted by the Special Meeting of IA-ECOSOC at Punta del Este, Uruguay, in August, 1961, requires participating Latin American countries "to introduce or strengthen systems for the preparation, execution, and periodic revision of national programs for economic and social development." They were to try to formulate long-term development programs within the next eighteen months. United States aid was made contingent upon incorporation of certain measures in the national development programs. Aid in programming and planning was promised by the OAS, CEPAL, and the Inter-American Development Bank. Nine experts were to be selected by the IA-ECOSOC, and attached to it, to provide experts for *ad hoc* committees to examine the national economic and social development programs. The committees were to "exchange opinions with the interested government as to possible modifications." Also, they were to report to the Inter-American Development Bank and to other governments and institutions that they might wish to render financial and technical aid. Finally, the Charter stated:[17]

> The recommendations of the ad hoc committee will be of great importance in determining the distribution of public funds under the Alliance for Progress which contribute to the external financing of such programs. . . . The Inter-American Economic and Social Council will review annually the progress achieved in the formulation, national implementation, and international financing of development programs.[18]

Mexico soon drafted a national development plan in response to the requirements of the Alliance.[19]

In accordance with the Charter of Punta del Este, the Secretary-General of the OAS in December, 1961, held a Round Table on Immediate Problems of Planning within the Framework of the Alliance for Progress. One result was a call for a February-March, 1962, meeting of experts and planning officials to Santiago, Chile, under the auspices of the OAS, CEPAL, and the IDB.[20]

The first annual OAS meetings to review the achievements of the Alliance for Progress were held at Mexico City in October, 1962. The countries presented reviews of their economic and social development. The Mexican account included a section on planning.[21] The meeting also considered the theory and practice of planning at considerable length.[22] It agreed to form a "Special Committee on Planning and Project Formulation."[23] The second annual meeting of IA-ECOSOC was at Sâo Paulo, Brazil, in October-November, 1963, at which the planning committee reported.

Considerable theoretical or descriptive material on planning is produced by Mexicans.[24] Some of it is printed in newspapers and popular magazines;[25] some in scholarly journals;[26] some in government periodicals that might be said to combine the political and technical functions of the two preceding types of publications;[27] and there are sections or passages on planning in books on public administration and on economic development.[28] There are, however, few book-length treatments of planning by Mexicans.[29]

It is likely that these materials contribute less to the knowledge of government officials engaged in planning or research to support planning than does the rich foreign literature on planning and allied subjects available in Mexico, as noted above. On the other hand, the domestic literature has, and will continue to, build interest in, and support for, planning in Mexico. In fact, it has been apparent for years in Mexico (as in the United States) that the supply of knowledge of planning theory has outrun the willingness of government to make use of it. Finally, the contributions of government officials to this Mexican literature on planning, does, presumably, assist in clarification of their own ideas.

With planning doctrine and economic techniques thus widely available in Mexico, there is little problem, as one Mexican official remarked to the present author, of importing ideas. It is a problem, rather, of deciding which ideas to use, and when, and in what fashion. For example, although Mexican interest has been growing in the French method of coordinating private and public planning, the adaptation of such methods to the Mexican scene raises serious technical and political problems. It also is a problem to find sufficient technicians to implement new ideas in detail. New techniques are, however, adopted quite quickly on some sort of scale. Input-output analysis, for instance, has been used in Mexican planning studies at least since 1955.[30]

Little is published, however, about the use of planning principles in the government. The Ministry of the Presidency publishes virtually nothing; there is little but summary reporting in the publications of the other ministries, even in sections dealing with their planning offices. There is, to be sure, much government publicity about programs and projects—often spoken of as plans—but it lacks detail as to the principles or techniques involved in developing them, except as they concern broad economic or social policy or objectives.[31] The same is true of most of the speeches and papers of government *técnicos,* even those delivered to academic audiences, which tend to be long on development principles, and short on planning doctrine.

The paucity of easily available data on the subject of planning formulation and operations in Mexico is one source of the widespread, and often stated, suspicion that planning doctrine is too thinly applied in the development of programs. This difficulty even afflicts Mexican *técnicos* when speaking of other agencies than their own, and leads to assertions that little or no planning could have been involved in the development of programs, even when the information available to the speaker clearly is rather weak for such generalization. Some of this, to be sure, is the simple resentment of the technician in the face of political decision-making. Another reason for a lack of good analysis of Mexican planning doctrine is wide difference of opinion as to what constitutes planning. The result of this is that much elaborate intersectoral or intrasectoral study is dismissed as not rising to a sufficiently comprehensive plane to deserve the term planning.

Much of the government and nongovernmental literature that touches on planning is (1) so general as to give little idea of actual planning in Mexico,[32] or (2) simply emphasizes the importance or value of planning as part of a general bias in favor of government intervention in the economy,[33] or (3) favors planning as necessary in a nation of limited resources,[34] or (4) concentrates on development generally, on economic policy, on government controls, with but incidental reference to planning as such. Mexicans have produced quite a lot of these various sorts of literature that engage in restricted, tangential, and meandering discussions of planning.[35]

It is not to be wondered, then, that some observers, possibly partly in irritation, assert that there is no official planning doctrine in Mexico, meaning by this that it is partial, not systematically applied, and often opportunistic or pragmatic.[36] The presence of doctrine also is obscured, it is said, by the tendency of the *técnicos* to "Mexicanize" foreign ideas before presenting them to the *políticos,* and by the practice of the latter of further domesticating them before presenting them to party and nation.[37]

Much doctrine in Mexico is, of course, implicit in action and in government economic policy. Thus it is evident that the government has in practice emphasized sectoral planning, and regional planning,[38] and has made its largest integrative planning effort in connection with public investment. On the other hand, there has been much study and action founded upon consideration of intersectoral problems, and national fiscal, tariff, price, and other policies involve such considerations. Expansion of manufacturing, import substitution, industrial integration clearly are much applied principles, through tax exemptions, loan policies, and other measures. Concurrent development of agriculture and industry certainly is a principle followed in Mexico on a scale unmatched elsewhere in Latin America. Some commentators might say that it has been policy to talk of raising levels of living as a basic principle of development, and, by implication at least, of planning; but that in practice it has not seemed quite so fundamental.[39] There can be no question of the Mexican government's extreme sensitivity to the balance of international payments, or of its ingenuity in adjusting (sometimes by planning) to alterations therein. Finally, recent years have seen a growing interest in the coordination of public and private planning—or at least of investment planning, but the government appears to be following its long-time tactic of proceeding slowly rather than presenting the private sector with large-scale demands.[40] Clearly, the decision will be political, rather than technical, although government publications are referring to French experience in this field. More of this deriving of doctrine from action is deferred to the final chapter of this book.

B. Study of Economics and Public Administration

In recent decades Mexico has greatly increased instruction in economics, business, public administration, and allied subjects. Of these, public administration is the least developed; and practical business subjects, such as accounting, have been better developed than formal and theoretical economics. On the other hand, instruction in the latter has improved in recent years. Furthermore, publication in economics has increased greatly since, as observed above, the establishment in the 1930's of journals devoted to the subject.

It seems a fair judgment that the Mexican system of training in economics turns out some excellent people, but not enough of high caliber, and that the excellence of the best people is partly due to the energy of this select group in pursuing its studies after graduation (at home or abroad). This is the more possible in that most of the best *técnicos* work for the government, but under such conditions as to encourage considerable outside work or study.

The most important institution offering instruction in economics is the National University in Mexico City. The quality of instruction in its School of Economics (Escuela Nacional de Economía) is a controversial matter. Opinions expressed in interviews with government officials dealing with economic matters ranged from "excellent" to "a joke" or "not serious." Although the School of Economics is an important supplier of personnel to the government, it is suggestive that a number of its most talented graduates elect to pursue advanced studies abroad. The school suffers from the common Latin American plagues of part-time faculty, part-time student body, and excessive preoccupation with political and ideological issues to the damage of technical studies.

The Monterrey Institute of Technology (M.I.T.) emphasizes business subjects, rather than economics. It has a reputation for better instructional practices than the National University, meaning that it is more single-mindedly devoted to its obvious instructional functions. The assistance funneled into M.I.T. by the United States Agency for International Development has been understood by Mexicans as a judgment against the National University. This judgment is the more bitter to graduates of the latter now in government service (and sometimes teaching part-time at the University) in that Monterrey is a center of conservative opposition to government policies.

The Polytechnic Institute in Mexico City teaches economics and business subjects. Its orientation is more vocational and less theoretical than that of the National University, and its student body comes from a poorer economic group. The state universities are not important suppliers of economists; their resources are small, and their degrees carry no prestige, though the government hopes to change this.

A recent study summarizes the views of Mexican—and other Latin American—government economists or *técnicos* as generally involving: (1) opposition to United States efforts to reduce trade barriers; partly on the grounds (2), much publicized by Raúl Prebisch through the Economic Commission for Latin America, that the terms of trade generally run against raw material producers and in favor of exporters of manufactures; but with (3) a large array of arguments in favor of industrialization for Latin America, and reduction of its reliance on raw material exports and imports of manufactures; (4) considerable reservation about the effectiveness of the price mechanism in the allocation of resources—e.g., on the grounds that monopoly pricing by wholesale food merchants keeps down the profits of agricultural producers and discourages investment in agriculture; and (5) a general belief that public investment is done more "rationally" than private investment.[41]

Although considerable public administration is taught in Mexico, much of it is handled incidentally to other subjects, and thus not taught systematically or in depth; and much of the rest is in-service training. Most institutions of higher learning touch the subject in some way, but much of the content is business administration. At the National University there is a combined curriculum in political science and public administration in the School of Political and Social Sciences; in the School of Commerce and Administration there is a curriculum in business administration; some attention is paid to administration in courses in economics, law, and engineering; and courses in economic and social planning are offered in the School of Architecture. The undergraduate teaching at the National University is good, but the graduate work in public administration has been of low quality. No other institution of higher learning in Mexico has a course in public administration, distinct from business administration.[42] Quite a lot of in-service training in special aspects of administration is available in Mexico.[43] Mexicans have access to international and foreign institutions for some training in the field.

The instruction outlined above is insufficient to Mexico's needs. Some observers believe that improvements in instruction and curricula in public administration in Mexico offer conspicuous opportunities for improvement of the performance of public agencies. This has an evident relevance to economic development planning, and the execution of plans. Several extra-Mexican institutions, convinced of the opportunity, are giving, or considering offering, aid in this field.

Research and publication in the field of public administration also are thin. Relatively little theoretical or descriptive literature is produced,[44] even though it is evident to informed persons that research leading to improvement of the performance of the bureaucracy is needed. On the other hand, more data on the theory of public administration is available than the government is willing to make use of.[45] Still, an expansion of knowledge in this field seems desirable.[46] But the difficulties of building solidly are illustrated by the experience of the Institute of Public Administration of Mexico. The Institute was founded in 1955,[47] by persons highly qualified to give impulse to such an enterprise, by reason of their training (some of it abroad), and their position in government. The *Revista* of the Institute endured only a few years (1956–58; but it was revived in 1964), and the other activities of the Institute have remained feeble. It has not been able to build the broad support for public administration instruction, research, and publication that its sponsors had hoped for.[48]

C. Public Agencies

1. *Some Problems*

Some difficulties of research and instruction in public administration in Mexico relate to the nature of its public service, others result from the state of information on the subject. Some fundamental data either are lacking, unsatisfactory, or difficult to accumulate. Even a list of public agencies is not easy to come by, and a really comprehensive and up-to-date description of the relations between agencies cannot be had. The *Federal Directory,* first issued in 1947, has been revised tardily and irregularly, and is difficult to obtain. The Institute of Public Administration in about 1960 issued a chart of government agencies, now out-of-date and unobtainable.[49] Apparently, there is no readily available and sufficiently comprehensive roster of important public officials, or count of the total number of workers in government agencies.[50] These lacks, together with the concomitant lack of data regarding the functions, pay, selection, etc., of public employees, restricts research in the field.

In addition, the apparently universal inclination of public agencies toward secretiveness is aggravated in Mexico by the fact that there seems to be a rather severe compartmentalization in the bureaucracy, a notable degree of department or agency autonomy, and a weak spirit of inter-agency cooperation.[51] At least one often is assured that this is the case—without, to be sure, detailed specification. How serious this is compared with other countries could scarcely be guessed. The common ascription of the condition to the fact that the President has relations with department and agency heads only individually cannot be persuasive without corroborative evidence. The political reasons for presidential preference for compartmentalization seems more plausible. In any event, it seems possible that the relative autonomy of major ministries and agencies creates one barrier to the rapid adoption of common statistical standards and procedures in the government (see D, below). This creates difficulties for researchers within and without the government. The degree of agency autonomy found in Mexico probably also is in part responsible for the fact that each acts in large part independently in issuing and distributing publications. The result is, predictably, unpredictability. Not only is it difficult to know what or when an agency is going to publish an account of some portion of what it has been doing, but getting copies of such reports can be a major operation. Finally, there is considerable resistance to the use of public administration knowledge that is available in Mexico.[52] Although this resistance is not unknown in government circles in other countries (the United States, for example), it should be set down as a notable barrier to public administration research in Mexico.

The strengths and weaknesses of the Mexican federal bureaucracy are apparent, understandable, and probably subject to change only slowly. Many of the upper-echelon administrators in the economic investigation offices are highly talented and well trained. Administrators in the lower echelons are less well prepared to perform their functions.

Personnel selection and job tenure policies are widely admitted to be susceptible of great improvement. On the other hand, it will not do to exaggerate the problems involved here. For one thing, regardless of the weak formal system for protection of tenure, in fact a large part of the bureaucracy is secure. The pay of public officials is low, and results in a huge amount of "moonlighting." Even quite important officials are expected to devote only part of their time to their official positions.[53] A small beginning has been made in administrative planning.[54]

Despite all the deficiencies of the current system, it must be observed that the bureaucracy accomplishes a great deal of necessary work, and does some of it very expertly indeed.[55] Technical, financial, and economic knowledge and engineering skills are notably present in critical places. No doubt more of these skills could be used profitably.[56] And certainly much of the routine activity of the government is carried on by a staff that is too large and is poorly trained. On the other hand, immediate drastic changes in the mass of the public service would create serious problems of expense and political friction.

Three other areas of government practice that especially relate to planning are: (1) the tendency in Mexico to create new government agencies to handle new functions, rather than fitting them into the existing departments;[57] (2) the efforts to create effective machinery for the integration and control of the government's multiplying entities; and (3) the creation by many agencies of their own economic study, programming, and planning offices, a development that seems not to have aroused much criticism. Finally, it should be noted that many of the criticisms of the Mexican public service mentioned above are levied against all bureaucracies, often with less foundation than the information on which this study is based.

2. *Efforts to Coordinate and Control*

The effort to coordinate and control the activities of government entities is here taken to mean their operating activities rather than their policy or planning functions. This effort at control took a new and more effective form with the creation in 1946 of the Ministry of National Properties (Bienes Nacionales) and Administrative Inspection. It had some success in establishing controls on purchasing, contracts, construction, inventories, and the like.[58] This ministry was replaced, by law of December, 1958, by the Secretaría de Patrimonio Nacional, with broadened powers.

The powers granted the Ministry of National Patrimony not only spelled out in more detail functions that had been handled by the Ministries of National Properties and of Finance,[59] but they were notably and clearly widened by extension to the decentralized organs and enterprises with state participation. Among the powers granted National Patrimony were: preparation of rules and procedures, and control and overseeing, both financial and administrative, of the operations of organs, institutions, or corporations that managed, owned, or exploited the property or natural resources of the nation; and inventory and overseeing of all real and other property and of natural resources in the public sector.[60]

The Ministry of National Patrimony by this law became an important element in the continuing effort to control the investments of government agencies, a subject discussed below.[61] As for its control over purchases, natural resources, and the like, the Ministry has much elaborated its methods of recording, supervising, and publicizing such activity.[62] There does not seem to be any detailed judgment available, however, as to the effects of these efforts.[63] Indications of continued struggle with what all modern governments find a never-ending problem is seen in a decree of March 8, 1965, modifying the Supervisory Committee of the Organs and Enterprises of the State (Junta de Gobierno de los Organismos y Empresas del Estado).[84]

It was at first asserted by critics of the law of December, 1958, that it gave National Patrimony such extensive powers of supervision over government dependencies that it would be involved intimately in the planning process with the Ministry of the Presidency set up by the same law.[65] There was some objection in the congress to giving the same functions to two ministries.[66] Subsequent developments indicate that this fear of conflict was not well founded. The Ministry of National Patrimony has defended itself against the charge of conflict by declaring that planning and control are related but distinct functions, for:

> It is not possible to control an activity that has not been planned. Planning is the function relative to the selection among alternatives, objectives, methods, and programs. By exercising control operations and activities may be supervised within agreed limits, correcting deviations from plans. Thus, control cannot exist if there are no plans that determine the standards for control.[67]

D. STATISTICAL, STUDY, AND PLANNING OFFICES

Many government offices prepare regular statistical series, or special materials.[68] The General Statistical Bureau (Dirección General de Estadística) of the Ministry of Industry and Commerce puts out a bibliography of national statistical sources, which includes the names of some of the offices putting out statistics.[69] This is the best lead to official government figures, but it is not exhaustive. According to law, the Ministry of Industry and Commerce is charged with setting up common statistical standards and methods for all government agencies. Only slow progress has been made in this regard since the law was passed in 1958.

The quality, quantity, and method of publication of official figures in Mexico are adequate, in spite of variations in method and in publication practice. Clearly, the government could not operate as well as it does without reasonably satisfactory information. Improvements in statistical series are effected frequently.[70] On the other hand, students and government officials appear reluctant to concede Mexican statistics anything more than adequacy. For one thing, the compartmentalization of the bureaucracy, to which we have referred, has encouraged secretiveness in the treatment of statistical information.[71] For another thing, some complaints are not so much about the inadequacy or inaccuracy of traditional figures on such things as government revenues or public investment, as about the absence or inadequacy of data requiring types of information-gathering not yet sufficiently elaborated by the government (e.g., on actual family income or expenditures, or the investment plans of private enterprise, or the skills of industrial workers). It is widely recognized that improvements in the statistical field are every day more desirable as the size and complexity of Mexican economic development operations increase.[72] Some of the most important and best statistics are compiled by the Bank of Mexico and by Nacional Financiera, and occasionally their figures conflict disconcertingly, a situation not unknown in other countries.

Many Mexican government economic study offices have for years produced studies for use in planning, and have produced plans, without being designated planning offices.[73] This was long the case, for example, in the complex organizations of the Ministries of Agriculture and of Education. Another example is the Bureau of Economic Studies (Dirección General de Estudios Económicos) of the Ministry of the Economy, long one of the most active research units in the government. Of its 361 investigations in 1957, 33 were specifically on planning activities.[74] Some of its work has involved cooperation with other ministries.[75] In addition to such study offices, there have been created in recent years rather numerous offices or staffs with the specific planning title. Indeed, it appears that no major unit of the government now lacks a planning office. Presumably this has resulted in part from the growing acceptance in Mexico of the administrative theory that planning should be done by staffs or agencies that have no other responsibilities. Mexican writers on public administration seem to agree on this general principle, while disputing many other aspects of the question.[76] One may also speculate that it has become "fashionable" to have planning offices (and computers and water-coolers).

The following table lists some of the more prominent planning and economic study offices:

TABLE 3
SOME MEXICAN GOVERNMENT ECONOMIC PLANNING AND STUDY OFFICES[77]

Ministries and Depts. of State	Planning or Study Offices
Presidencia	Dirección de Planeación Oficina del Plan General del Gasto Público
Industria y Comercio	Dirección General de Estudios Económicos Dirección General de Estadística
Recursos Hidráulicos	Dirección de Planeación, Estadística e Información Dirección de Estudios y Proyectos Comisión de Estudios del Río Balsas Comisión de Estudios . . . Grijalva Comisión de Estudios . . . Papaloapan
Patrimonio Nacional	Depto. de Investigaciones y Estadística, in Junta de Gobo. de Organismos y Empresas . . . Depto. de Estudios Técnicos y Económicos, in Consejo de Recursos Naturales no Renovables Depto. de Investigaciones y Estadística, in Dirección General de Urbanismo, Ingeniería y Arquitectura
Hacienda y Crédito Público	Depto. de Planeación Presupuestal, in Dirección General de Egresos Deptos. of Estudios Económicos, of Estadística, and of Estudios Especiales, in Dirección General de Estudios Hacendarias
Obras Públicas	Dirección de Planeación y Programa
Agricultura y Ganadería	Dirección General de Economía Agrícola
Comunicaciones y Transportes	Depto. de Planeación
Other Agencies:	
Depto. de Turismo	Dirección General de Planeación y Recursos
Depto. del Distrito Federal	Subdirección de Planeación y Programa, in Dirección General de Obras Públicas
Comisión Federal de Electricidad	Depto. de Planeación

The evidence available on these and similar offices suggests that they generally concentrate on the relatively limited concerns of their agencies—that is, that they chiefly do regional, sector, or subsector planning or studies. Such activity is, of course, increasingly important for its own sake, in view of the great expansion of the Mexican economy in recent decades. Furthermore, the increasing quantity and improving quality of sector planning studies must have important effects upon the work of agencies engaging in cross-sectoral or aggregate planning.

Indispensable as these sector research and planning groups are, technical staffs with broader interests obviously are needed. The need has been filled in large measure, for more than two decades, by the Bank of Mexico and Nacional Financiera. The Ministry of Finance does important research, but it is financial, rather than broadly economic or developmental, so that it assigns much of its research to the Bank of Mexico.[78]

Students of Mexican economic policy long have recognized that the Bank of Mexico and Nacional Financiera possess the broadest collections of materials, the most notable concentrations of technical personnel, and the most important study and planning assignments (aside from finance) in the fields of economic development. Technical studies (as of railways or petroleum) of a routine nature, or at project level, are well handled in other government departments or agencies. But national questions, or questions involving integration of sectors, or matters requiring the use of new concepts or methods, have fallen rather to the staffs of the Bank of Mexico and Nacional Financiera. Although some tension and competition exist between the staffs of the two institutions, it is not disabling, and may be declining. Even the recent establishment of the Ministry of the Presidency, with the stated function of handling national planning, has not much, if at all, reduced this activity in the two banks. Much of the economic study and planning activity of these two institutions is little known or not at all known outside restricted government and business circles.[79]

The Bank of Mexico's investigative activity was considerably expanded when, in 1941, at the suggestion of the Bankers Convention, it established its office of Industrial Investigations. This office was set up specifically to fill institutional or functional gaps that tended to retard economic growth. As a consequence of this purpose, the office often worked in cooperation with other agencies. Other offices in the Bank today include: Estudios Económicos, Estudios Económicos Regionales, Instituto Mexicano de Investigaciones Tecnológicos, Investigaciones Industriales de Productividad Nacional, and a library and bibliographical service. Bank of Mexico studies have been highly varied, ranging from natural resources to all the major sectors of production. Among recent activities are studies in productivity, emphasizing the importance of technical training; and on the promotion of exports and the substitution of imports.[80]

Nacional Financiera includes offices with the following titles: Industrial Programming, Economic Investigations, Statistics and Economic Development, Special Studies. This institution's role as a development bank gives it a strong interest in economic planning and in studies in support thereof.[81] It has sponsored research and publication on some important economic subjects. Although there is some public knowledge of the study function of Nacional Financiera, and even more of its policies and actions with regard to its own investments, there is little direct information on its influence on broader policy or planning.[82]

E. SOME ASPECTS OF IMPLEMENTATION

The viability of the Mexican sociopolitical system is explicable in part as a triumph of communications and the mobilization of influence by the PRI and the government. Certainly no aspect of the activity of the establishment is so galling to the opposition as the ability of the former to maintain a workable national consensus with a minimum of the violent frictions so necessary to the hopes of the latter. The general importance of this communications system to economic development and planning is clear, but in the present state of Mexican studies we are somewhat frustrated by a shortage of detailed data based on sophisticated social science investigation and dealing with conflicts of goals and values, organized interest groups, the conditions of discussion and publication, information networks, communications techniques, and methods of propaganda, bargaining, and pressure.

Mexico is like many other countries in that: (1) debate on economic policy is affected by conflicts of goals and value systems; (2) it often is difficult to identify the points at which affection for values shades into attachment to material interests; and (3) many statements on public policy either are inadequately linked to economic reasoning, or the reasoning is so obscure as to be either ambiguous or invisible to the observer. On the other hand, it is uniquely Mexican that conflict over goals and values is tied to debate over the condition of the Revolution—ongoing, moribund, or defunct. The fundamental, as opposed to the ostensible, or the public, attitudes toward policy in Mexico are as much obscured under the poncho of the revolutionary shibboleths as they are in the United States under the mantle of the American Way.

Although the subject of values has not been studied in the Mexican environment—at least in its economic connotations—in the detail it deserves, we may mention some areas of disagreement. Possibly the most important is the question of whether "social" or "economic" values are to have precedence in determining policy.[83] This must be accepted as a matter of some practical importance in contemporary Mexico, however it may be viewed as a useful subject for theoretical discussion. It colors debates over investment priorities, the relative importance to growth of expansion of production facilities (investment) or of increases in consumer purchasing power (wages), and the relative importance of short-term as against long-term goals. Another conflict relates to the aims, efficiency, and social utility of the public and private economic sectors. Some intellectuals even carry into this discussion a repugnance for the personal habits and taste of the new rich of Mexico.[84] A special form of the public/private debate revolves around the supposed merits—social, economic, and apparently metaphysical—of communal farm land ownership. This is a subject as productive of obscurantism and sentimentality in Mexico as the present legends of the blessed on the American frontier and the myth of the selfless socialist brotherhood in Communist lands. A third conflict is over the value of agricultural as against industrial development, not so much as an economic question as in relation to the supposed social values of different types of occupational activity and of rural as opposed to urban residence.[85] Finally, we may note the conflicts and ambiguities of values in connection with nationalism or *Mexicanidad*.[86] This is related to such important policy questions as the amount of reflection to be permitted to modify the passion swirling about the notion of "nonrenewable natural resources," and whether the animus against foreign capital is to be indiscriminate or selective. In any event, humanistic, "revolutionary," and other sociopolitical value clusters produce in Mexico attitudes toward and statements on economic policy that suggest difficulties of communication between groups.

It is through organized interest groups, of course, that the most effective expression of goals and values occurs. Although such groups are numerous and important in Mexico, the study of their activities by social scientists is barely in its infancy. The PRI and the government obviously are highly organized interest groups. Although the two institutions have much in common (including rather considerable numbers of personnel), their interests are not identical on all questions and at all times. Thus, implementation activities can by no means always be identical for mobilization of the support of the bureaucracy and for that of the PRI. Furthermore, neither government nor PRI is monolithic in its interests. There is considerable competition and conflict of interest between various elements of the government, and implementation of development plans must deal with this fact.[87]

As for the PRI, it is a congeries of interest groups, and they struggle for power and favor within the party.[88] Large numbers of leaders of party affiliates jockey for attention and preference for themselves and their organizations. The peasants and small farmers, industrial labor, small businessmen, and civil servants largely are involved in the sector apparatus of the PRI.[89] The military's lines of communications are within party and government, even though there is no longer a military sector of the PRI. Not only must the national party leadership acceptably resolve the many tugs-of-war between party affiliates, but they must repel, capture, or otherwise effectively dispose of the attempts of non-party groups to influence PRI members, or even to draw them into non-party organizations, with or without resignation from the PRI.

The minor political parties, especially PAN, constitute interest groups, and maintain communications networks and engage in efforts to win popular support or to wring concessions from the establishment. The Church has its own organization and interests. Important Church elements often collaborate with rightest parties; but there is also a liberal element among the religious, and they and their supporters engage in efforts to gain favor.

Intellectuals in Mexico may be regarded here as an interest group both because of their affection for certain types of employment and for government support of artistic and intellectual endeavor, and because efforts on the part of the establishment to mobilize their support often require a specialized type of communications effort. One must beware of exaggerating the importance of such efforts. Considerable numbers of Mexican intellectuals are satisfied with the establishment,[90] even though some of them find it pleasant, or necessary to their connections with the intellectual community, to veil their complacence by occasional assumption of the standard stance of the intellectual in at least partial repudiation of the values and deeds of government and business. An important aspect of this is the fact that large numbers of intellectuals are government employees. If their connection is primarily with the National University, they are in some measure protected by its freedom from government interference. But if they work for noneducational agencies of the government—and the majority of well-trained Mexican economists do—their freedom to adopt "intellectual" stances, insofar as those may be at variance with government and party positions, is more limited. Finally, many intellectuals are so little, or so loosely, or ineffectively, organized that they can be considered an unorganized "public" rather than an interest group.

In Mexico's regulated market economy private enterprise essentially does its own planning, within the limits imposed by government and by prudence in the face of government suggestion. Communication between government and private enterprise is, therefore, a critical element in efforts to plan economic development. The OAS group studying the Mexican Plan of Immediate Action in 1964 emphasized the importance of improving the confidence of private enterprise.[91] Recognizing this necessity, the government consults private enterprise a great deal—both officially and unofficially. Some of the most important communication lines between the two sectors run into and out of the business associations. Although the organization and role of private business associations in Mexico have been little studied in depth, enough is known about them to permit presentation of some statements, with greater or lesser degrees of confidence.

First, the business community is highly organized, in large measure as a requirement of law, and to some degree both the terms of organization and the activities of the bodies are controlled by the government.[92] This is, however, far from making the associations creatures of the state. Second, the government assiduously seeks the views and courts the cooperation of the associations, even in connection with actions it knows the associations oppose. Much of this consultation is unpublicized, but the government also carries on a highly publicized dialogue with the business associations, especially at their annual conventions.[93] Third, the associations generally are fearful of government intervention in the economy, but some of them approve of certain types of intervention, so that the view of the business community is not monolithic, and it has, furthermore, changed to some extent in the course of time.[94] Fourth, the present business associations are not very old.[95] Fifth, the business notion of "planning" is for private enterprise to play the leading role,[96] although there may be some recent increase of willingness to consider the sort of collaboration with government in planning that has been accepted by business in France.[97] Sixth, the associations are not part of the PRI and are not likely to be in the foreseeable future. Seventh, there is reason to be wary in interpreting the public statements of spokesmen of the associations, and those of government officials in addressing the associations. We have observed in this connection that leftist critics of the government assert that much of the public relationship between it and business is a charade put on to screen the intimacy of the collaboration between them.[98]

The conditions of competition for influence in Mexico are affected by some features of the cultural environment that must be summarized here:

1. *Popular Attitudes toward Major Contestants for Influence*

The government (hence the PRI) benefits from the fact that there is wide popular belief in the value of government action. The business community not only labors under this disability in its efforts to mobilize support against government intervention in the economy, but also under the disability that there is little popular emotional attachment to business leaders, achievements, or philosophizing. The intelligentsia may be guessed to have less influence than in France, more than in the United States, much less than they consider they are entitled to, and a great deal less than some commentators seem to imagine.

2. *Popular Social Conditions*

Much of the population is either illiterate or has had little schooling. The rural poor are much isolated by poverty, poor communications, and a traditional diffidence and apathy toward public affairs. The urban poor apparently must be described either as not very demanding or as rather optimistic about their chances of improving their condition.[99] One is tempted to speculate that optimism, increased achievement motivation, and social mobility are bolstered by the swarms of United States tourists in Mexico. All of these social conditions are favorable to the efforts of government and PRI in the competition for popular support.

3. *Politicogovernmental Conditions of Discussions*

The virtual one-party system relieves the PRI of the problems of debate that exist when there is meaningful party competition. The great power of the executive branch of the federal government relieves it of the threat that opposition efforts will be led by or coalesce around the legislature or the judiciary. This means that interest groups lobby with agencies of the executive branch but not with the Congress. Although judgment is more difficult with regard to freedom of discussion, protest, and petition without fear of arbitrary arrest or physical coercion, it seems to an outsider that this type of fear plays a minor role in the effort to mobilize influence in Mexico. Even more difficult is judgment as to the effects on communications of the heavy influence of government and PRI on the media of public communications. Speech and publication are free enough in Mexico so that a great variety of views is published, especially in the capital. There is sufficient variety so that the government and party must make lavish outlays to uphold their views before the public. Although the government does exercise great influence on the press, and manipulates and interferes with publications, it also cherishes a domestic and international reputation for the maintenance of free publication. On the whole, therefore, the establishment prefers to answer criticism, rather than to smash the critics.[100]

The PRI long has exhibited a conviction that there is political mileage in the terminology and a popularized concept of planning. We have commented on the party involvement in two Six-Year Plans, and their use in the presidential elections of 1934 and 1940. The intentions of Alemán and Ruíz Cortines, in running for the next two terms, were widely described as plans in meetings and speeches all over the country and in floods of campaign literature issued by the PRI. López Mateos, in preparing for the election of 1958, made use of a Council on Economic and Social Planning, through which he met business elements not formally represented in the structure of the PRI.[101] As early as 1960 the PRI decided to pour considerable effort into a party "planning" campaign, through Popular Programming Committees to help set the aims of the next administration. These committees met throughout the country. In January, 1963, the PRI's First National Programming Conference was held, with representatives from various echelons of the party and all states of the republic, including officials of the PRI's Instituto de Estudios Políticos, Económicos y Sociales. It assertedly began to prepare state and regional development plans for later incorporation into the government program for the next administration. The PRI issued a statement that pointed out that programming for economic development was common in democratic countries, that both public and private activities should be included, and that "it is necessary that all sectors of the population collaborate" in this effort.[102] Later in 1963 the results were published. This was, of course, campaign material. It poured praise on the development of the country since the Revolution, celebrated the value of planning and programming, uttered the predictable generalities about each major economic sector, demanded more social planning, and said this result of much popular consultation had been contrived to serve as a base for the plan of government of the party candidate.[103]

It is clear from what has been said above that Mexican public men exhibit none of that timidity about uttering the terms "plan" and "planning" that is a condition of survival in national politics north of the Rio Grande. Thus, to the north of the border more planning is done than is publicized, while south of it more is proclaimed than occurs or is intended. Speeches and the press in Mexico teem with references to and discussions and celebrations of planning as such, and of portions of plans at various government levels. Even the pro-government press gives some space to criticism—though rather general—of various aspects of government plans.[104] The opposition press violently objects both to known government plans and to the supposed lack of sufficient planning.

The annual messages of the presidents to the congress are an important device for dissemination of the plans and philosophy of planning of the establishment. In his 1963 message,[105] President López Mateos asserted that improvements in levels of living required rigorous planning by government, so that government activity had been subjected to such plans as "the Eleven Year [plan] on matters of fundamental education, that of overall agricultural development, that of industrial promotion, and those of regional development"; he noted that modern conditions required programming that involved both public and private activities, and that government must pursue social justice by such means without adhering to outmoded ideas; he declared that he favored public and private cooperation, but that the country would resent it if the private sector did not do its duty in investing in the future of the country; included was the following passage, which is an eloquent expression of the point of view of the PRI and the government:

> Those who in other times believed that to have their activities subjected to plans and programs would bring a decline in their liberty, have learned that it is necessary in order to have the most efficient and creative force for . . . the benefit of the Mexican population and the aggrandizement of the fatherland.

Important also are the speeches of government officials to the annual meetings of business associations, which we have mentioned. Very recently, they have played a role in the government effort to persuade private enterprise to improve the integration between public and private planning, especially of investments. The mobilization of support for this closer public/private tie, called for in the Plan of Immediate Action for 1962–64, is possibly the most important implementation effort being conducted by the government in connection with planning. The press has been used by the government in an effort to develop general support for a more complaisant attitude on the part of private enterprise.

The tireless attendance of Mexican national government and party officials at regional and state celebrations often is used to propagandize plans and the planning function. Speeches at the dedications of public works serve the same purpose. Recently, there has been a proliferation of plans at the state level, celebrated at the inaugurations of governors, and applauded in person by the most eminent representatives of government and PRI.[106] This state-level activity may make mobilization of support for national planning somewhat easier; or it may increase and complicate the uneasiness of business interests. Finally, we may remark on the involvement of government technicians in economic development and planning discussions in academic and other intellectual surroundings. All these publicly visible means of promoting approval of or acquiescence in government planning constitute a sizable effort.

To the outsider, it thus appears that the always lively debate in Mexico over economic policy now includes a fairly notable component on planning. It has been asserted, however, that public discussion of planning in Mexico is too infrequent and too generalized—chiefly because of government secrecy—to affect significantly government policies in that connection, and that planning would be done more carefully, rationally, and effectively if such public debate were increased.[107] A project for a new planning law in 1963 declared that publicity on planning was needed to ensure both public support and proper government coordination.[108]

VI

Sector and Regional Planning

A. Introduction

Many less than nationally comprehensive (sector, regional, state, municipal) plans, and studies or programs involving some approach to planning activity, are drawn up by public agencies in Mexico. Some are essentially engineering or physical plans—for projects that are somehow selected, assertedly on occasion in the absence of criteria that critics consider indispensable to the veritable planning process. In any event, critics sometimes dismiss as simply "engineering plans" activity that can be shown to have involved economic and social factors. Much of this work is so well done that many analysts consider the quality of Mexican sectoral planning an important factor in her relatively satisfactory rate of economic growth in recent decades. A prominent Mexican *técnico* recently put it that although Mexico has not had "formal or integrated economic planning in its technical sense," the government "has drafted sectoral plans of great scope for some public activities."[1]

Data have not been found for this study to permit systematic discussion of criteria of project selection or problems of project coordination. Little information is available on planning at the enterprise level, in either public or private enterprises. Much information is available on the construction, cost, characteristics, economic and social effects, and other aspects of projects; on government policies and actions that affect them; on statistics of growth, and kindred subjects relating to sector and enterprise activity; but there is little on planning as such.[2] The information available suggests respect for the judgment reported in the preceding paragraph. There is no mystery about the paucity of information on sector planning. Much of such activity does not reach print, but circulates in typescript or mimeograph, or remains in working files.

Programs that result from sectoral planning are drafted and given publicity with little need for reference to the planning function. Even that published material that contains modest discussion of planning is not widely circulated. Thus, in some areas where there has been large growth, it is not clear how much of that growth resulted from planning, and how much was due to opportunistic (and possibly quite intelligent) response to circumstances, or to sheer luck.

Some *técnicos* in Mexico would like to see more material on sector planning made available, because they suspect that it would reveal mistakes that wider and better-based discussion might help to avoid in the future. On the other hand, few other Mexicans seem much interested in sector planning. Politicians, publicists, and humanists who criticize the national government's planning seem to shy away from the details of planning for chemicals, petroleum, electric power, irrigation, transportation, and the like. Presumably this is because criticism of sector planning in this sense requires a detailed technical knowledge they do not possess, or because it does not make good material for public controversy. Instead, public criticism tends to pry at what seem to be the obvious cracks in "agricultural" or "industrial" planning, as supposedly evidenced by such conditions as inequitable income distribution, or geographic concentration of manufacturing production.

There has been considerable government sectoral planning in connection with electric power, petroleum, transportation, and irrigation. There is heavy government ownership in these fields, and they account for the bulk of investment in economic development from the federal budget. In addition to these sectors, in which there has been important activity for years, the government produces many programs for development in aspects of agriculture or manufacturing—from expanding or lowering coffee production, to the recent remarkable development of chemical production, to the new automotive industry. The three instances just mentioned are examples of government activity involving coordination of policies and agencies that may be included under the definition of planning.

Coordination in some sense of sector plans is theoretically one of the duties of the planning office of the Ministry of the Presidency. It presumably manages some measure of coordination by way of its function of coordinating investment budgets, and through the regional planning the Ministry has undertaken. It should be observed that even if the Ministry wished to make a maximum effort to coordinate sector planning, several factors would restrict its efforts. For one thing, the law of December, 1958, setting up the Ministry's planning functions, not only left some planning functions to designated agencies (the Ministries of Public Works, of Communications and Transport, and the Agrarian Department), but it stated that the President could relieve others from the Minister of the Presidency's supervision.[3] For another thing, the only partially revealed history of that Ministry since 1958 indicates, as we would expect in the Mexican government—or most any, for that matter—that the more important agencies will resist too much effort at supervision or the capture of functions by the new ministry. Further, a major effort at coordination probably would be duplicative to some extent of such work now done in the Bank of Mexico and Nacional Financiera, and would arouse resentment in those agencies and in the Ministry of Finance, with which they work closely. In any event, such an effort would be beyond the personnel capabilities of the Ministry of the Presidency, and it would not be likely to be able to capture the requisite staff from such agencies as the Bank of Mexico, Nacional Financiera, the Ministries of Hydraulic Resources, Communications and Transport, or Public Works, or from Petróleos Mexicanos or the Federal Electricity Commission.

In any event, coordination of sector plans, by whatever agency, means that the coordinators in large part depend on the technical studies of the great federal agencies that are responsible for the selection of sites, location of raw materials, drafting of construction plans, estimating costs and schedules. The coordinators will also, no doubt, depend in part on those agencies for economic studies on such matters as the projected contributions to the national economy from the works recommended, and for interagency and intersectoral study and coordination. We have noted that a number of agencies produce such studies: e.g., Estudios Económicos of the Ministry of Industry and Commerce, the Ministry of Hydraulic Resources, Nacional Financiera, and the Bank of Mexico.

Finally, a word should be said about the agricultural and industrial sectors as a whole, and about coordination within sectors. No one outside the government seems to want to state that there is an overall agricultural or an overall industrial plan. And within the government, the *técnicos* tend to scoff at the idea. On the other hand, upper-echelon government and party figures sometimes assert that the government has such agricultural or industrial plans, and even attach resounding names to them. What they mean is that the government has a congeries of agreed-to and often individually considered policies and programs and goals (general and specific), more or less interlocked, for the development of agriculture or manufacturing.

As to how much these policies and programs are "coordinated" or "integrated," little public information exists; however, we are assaulted with many assertions that there is little of either. Highly competent analysts have judged for years that there is too little such coordination in Mexico. Unfortunately, less competent witnesses sometimes give the impression that no such coordination exists. Given the competence of the Mexican government, its fixation on economic development, the complexity of the Mexican economy, and the good growth rates achieved in a number of publicly dominated sectors, it is not possible to believe that no such coordination has existed. Furthermore, the government is known to plan the coordination of many fiscal and other measures for the promotion of selected agricultural and manufacturing fields, in pursuit of a number of well known objectives. There is a Special Commission on Foreign Financing, headed by the Minister of Finance, and with the other members the Directors of the Bank of Mexico and of Nacional Financiera; internal private credit is managed through the Bank of Mexico; and internal public credit is managed through a Coordinating Committee of National Institutions of Credit, headed by the Minister of Finance.[4] We know also of a number of other interministerial committees with coordinative functions, such as that created in 1964 to plan for the sugar industry, and consisting of representatives of the Ministries of Industry and Commerce, of Finance, and of Agriculture. Some other such coordinative bodies are mentioned below.

B. Agriculture

There is no single government plan for the entire agricultural sector of the economy, or even for public-sector activity. There is, nevertheless, considerable government decision-making regarding agriculture that involves goals, futurity, and an approach to comprehensiveness, that may be called planning. It should be borne in mind that: (1) some government agencies typically produce plans or executive programs that affect parts of the agricultural industry;[5] (2) there is considerable coordination of studies and policies between agencies, but many observers believe that it should be much extended and improved; (3) as in so much else of Mexican development policy, a critical area of decision-making relates to credit and investment, and involves agencies with cross-sectoral interests as well as those with primarily agricultural orientation; and (4) there is so much government action affecting agriculture in Mexico that some observers find it heavily planned,[6] even if the planning is not, in their judgment, well integrated with all aspects of development. Three other observations should be made: (1) although it is widely agreed that there is no well integrated national agricultural development plan, the government sometimes asserts that there is;[7]

(2) much of the demand for a national agricultural plan is either simply politics or just simple;[8] and (3) although much planning and operational responsibility falls to the Ministry of Agriculture and Stockraising, and to the Department of Agrarian and Colonization Affairs, many other agencies also are involved. In regard to these last, it will be noted that many have intersectoral responsibilities, such as the Ministry of Finance, government banks, and the Ministries of Hydraulic Resources and of Communications and Transport.[9]

In any event, Mexican agriculture is controlled, channeled, and influenced in many ways by the government. It is not clear that an integrated national agricultural plan would have brought better results than the conglomeration of policies, actions, and partial plans that Mexico (as the United States) uses.[10] Furthermore, data are lacking for a total agricultural plan.[11] Important gains in productivity could be achieved by relatively simple improvements in agricultural technology, whether or not as a part of an integrated national plan.[12] There is quite an elaborate institutional structure for the dissemination of new agricultural methods.[13] And the political problems involved in Mexican agricultural planning can scarcely be judged effectively by foreigners. For one thing, a blue print for all agriculture might make too visible the fact that capital resources are channeled heavily to non-*ejidal* agriculture. There is, nevertheless, reason to believe that agricultural planning by the government may be soon either more centralized or more publicized, both because of increasing public criticism of the condition of the rural community, and because Gustavo Díaz Ordaz during his campaign for the presidency in 1963–64 often stated that the agricultural community probably required more attention than any other. To be sure, he also said that the solution to the rural problem lay partly in increasing the movement to industrial towns.

C. MANUFACTURING

Much the same points made in connection with agricultural planning may be made with reference to planning for the development of manufacturing industries, except that there is no humanistic interest in "total" or integrated planning for manufacturing comparable to that interest in agriculture. Although there is no over-all government plan for the development of manufacturing,[14] planning and quasi-planning activities affecting manufacturing are carried on in a number of agencies, including the Ministry of Industry and Commerce, the Ministry of the Presidency, Nacional Financiera, and others. The Bank of Mexico's Department of Industrial Investigations has existed since 1941. A good part of the planning relates to specific manufacturing industries, and most of that consists of a combination of measures to encourage investment by private interests, with provision of economic infrastructure to serve the manufacturers.

To some observers this method of attacking the problems of manufacturing development does not deserve the name of planning. Thus Mosk wrote in 1950 that although there was government talk of its "plan of industrialization," this was not, in his view, to be taken literally. He considered that the only overall government "plan" was to encourage private investment, Mexican and foreign, to build new plants.[15] Furthermore, Mosk considered that there was only one national plan for the development of an individual manufacturing industry—cement.[16] Mosk would no doubt have found little planning in connection with President López Mateos' statements to congress in September, 1962, on a "plan of industrial promotion," since it was clear that López meant by this essentially a strategy of encouraging and to some extent channeling private investment in industry.[17]

Although such views still are current, they are less common. Observers are beginning to construe the term "plan," and especially "planning," less narrowly than a decade ago. They certainly tend to point out that there has been much promotion of other industries than cement, and in a fashion that bears some resemblance to planning.[18] Further, as in the case of agriculture, it will not do to ignore the coordinative and continuitive aspects of national policy and action to promote manufacturing. This includes the long-continued use of tax exemptions, protective tariffs, import licenses, credit policies, and other devices, in pursuit of such accepted principles as import substitution, Mexicanization,[19] and national economic integration. In connection with this last, an interesting use has been made by the government since 1961 of a list of 500 industrial products it claims offer good opportunities for private investment, and which it states are necessary for a properly integrated national manufacturing industry.[20] It should be noted of government promotion of manufacturing that there is constant criticism that there is too little coordination of such activity. The OAS group studying the Plan of Immediate Action in 1964 advised improvement of coordination of the industrial promotion of Nacional Financiera, the Bank of Mexico, the Ministry of Finance, and the Ministry of Industry and Commerce, in order to formulate a development program for new industries and for modernization of existing ones with the collaboration of the private sector.[21]

Certainly, much development in the basic iron and steel industry has been due to government action, including ownership of some production facilities. Also, some would say that government has for some years helped plan development of the private automotive industry, at first in connection with the assembly of largely foreign-made components,[22] and since 1962 by forcing the manufacture of more and more components in Mexico.[23] This has led to considerable new foreign private investment.[24]

Nacional Financiera's industrial investment is to some degree—perhaps largely—guided by such principles as improvement of the balance of payments, development of industrial integration, the growth of productivity, the development of savings, and raising the employment level.[25] Because of its large role in manufacturing investment, Nacional Financiera has in some measure served as a centralized planning, study, and policy-making institution.[26] Certainly it—and other agencies—have been much concerned with the study of manufacturing, especially of certain aspects.[27] Mexican private industrial associations at least furnish data that is useful for planning purposes.[28]

It must be noted in connection with government studies of manufacturing activity in Mexico that it often is complained that they are based on too small a percentage of the activity occurring in the field under study. It must also be noted that, as in the case of agriculture, there is some Mexican opinion in favor of more far-reaching planning for manufacturing development. In June, 1962, for example, the Fourth National Congress of Mechanical and Electrical Engineers had as its theme "Planned Industrialization through the Use of Human and Natural Resources." One proposal at the Congress was that a Subsecretary of Industrialization be appointed in the Ministry of Industry and Commerce to coordinate the development plans of the states, and to formulate an industrial development plan of national scope, taking into consideration the location of resources, and avoiding further concentration of manufacturing in congested areas. There are frequent suggestions that the government "Plan" the geographic dispersal of industry.[29]

D. IRRIGATION

Post-Revolution irrigation activity dates to the 1926 Irrigation Law and the National Irrigation Commission set up in the Ministry of Agriculture and Development. Irrigation development was slow to 1946, when the Irrigation Commission was merged in a new Ministry of Hydraulic Resources. Under this agency irrigation works have been constructed at a greatly accelerated rate, and Mexico has become a world leader in such development. In recent years the Ministry of Hydraulic Resources has received a major share of federal budget allocations. Furthermore, a high proportion of government expenditures on agriculture are in irrigation.[30] The value of this effort, however, is disputed, and the difficulties of computing returns on investment in irrigation are considerable.[31] In addition, many political factors operate in connection with irrigation policy—in Mexico as in the United States.

The World Bank in 1953 criticized irrigation work in Mexico as not having shown adequate returns, partly because of investment in large projects not yet showing much yield, insufficient attention to auxiliary distribution works, and too little effort to improve farming methods in the irrigated areas.[32] All these criticisms are heard today in Mexico. One often hears the comment that planning conspicuously is lacking when millions are spent for impressive-appearing dams whose effects are seriously inhibited by the failure to make small auxiliary efforts in education or technology. Suspicions are also voiced that many dams and irrigation works were built in poor locations as the result of inadequate investigation. Drought in the Laguna area currently has drastically curtailed the usefulness of the irrigation system built there some years ago, and the result is assigned to what assertedly were inadequate rainfall statistics used during the planning stage. Of course, in the absence of adequate data, planners must make some guesses. Further, some of the other criticisms mentioned above are not directed at irrigation planning per se, but at total agricultural production planning.[33]

Thus, it appears that many of the criticisms of irrigation planning should be directed not at the Ministry of Hydraulic Resources but at the President of the Republic for not providing more coordination in the field of agricultural development. But, in fact, as World Bank experts found in Mexico in 1963 in considering the Plan of Immediate Action for 1962–64, it is difficult to determine the real returns obtained from Mexican irrigation projects.[34] In any event, the approach of Hydraulic Resources to its activities is quite broad, as indicated by its planning activity in a recent year.[35] Under the heading "Planeación General" it reported formulation of studies, plans, and projects (agricultural, pastoral, commercial, industrial) looking to the maximum use of natural resources, to get the highest return with minimum effort; it worked on Irrigation District plans;[36] and did studies on the integral planning of the southeast.

Under the heading "Planificación" it noted that irrigation alters population projections, and requires planning or replanning of communities; it stated that it had made a plan for a specific small region, "and continued study of the necessary data that will permit formulation of a concrete plan of works with priorities." Under "Estudios Económicos y Estadística" it reported: socioeconomic studies of eight separate states;

socioeconomic studies of entities of the republic, to permit "integral planning" of irrigation works; studies of investment needs; population studies in irrigation districts; studies relative to the "economic planning" of the zones of influence of irrigation districts; a study of the activities that the Ministry should coordinate with other dependencies of the government relative "to planning the integral development of Mexico." Even in the absence of access to these studies one feels confident that the staff has some understanding of what may be involved in planning.[37]

The Ministry of Hydraulic Resources has developed a plan for irrigating additional lands and forming new irrigation districts in the years 1962–85. Under this plan the total area irrigated is to be increased from some four million hectares to a total of 5.9 million. This will require an investment of 10.72 billion pesos. The plan includes rehabilitation of existing works, control of salinization, and increases in the extension services and credit agencies that serve the irrigation districts.[38]

E. TRANSPORTATION

Railway and highway building and maintenance are carried out on a large scale by the Mexican federal government (plus some by the states). A large fraction of the federal budget, and of federal investment, has for years gone into various aspects of transportation. There is general satisfaction with the wisdom of the decision to concentrate on transportation as a critically needed support for economic development. Apparently, there is no wide disposition to claim that the large public investment in transportation has been badly mismanaged; but there is considerable disposition to argue that: (1) it could have been handled better, so that economic development would have been significantly affected, but this view tends to be expressed in quite general terms; (2) the coordination of highway and railway development could be improved —without much statistical base for this; (3) some decisions (for example, to build super-highways) are based on considerations too little related to national economic development; and, growing out of other criticisms, (4) the most important requirements to improve transportation planning are more centralization of planning, its better relationship to total government economic development policy, and more resistance to political influence in decision-making.[39]

Some of the criticism of national transportation planning clearly relates to the sort of politically oriented decision-making that is well known in the United States in connection with transportation policy. Some other criticism appears to result from frustration with the fragmentation of authority in the government, and with the large amount of coordinating activity required in so complex an establishment. There was especially heavy criticism of Mexican transportation planning in the first years of greatly expanded effort after World War II. Some of these complaints have been met, at least in part, during the last decade.

National transportation planning is carried out in several places, including the Ministry of Communications and Transportation, the Ministry of Public Works, the Ministry of the Presidency, the Bank of Mexico, and Nacional Financiera. Planning studies done in transportation in Mexico involve consideration of the objectives of improving levels of living, stimulating the least productive zones of the country, raising production and the development of activities that the country requires for balanced development. Consideration is given to the development of a national transportation net. The government is well aware of the difficulty of balancing railway against highway development. A large corps of technicians devotes its attention to making investment plans, cost analyses, and traffic volume projections.[40]

F. Electric Power

After 1945 the Federal Electricity Commission (CFE) did an increasing amount of planning and development work, as electric power generating and distribution facilities in Mexico grew much more rapidly than GNP, and especially in the public sector. The more rapid growth of public electric power was due to government policies, especially on prices, that made it difficult for the private companies to make profits and attract capital. The provision of public funds to build new public facilities, the sale of public power at low prices, and various forms of subsidy of private power, meant that the rest of the Mexican economy was subsidizing the electric industry. The heavy costs of these policies led to the appointment in 1953 of a government Committee for the Study of the Mexican Electric Industry (CEE-MEX). After four years of study CEE-MEX recommended that the state virtually give up investing in electricity and adopt pricing and other policies that would make massive private investment in the industry attractive. The report was shelved for a combination of political and economic reasons, especially political. The government soon thereafter "solved" the problem by buying out the private companies in 1960–61. One of the first acts of the new government thereafter, of course, was to raise rates for the nationalized industry. In accordance with the common Mexican government practice of dispersal of authority, the electric industry was not centralized and integrated, although the bulk of it remained under CFE.[41] There is no definitive argument that nationalization of electric power was or was not rational.[42] Politically, it seemed inevitable. Economically, about all the analysts seem able to say is that it would be nice to have the investment burden in electric power assumed by private sources, so that public funds could be used for other purposes; that subsidized low prices to Mexican manufacturers have some justification; and that the efficiency of the public as opposed to the private entrepreneurs in electric power is a critical question.

This history indicates that for two decades the government has been heavily engaged in an activity requiring much expert physical and engineering planning.[43] The CFE long has had a planning division,[44] with a large number of technicians and economists, and has produced many studies and development plans.[45] Some years ago it could be asserted that its "planning . . . has developed further than that of almost any other sector of the economy."[46] The government electric expansion plan announced in 1962 for 1962–64 was to be handled largely by CFE, and to raise national capacity from 2.455 million to 4.688 kilowatts. At the same time, planning was being carried on for expansion to the year 1970.[47]

CFE planning must have been reasonably well done, judging from the relative lack of criticism of its technical activity, from its success in obtaining credits,[48] and from the fact that manufacturing growth has not been slowed seriously by electric power deficiencies. There long has been complaint about the concentration of electric power facilities around a few urban and industrial centers, but the decisions to permit population and plant concentrations that require power are not made by the CFE. The criticisms of dam site selections might be directed rather at the Ministry of Hydraulic Resources than at CFE, since it is declared Mexican policy that irrigation takes precedence over power in cases of conflict. Finally, several Mexican *técnicos* said in personal interviews that electric power development in Mexico is poorly integrated, but agreed that the figures to support this view firmly are not available.

G. PETROLEUM

Pemex, the national petroleum monopoly, engages in large-scale development.[49] It sometimes is suggested that the activities of Pemex are not well planned, but few data are offered to substantiate the claim. Many of the complaints about Pemex relate, in fact, to questions over which it has little or no control: for example, low prices for products, reluctance to permit much foreign capital into the country (except as credits), even in exploratory and development drilling; the failure to produce a larger surplus for sale abroad, to earn foreign exchange that could be used for petroleum or other development. Pemex has no control over the heavy taxes levied on it, or over domestic pricing policies for petroleum products, or over general foreign investment policies. There is disagreement as to whether these policies have been "unrealistic" and "uneconomic." They have restricted investment in petroleum, and have kept production lower than it might have been. On the other hand, production and national markets for petroleum products have expanded rapidly in recent years, and low pricing policies have aided industrial expansion.

The World Bank found in 1953 that in spite of insufficient funds Pemex had been able to keep pace with domestic demand, to improve internal oil transportation facilities, and to avoid net imports of refined products. It also asserted that for the Mexican economy as a whole the petroleum problem was not insoluble or even especially difficult, consisting in essence of the diversion as needed of investment to petroleum from less urgent sectors.[50]

In 1942 Pemex created its Coordinating Department of Technical Studies, which was in charge of originating and developing technical programs, and of approving investments. It had close liaison with the Pemex Department of New Projects, which did engineering studies. The latter also supervised the execution of approved projects, most of which are done by contract with private companies. Pemex has planned within a framework of agreed objectives. It tries to develop the industry in all of its branches, with the twofold aim of keeping production well ahead of demand, and building some surplus for export to get foreign exchange for the purchase of new equipment. It tries to adjust the structure of the industry to meet geographic and functional alterations in demand. It tries to modernize the industry by the adoption of new technology. It has tried to avoid duplication of activities, and to base expansion programs on criteria of productive and distributive efficiency and national need, rather than on motives of immediate profit.[51]

H. Other Sectoral

The mining industry is privately held, mostly by foreigners. There thus has been little or no government development planning for mining, but its taxing and other policies have been a critical factor in determining the history of the industry. The chief effect of these policies, according to the World Bank report of 1953, "has been to discourage new investment in the industry." It also pointed to the need for better transportation and power development in aid of mining, the lack of sufficient geological data, the need for better coordination of agencies dealing with mining, the desirability of a review of official mining policy and of formulation of a program to stimulate development, which, in any case, "would take years to put . . . into effect."[52] Recent government actions (especially since 1960) to speed the "Mexicanization" of mining, with continuing inhibitory effects upon private investment, are continuing evidence of general government satisfaction with long-term policies.[53]

A number of government agencies do engage in study of the industry,[54] and in recent years there has been some increase in awareness of the need for more coordination of policy in relation to mining. The government has not felt, however, an acute need to plan in the field, because: (1) immediate domestic needs for minerals are being met fairly satisfactorily, and the prospect of future difficulties has been pushed aside; (2) there has been reluctance to interfere with the especially heavy taxation of the largely foreign-owned companies, although there was a recent reduction; (3) there is a desire to force the foreign companies to sell majority interest to Mexicans; (4) mineral export revenues remain a large, though declining, share of exports by value, and increases of exports do not appear easy to arrange in the present state of world production and demand; and (5) when special conditions arise in connection with the preceding, the government can make arrangements to exploit them, as in recent actions which have resulted in a spectacular increase in Mexican sulphur mining and exports.

The López Mateos administration created a Tourism Department to promote the growth of an activity that is most important to the Mexican balance of payments and to investment for economic development.[55] The Tourism Department's Bureau of Planning (Dirección de Planeación) has been developing national tourism plans in collaboration with the Ministry of the Presidency. A nine-year plan for 1962–70 was announced in 1962. It set up eight tourist zones, and provided for the coordination of the efforts of government agencies in developing tourist facilities. It also provides for improved data collection, better transportation, and the coordination of public and private action.[56]

Partial or sector economic and social planning is done in a number of other fields for which little information was available for the present study. The government is helping massively to guide the development of the chemical industry.[57] Nacional Financiera has been prominent in the financing of chemical projects. Some of these are quasi-governmental, but much of the chemical industry is in the private sector. Sector planning is involved in Pemex's reservation to itself of the manufacturing of base materials in the petrochemical field, supplying them for elaboration to private companies. Pemex also creates facilities for the elaboration of finished products where the base products are thought to be not sufficiently exploited by the private sector.[58]

Social planning has been done in Mexico for some years, and on a considerable scale, especially in public health fields and in education. Recently, increased attention has gone to the planning of housing, mostly in the public sector, but hopefully with some influence on private activities. In 1960 an eleven-year plan was drafted for elementary education in 1960–70. It has the goals of both increasing enrollments and expanding the average number of years of training actually received.[59] The connections between social and economic development are well understood in the Mexican government,[60] but political expediency or necessity dictates much obfuscation of this understanding in public debate.

I. Regional, State, Municipal Planning

Federal study and action in relation to regional problems goes back to the 1920's.[61] The notion of regional planning was not highly publicized, however, until creation of the first river basin authorities in 1947. Theoretical literature on regional planning became more abundant in the 1950's and 1960's, possibly in part because of widespread receptivity to regional planning as somehow especially liberal and Mexican. Regional planning appeals to the understanding that there are "many Mexicos," to the view that the hinterland should be better developed in relation to the Federal District, and to the belief in political federalism as against centralism. Use of the regional approach appeals to the Mexican interest in irrigation and development of hydroelectric resources. It is useful to the national leadership as a device for translating its remote power into more intimate localized activity, giving the regional citizenry a sense of enjoying special attention. It appeals to state and local politicians both as a practical means of concentrating funds in their home districts, and because it dramatizes the aid they are securing for their constituents. It is easy to understand why many private local interest groups welcome regional programs.

The more technical appeal of regional development and planning includes a belief that it represents a mechanism of relatively coordinated attack on development that is difficult to arrange on a national level, both for political and for technical reasons. It has been defended on the grounds that Mexico can usefully be considered from the geographic point of view as a system of "natural regions,"[62] culture regions (European and Amerind),[63] and narrow, nearly self-contained market areas.[64] One of the purposes of concentration on regional development is the ultimate improvement of interregional connections, the achievement of national economic integration.

One of the most recent Mexican expositions of the theme of regional development emphasizes the need of reducing the imbalance between the metropolitan zone of Central Mexico and the rest of the country. This imbalance is viewed as resting in important measure on the superior transportation connections of the Federal District, and on the railway rate structure, which favors primary materials, encouraging manufacturers to concentrate their facilities in the capital area. The central area also has the most experienced and best-trained labor force, partly because social security and other state benefits are concentrated there. Furthermore, the national tax structure is such that it is difficult for the state governments to find funds for local modernization programs in the face of federal favor for the center. Credit facilities are heavily concentrated in the Federal District. The system of centralized administration of permits and registration for industry favors the center. Even though all these conditions cannot be corrected quickly, and in any event all regions cannot be made to progress at the same rate, plans should be developed to accelerate the development of the noncentral regions—so the argument runs.[65] On the whole, it must be said that some of the Mexican faith in regional development is not supported very persuasively from the technical point of view,[66] but possibly this is not important in view of the practical value of regional planning and development in the actual political circumstances of the country. Regional plans and programs are useful for the mobilization of support and resources. In the end, regional activity is important as it affects sectors of the national economy.[67] The OAS group studying the Plan of Immediate Action said approximately this in 1964, and also advocated regional plans to create local conditions that would promote decentralization of industry, and especially establish industries making use of agricultural and pastoral products.[68]

The first two river basin authorities, created in 1947, were the Commissions of Papaloapan and of Tepalcatepec. Since then several others have been set up.[69] In addition, since 1959 there has been a new orientation of regional planning in the Ministry of the Presidency.[70] For one thing, it has drawn up plans within the framework of a new Southeast Regional Program, involving the states of Tabasco, Chiapas, and parts of Oaxaca and Veracruz. Planning studies and field surveys have been carried out by economists, engineers, and other technicians from Nacional Financiera, the Bank of Mexico, and the Ministry of Hydraulic Resources.

The river basin authorities have concentrated on flood control and irrigation, which explains their creation as semiautonomous agencies of the Ministry of Hydraulic Resources. They have had considerable planning to do in connection with this activity, and there apparently is rather widespread dubiety as to the methods by which the dam sites were chosen. Data for definitive judgments, however, appears not to have been developed. As to the other functions of the river basin authorities, they tend to be connected with agriculture, and with social development for largely agricultural populations.[71] The industrial interests of the river basin authorities are relatively unimportant.

Although solidly based judgments as to the overall performance of the authorities is difficult to find,[72] Thomas Poleman has published a good study of the Papaloapan Project.[73] He tells us several things of interest for our present purpose. First, although he declares that the experience of the Papaloapan Commission shows the value of regional development in Mexico, he apparently has not the data required to demonstrate this convincingly. Second, he declares that the Papaloapan Commission did not really plan; instead, "much of its program evolved through trial and error." The Commission had little data and was forced to act hastily. This was especially unfortunate for experimental work in a tropical area. Third, the activity of the Commission depended on the attitude toward it of the federal government, which fluctuated considerably. This was especially important because the Commission was not independent, on the model of TVA, but the creature of the Ministry of Hydraulic Resources. Fourth, because of this it only had control of its own projects, and other government agencies continued to operate projects in the area. Although the Commission theoretically had a coordinative role, it had no power to impose it. Fifth, the project was begun primarily to control floods, and it did little else in fact. In 1957 and thereafter its functions were cut drastically. For all the considerable value of the Poleman study, it tells us that the regional method as seen in the Papaloapan basin was valuable, without telling us why. The Commission in 1958 published an evaluation of its investments, which included statements on objectives and methodology, from which some notion of planning activity can be derived.[74] No assessment of these claims could be attempted for the present study.

Not only are judgments on the river basin authorities difficult to assess, but some sizable regions of Mexico—for example, the northwest—have enjoyed rapid development with federal government aid without use of the regional authority device. The coordination of regional planning now assigned to the Ministry of the Presidency may reduce the frequently heard criticism that even some of the best regional planning in Mexico has been in part wasted because the activities promoted would in fact be more suitable for another region of the country.

A Frontier Program (Programa Nacional Fronterizo) was announced in 1961. Operating as a decentralized agency, and calling on other government offices for aid, it plans modernization and development of the northern border areas, and their better integration into the national life. It focuses attention upon the major northern border towns. The Frontier Program has an investment budget which rose from 33.2 million pesos in 1961, and the same in 1962, to 89.3 million in 1963. Its activities include stimulation of local manufacturing and the flow of Mexican manufactures to the area from the interior. These efforts are designed to reduce the heavy Mexican border purchases in the United States. The Program also is taking steps to improve tourism in the area, where it already constitutes over one-half the total foreign tourism by value in the entire country. The Program and the Ministry of National Patrimony have been active in promoting zoning plans for the major border towns. The Program is receiving some research aid in planning its activities from the Office of Regional Economic Studies in the Bank of Mexico.[75]

State and municipal planning done by those echelons of government in Mexico has been increasing.[76] Presumably, this builds some support for national planning. State governors now make great efforts to convince their constituents that they have development programs, if not plans.[77] Officials of the national government and of the PRI go to the hinterlands to lend their presence to public celebrations of state development activity, and to emphasize federal collaboration. The states have enough in the way of development plans of their own so that in 1962 a professional group suggested that a Subsecretary of Industrialization be appointed in the Ministry of Industry and Commerce, in part to coordinate the development plans of the states. The federal government does planning for cities and for states. It is especially involved in urban planning for the capital city. We noted above that the Frontier Program engages in urban planning and development. For the states, we noted above some government planning activities. In addition, for many years states have received aid from the federal government in making economic and technical studies. A recent development in this regard has been the preparation by the Bureau of Economic Studies of the Ministry of the Economy (now Industry and Commerce) of quite sophisticated planning studies for states.[78] Urban zoning plans are being prepared in considerable abundance in Mexico,[79] many of them in the Ministry of National Patrimony.[80] The growth of urban population is increasing the desirability of and interest in municipal planning.[81]

VII

Approaches to Integrated and Comprehensive Planning

The Mexican government has made what may be described as at least approaches to cross-sectoral and aggregate planning. Some of these have involved policies and decisions relating to the supply or distribution of credit or manpower, or to the attainment or maintenance of general levels of output, or price levels, investment, or the international balance of payments. Such objectives, on which we have commented above, were pursued for some years without centralized planning institutions or integrated national planning covering all factors and objectives. These are the activities—involving foresight coupled to goals, policies, and actions—which constituted at least approaches to cross-sectoral or aggregate planning.

In addition, we have noted the pressures in recent years for the formalization and centralization of planning. The first sizable approach to such institutionalized and centralized planning on a cross-sectoral or aggregate basis was in connection with the coordination of the investments of public agencies. This began in the early 1950's and continues today. It has helped induce a more intensive examination of all aspects of national planning. Also, there has been important recent effort to find more effective means of coordinating public and private investment. This effort, bearing at least some resemblance to the philosophy of the current French system of national planning, may determine the essential direction of Mexican development planning.

A second approach to formalized, centralized, and more nearly comprehensive national planning dates from creation of a national planning office in the new Ministry of the Presidency, by the law of December, 1958. The same law also created the Ministry of National Patrimony, with some functions important to the implementation of plans.[1] The

Ministry of the Presidency was the first Mexican agency publicly and unequivocally assigned something approaching responsibility for national planning—or at least the adjustment of various plans into a national plan. Not surprisingly, it encountered resistance from older departments and agencies.

The next development was the preparation in 1961 of growth goals and sectoral projections for 1961–70. (See Chapter IV.) It was largely on the basis of these studies that the Plan of Immediate Action for 1962–64 was prepared, and submitted to the Organization of American States in 1962 under the provisions of the Charter of Punta del Este and the Alliance for Progress.

A. INVESTMENT COMMISSION OF 1954–58

In later years, an official of the Investment Commission observed that until 1953 Mexico's only public investment policy was one of maximum activity by individual agency heads without reference to the activity of other agencies.[2] Although this description is helpful in suggesting the usefulness of more coordination of public investment, it was an exaggeration. As will be observed below, when an agency for coordination was established, much of its policy and activity was predetermined by the existence of long-established investment policies that could not be altered drastically, and that apparently were accepted by the new agency with little or no belief that they were mistaken. Another judgment, of the same year, in the important World Bank report on Mexican economic development, written by two Mexicans and two World Bank officials, strongly recommended more integration of investment and of planning generally. The Mexican federal government, as we have indicated above (Chapter IV), had made some tentative moves toward integration of planning before 1953, and in that year created the Investment Committee. This last soon was merged into the Investment Commission (Comisión de Inversiones), created by presidential order in September, 1954. It was a direct dependency of the presidency, with the organization shown:[3]

The Commission was to send to the executive annual recommendations for coordinated investment programs, with indicated priorities; it was to study investment projects; and it was to make economic studies necessary for its function of coordinating projects. The Commission's studies were limited exclusively to the economic and social aspects of projected government works, and to problems of coordinating such projects, leaving everything concerning the technical aspects of projects to the dependency in charge of the project.[4]

TABLE 4

FUNCTIONAL DIAGRAM OF INVESTMENT COMMISSION

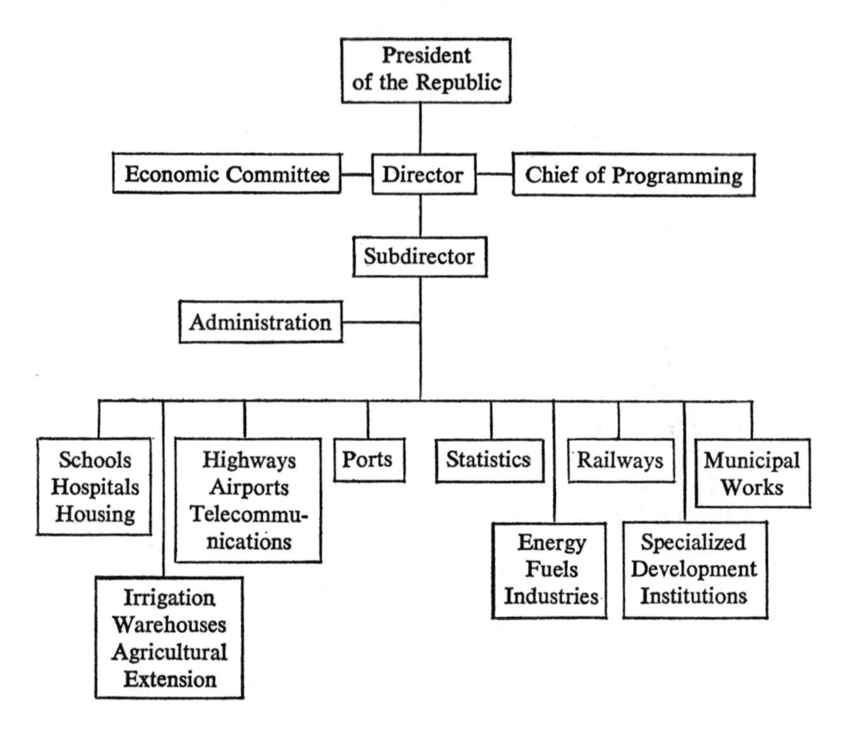

Annual programs for investment were prepared by government agencies and submitted to the Commission, which coordinated them, assigned priorities, and sent the consolidated program to the President. The latter reviewed the program, in consultation with government and party officials, and in the light of political as well as economic considerations. The plan, as revised at the presidential level, was returned to the Commission, which then sent to each dependency of the government the approved program. Changes were permitted after completion of the approval process outlined above. For this purpose, the Commission received petitions of modification from agencies, to pass on to the President with recommendations.[5]

The Investment Commission tackled the difficult and critical question of national priorities by adopting the following investment criteria: (1) the productivity of a project—the cost-yield ratio; (2) the degree of coordination with other projects; (3) the social benefit involved; (4) the stage of construction of unfinished works; (5) protection of investment already made in works under construction; (6) amount of employment to be generated by the project.[6] All of these, of course, represented principles well known, and often applied, in Mexico. Actually, most of the annual program each year consisted of the continuation of projects, so that these criteria did not apply to all expenditures during a given year.[7] Furthermore, there was continuity in sectoral distribution imposed by the accepted general policy of giving investment preference to irrigation, energy development (electric power, petroleum), and transportation.[8]

Control of the approved programs was exercised through the Ministries of Finance and of National Property. The former, through its Pay Office (*Dirección de Egresos*), strictly controlled such funds from the regular budget as went to agencies for investment purposes, requiring that the contemplated use be listed in the annual program authorized by the President. The Ministry of National Property would not approve contracts or supply orders for public works that had not been studied by the Investment Commission; and without this approval, the government agencies, and private contractors working for them, could not get funds from the Pay Office of the Finance Ministry.[9]

The Investment Commission made inspection trips to construction projects. It began an inventory of public works in progress, giving location, date of initiation and of probable completion, total cost, and other data. It was expected that this inventory would help in making up the annual investment programs, in the supervision of works in progress, and in the process of coordination. The Commission made studies of such basic problems as the proper level of public investment compatible with monetary stability, with the research aid of other agencies, especially the Ministries of Finance and of the Economy, the Bank of Mexico, and Nacional Financiera.[10]

The Commission may thus be seen as a rather important part of a trend in Mexico toward more integration of public economic development activity, and toward more centralization of control over government entities. It also played a role in a trend toward longer-range planning. The World Bank criticized its early concentration on short-term investment programs. In 1956 the Commission extended its investment planning to a two-year period (1957–58).[11] The Commission also has been criticized for not setting up overall sector priorities, on the grounds that the failure to do so gave a privileged position to agencies that could present their projects best, or which could bring the most pressure to bear on the President.[12] This may, however, be unfair, in view of the short-range problems the Commission had to face in its early days. Although it did develop strength during its short history,[13] the Commission was not meant to be a national planning office. It has been called "a public-interest watchdog . . . in the sense that it had a limited veto power over the overall investment programs of the autonomous agencies and state enterprises, by being able to deny them access to the federal funds on which practically all of them depend heavily."[14]

B. Ministry of the Presidency

1. *Creation of the New System*

A law of December 30, 1958, at the beginning of the López Mateos administration, created a national planning office, and put it in a new Ministry of the Presidency.[15] The law also had provisions designed to promote coordination of public investment, and to improve centralized control of public property, resources, and business procedures, all of which also had been promoted by the preceding administration.[16]

The law did some of this by creating a new Ministry of National Patrimony (*Secretaría de Patrimonio Nacional*) in place of the Ministry of National Property, with considerable powers in connection with the execution of development projects. This led to some objections that a conflict of authority was being created.[17] Four years later the Ministry of National Patrimony was sufficiently sensitive about the issue to declare that the conflict did not exist,[18] and to point out the important role of National Patrimony in the implementation and control of plans.[19]

The law of December, 1958, provided that the Ministry of the Presidency would: (1) study and formulate presidential orders to ensure their execution; (2) "receive data for the purpose of drawing up the general plan of public expenses and investments"; (3) "plan works, systems, and improvements of the same," and "plan the promotion and development of regions and localities specified by the president"; (4) coordinate all the public investment programs, and study modifications therein; (5) "plan and oversee public investment," including that of decentralized organs and enterprises with state participation; (6) register laws, decrees, orders, and resolutions of the executive power and the president; and (7) "anything else set down by law or regulation or ordered by the president."[20]

The presidential explanation of the reason for this move was that the office had been operating with this name without being under the law (i.e., the ministry law of 1946); and its function would be "planning, coordination, and oversight, but not properly execution"; and "it will look after the programming of the general and specific activities of the federal government that will be executed by the ministries, thus widening the radius of influence of the President of the Republic."[21]

This was, however, very general, and left much to be spelled out later.[22] In addition, other areas of possible confusion lay in the provisions of the law that: (1) some ministries and departments retained functions that would require them to engage in planning activities;[23] (2) there would be, as under the old law, "interministerial commissions," transitory or permanent, for interagency coordination.

As might be expected, the new Ministry of the Presidency met some resistance from older agencies.[24] This would be expected in any event, and apparently it was exaggerated by the vigor with which the new office set about its functions, before it had the staff and experience to advise older agencies usefully. The process of adjustment is suggested by the number of regulations issued after 1958 to try to spell out the new ministry's functions, and by the creation of interministerial committees, often an indication of unresolved conflict between departments.[25] It also was indicated by the air of mystery that surrounded the Ministry's organization and activities, and by its lack of publication and public reportage during its early years. And, finally, the fact that the Plan of Immediate Action for 1962–64 was not prepared by the Ministry of the Presidency indicated that it had fallen far short of capturing all the central planning function of the federal government.

Within the next few years after 1958 the Ministry created four offices to deal with its new functions: the Bureaus (*Direcciones*) of Public Investments (*Inversiones Públicas*), Planning (*Planificación*), Supervision of Investments and Subsidies (*Vigilancia de Inversiones y Subsidios*), and General Plan of Public Expenditures (*Plan General del Gasto Público*). The Dirección de Vigilancia de Inversiones y Subsidios had functions that tended to overlap those of the Ministry of National Patrimony, and the lines of responsibility had to be delineated more sharply in February, 1961.[26] The Dirección del Plan General del Gasto Público was created early in 1963.[27]

2. *Investment Coordination and the Ministry of the Presidency*

The Ministry was able to pick up the work of the now superseded Investment Commission without much difficulty. A presidential order of June 30, 1959, required all government agencies (ministries and departments of state, decentralized organs, and state participation agencies) to draft investment programs. It specified content, form, principles on which they were to be founded, and required that proposals on financing be submitted. It set dates for submission of programs for 1960 and for 1961–64. The Ministry of the Presidency was to coordinate and rank the programs for submission to the President of the Republic, and the latter would authorize the annual programs through the former. The Ministers of the Presidency and of Finance were to supervise execution of the investment budget, although supervision of the investment system as a whole remained with the former. Enforcement measures were included in the order, providing for assistance from several government agencies.[28] Evidently the system still required readjustment or reinforcement, because an order to the Ministers of the Presidency and of Finance, October 29, 1959, amplified the rules for modification and final approval of investment programs. It also required government dependencies to provide the Ministry of Finance with the names and assigned work of contractors.[29] A presidential order of February 11, 1961, provided for coordination in connection with investments between the Ministries of the Presidency and National Patrimony.

The Ministry of the Presidency does, at any rate, seem to have begun promptly its coordination of public investment programs, and to have continued under one arrangement or the other to the present. In February, 1960, President López Mateos announced through the Ministry of the Presidency the figures on the 1960 investment program, and asserted it had been coordinated and given project priorities.[30] The same thing was done in succeeding years.[31] It was announced in 1960 that the Ministry of the Presidency was going to coordinate the investments of the states of Mexico, an activity which would be independent of coordination of the federal investment program.[32]

Evidence is not available to permit a judgment as to either: (a) the extent of control established by the Ministry over the several score government agencies that plan and execute investment programs, or (b) the usefulness of such coordination as has in fact been established. The view is common, however, that considerable public investment activity still escapes close coordination by the Ministry.[33] A government announcement in February, 1963, regarding the necessity of obtaining Finance Ministry approval of external credits for government agencies indicated the continued difficulty of getting obedience to such regulations.

It seems to be a common judgment among persons in some position to know, that these coordinated public investment programs are budgets rather than planning documents. That is, although sector planning is done at the agency level in connection with preparation of agency investment programs for submission to the Ministry of the Presidency, the latter has not had the staff to do much national planning in support of investment programming or in connection with the setting-up of investment goals. On the other hand, there is reason to believe that the Ministry from the beginning of its operations used principles of the sort known to have been employed by the Investment Commission of 1954–

58,[34] and which is widely conceded to have clearly established a role as a planning institution. In any event, the investment coordination function of the Ministry of the Presidency cannot be considered as entirely separate from what the law denominated as its "planning" function.

3. *Planning and the Ministry of the Presidency*

Although, as we have seen, a Planning Bureau, distinct from the Investment Bureau, early was created in the Ministry of the Presidency, the former had little life for some two years.[35] The language of the law of December, 1958, certainly called for a national planning office. As early as May, 1959, the Ministry of the Presidency, in announcing the creation of three bureaus of Planning, Investments, and Inspection and Control, stated that they were to be provided monthly by other offices of the Ministry with statistics from various government agencies.[36] There is reason to believe, however, that the information that came into the Ministry was inadequate, and that the staff, would not have been able to handle it if it had been even approximately sufficient. It certainly is clear that the Ministry encountered difficulties in its relations with other elements of the government.

In August, 1961, a presidential decree was issued which seemed to summarize both the planning interests of the government and the problems it was encountering in putting the new system into effective operation. The decree stated a need for coordination for investment purposes between federal agencies and local governments and private groups. It also stated a need for better executive coordination between federal entities and the Ministry of the Presidency, to include provision to the latter of better data on the programs of all government agencies and of the municipal and private sectors. So all federal agencies were ordered to intensify their efforts in promoting economic and social development, calculating investment needs, drawing national plans and fixing concrete goals for the benefit of the community, do regional or local planning where government aid was needed urgently, promote federal coordination with state and municipal government and private enterprise, and promote needed modifications in public administration.[37] This grab-bag of exhortations may be interpreted as suggesting that a great deal remained to be done in erecting planning machinery in Mexico. Other presidential orders, July 9, 1961, and March, 1962, lent strength to such an interpretation.[38] On the other hand, these orders indicated the Mexican government's understanding of and attachment to various facets of national planning.

In 1962 an OAS document, presumably based on material provided by the Mexican government, put neatly the problem of the new planning institution in Mexico by stating that the Ministry of the Presidency in its early years had to "define better the relations" between its public Investment and Planning Bureaus and "other official agencies."[39] Early in 1963 some changes in the Ministry of the Presidency were made that seemed to indicate a continuing effort to expand and define its activities.[40] In 1964 the Congress was considering a new national planning law that presumably would make another effort at redefining or restructuring the planning apparatus.

In its early days the Ministry's Dirección de Planeación did not try to concoct a national development plan with its limited staff, but began with the study and formulation of a plan for the economic and social development of Yucatán.[41] From this it moved on to the preparation of plans for the states of Tabasco, Chiapas, and the Isthmus of Tehuantepec area. It thus began to exercise a planning function that previously had been exercised both by autonomous commissions and by other government agencies (e.g., Bank of Mexico, Nacional Financiera, and the Bureau of Economic Studies of the Ministry of the Economy and its successor the Ministry of Industry and Commerce). It is not clear to what extent this will inhibit regional planning in the older agencies.

The Planning Bureau also began preparing sectoral development plans, beginning with tourism and the steel industry. It operated in this field mainly by setting guidelines to be followed by individual government agencies in preparing sectoral plans. The agency draft of a sectoral plan is then coordinated by the Planning Bureau of the Ministry of the Presidency with other sectoral, regional, and national plans, and checked against the national policies and financial resources.[42]

It was evident that a new planning institution was in operation, but it was not clear how much its activities had affected those of older agencies operating in the same fields, or whether coordination of sectoral or regional plans had been increased or otherwise improved. The Pan-American Union in 1961 asserted that not only was there no formal coordination of the public and private sectors in Mexico in connection with Mexico—assertedly one of the main objectives of the new system—but that there was no coordination of regional plans at the national level.[43] Neither was there much reason to believe at that date that long-term planning had much advanced beyond the situation in 1959 when the "plan" for the six years of the López Mateos administration may simply have consisted of a more or less coordinated set of sectoral plans and a set of general economic and social objectives and principles.[44]

In February, 1962, President López Mateos announced creation of an

Interministerial Planning Commission, made up of representatives named by the Ministers of the Presidency and of Finance, who were to organize out of their personnel a "technical office" to formulate national plans for economic and social development. Since the Ministry of the Presidency had few technical personnel, this meant that the Ministry of Finance would dominate the Commission. In fact, later in the year, Mexico reported to the Economic and Social Council of the OAS that the Commission was created "to facilitate the elaboration of general and sectoral development goals under the technical direction of the Ministry of Finance and Public Credit, with the collaboration of Nacional Financiera and the Bank of Mexico."[45] The President, in his annual message of September 1, 1962, stated it somewhat differently in declaring that the Commission was intended to bring together the functions of the Ministry of the Presidency in connection with planning and the programming of investment, and the functions of the Ministry of Finance relative to budget, money, and credit.

It is not clear why the Interministerial Planning Commission was created. Possibly it was due to the inadequacies of the Ministry of the Presidency, and the difficulties it had in gaining cooperation from older agencies. It would be in accordance with experience in most governments if the latter had resisted diminution of their role. The Commission may have been created primarily because of the need to produce quickly a plan that would satisfy the requirements of the Alliance for Progress. It is easily conceivable that one of the motives for creation of the Commission was the distaste of Mexican presidents for being committed to extensive specific plans, and this was thought of in part as a way of avoiding the development of such plans. All the above speculations have been advanced directly to me by Mexicans.

In any event, creation of the Commission strengthened the planning responsibilities of those government agencies with the greatest personnel resources and experience for this type of activity. The decision also was consistent with the customary heavy reliance of the presidency on the great technical resources of the Ministry of Finance and the autonomous state financial institutions allied with it, and with their great prestige in Mexico. It is not clear whether these institutions had adopted the position that they should continue to share in the planning function under all circumstances, or whether assertion of continuation of their role developed out of the weakness of the planning staff at the Ministry of the Presidency. In any event, how much the Ministry of the Presidency develops its planning function depends on the support that the President of Mexico decides to give to it. Finally, we may observe that the failure to include on the Interministerial Planning Commission the representatives of other agencies that might well argue the plausibility of their inclusion also was consistent with Mexican government practice.[46]

The Interministerial Planning Commission was to: calculate the amount, structure, and financing of revenues and of national income necessary for development that would be adequate to raise living levels; try to integrate public and private development efforts; plan on both long-term and short-term bases; align its labor with earlier presidential orders; and send its plans to the President of the Republic. In short, it was to try to do what the law of December, 1958, had called for, and what a succession of presidential orders subsequently had declared ought to be done, chiefly by the Ministry of the Presidency. The Commission began operations on March 1, 1962.[47]

C. Plan of Immediate Action for 1962–1964/65[48]

We have given above (Chapter IV) the general history of the *Plan de Acción Inmediata para 1962–64* (later extended through 1965). The procedures of the Interministerial Planning Commission in drafting the Plan have not been made public. It is known, however, that it was done by a small group of men, and that Víctor Urquidi of the Bank of Mexico was prominent among them. It was based on the longer-range planning studies that we have mentioned above. Although the text of the 1962–64 Plan was not available for this study, the lengthy analysis and commentary of the OAS Committee appointed to study the Plan was used. On the whole, the OAS Committee approved of the Plan.

1. The Plan postulated an average annual growth of GNP of 5.0 per cent in 1961–65, which would require an annual rate of growth of 5.4 per cent in 1963–65, because of the economic slowdown in the earlier years. These rates seemed reasonable to the OAS Committee in the light of Mexican experience. (See Chapter III, B, above.) The goal was in fact achieved in 1963 and exceeded in 1964. The Plan recorded a hope that growth might be raised to an average of 6.0 per cent annually in 1966–70. It will be observed in Table 5, below, that the Plan, and projections for the next five years, provided for continuation of the relatively faster growth in most other sectors than the agricultural that has been a much contested feature of development in Mexico. The OAS Committee's reaction to this was on the one hand to make many recommendations for the increase of agricultural productivity and for improvement of rural social conditions, but on the other hand to agree flatly that the solution to the rural social problem was largely a matter of getting people out of agriculture.

2. The heart of the Plan was investment. In fact, when data were

TABLE 5

PROJECTION OF RATES OF SECTORAL GROWTH, 1961–70[49]

Sector	1961–65 (%)	1966–70 (%)
Agriculture and Stock	4.5	5.5
Agriculture	4.3	5.1
Stock	4.6	6.1
Manufactures	6.9	7.1
Mining	2.6	5.3
Electric Energy	10.0	10.0
Petroleum	6.8	7.0
Construction	8.5	7.2
Transportation	5.9	7.2
Commerce	4.9	5.9
Public Sector and "Other Activities"	6.1	6.6

released on the plan, criticism was heard that it was merely a gloss on a public investment budget.[50] The strategy was to increase public investment, expecting that this stimulus to the economy, with other measures, would reactivate internal demand and create conditions more attractive for private investment. The OAS Committee approved this strategy.

a. Investment in the Plan may be summarized:[51]

(1) Total gross investment in 1962–64 of 80 billion pesos, accomplished by increasing the rate of investment, and by raising the public share of investment to about 50 per cent. Both the drafters of the Plan and the OAS Committee hoped that the private share of investment would return in later years to the average of the 1940's and 1950's. By late 1964 some 98 per cent of projected public investment had been arranged.[52]

(2) About 16 per cent of total financing of the Plan was to come from external credits. This followed a trend, as we have noted, that was foreseen as long ago as 1953 by the World Bank. The OAS Committee recommended that reliance on foreign credits be reduced, partly through better savings and taxation measures in Mexico. On the other hand, the OAS Committee approved the external credits planned as having "the double mission" of stabilizing the economy and of acting as a catalytic agent for obtaining increases of national saving. It also asserted that external credit would facilitate the continuation of the process of internal reforms necessary to stimulate even more the development and transformation of social structures.

(3) Of the 40 billion peso public investment, 22 per cent was destined for social development in 1963–65, compared with 20 per cent in 1960–62. The increase was in accordance with the aims of the Alli-

ance for Progress, promised some relief for pressing social problems, and provided the PRI with material for the presidential campaign of 1963–64. Opposition elements, of course, claimed that the increase in social expenditures was too small. The OAS Committee did not go that far; it found the increase admirable, stated that even more was needed, but did not suggest that some other sector be cut to provide it.

(4) The economic development portion of public investment was destined thus in millions of pesos: 11,429 (28.7 per cent of the Plan's total public investment) for industrial development, 11,383 (28.6 per cent) for communications and transportation, and 7,078 (17.8 per cent) for agricultural and pastoral development. This last represented a rise from some 16 per cent in the immediate past.

(5) The increased percentages of public investment for social and agricultural (many critics thought of this largely in social terms) development were obtained by reducing the proportions of public investment devoted to transportation, communications, electric power, and petroleum. Expenditures in those fields continued, however, to account for a large part of public investment. The OAS Committee put it that sector distribution of investment in the Plan remained much as it had been in recent years, but with a gradual modification. It considered that this modification could be continued, because the economic infrastructure of the country had been laid soundly. The OAS Committee also observed that the increase in social and agricultural/pastoral expenditures would not only improve the income of those population groups most needing it, but would strengthen internal demand.

There is no way of knowing how much these redistributions of projected public investment were due to the reduction of need in the fields cut, after decades of emphasis on their growth in public investment budgets; or on a decision that the time had come to devote more funds to agriculture because it had grown less rapidly than manufacturing; or in response to the cries of critics that income distribution was so weighted toward profits as to show clearly the probusiness and anti-Revolution bias of government and PRI; or to a wish to promote redistribution in order to increase purchasing power as an aid to Mexican production and employment; or because of the difficulty of keeping up with the food requirements of a rapidly increasing population; or because of the difficulties faced by export agriculture in recent years, which reduced its attraction for private investors; or because the Alliance for Progress stressed social and agricultural development and reform; or simply out of that obvious political prudence of Mexican leaders that becomes especially evident as presidential elections near.[53]

(6) The 40 billion pesos of private investment were destined (the

planners hoped) thus (in billions): 16.0 (40.6 per cent) to manufacturing industry, 13.0 (33 per cent) to construction industries, 5.6 (14.2 per cent) to agricultural and pastoral activities, and 3.8 (9.6 per cent) to transportation. The 16 billion pesos of private investment in manufacturing industry were supposed to be distributed thus (in billions of pesos): steel, 3.7; automotive, 2.5; manufactures of machinery and equipment, 3.2; chemical and chemical-pharmaceutical, 1.7; petrochemicals, 1.0; textiles, 1.0.

With some justice and some exaggeration the Mexican government in October, 1962, stated that the work of the Interministerial Planning Commission constituted a "new stage of planning" in Mexico, in which "the probable volume and composition of private investment" would be taken into account.[54] Although the Plan surely did take such investment into account, it contained little in the way of tactics to ensure the result hopefully projected. This became one of the most frequently criticized elements of the Plan. The OAS Committee stated that private investment was the least precise element in the entire Plan, because of lack of government control over actual private investment, and because the government's data on private investment plans were defective.[55] The OAS Committee stressed that the importance of private enterprise in Mexican development made it necessary for the government to improve business confidence, and to promote more active participation of the private sector in capital formation.

Critics did not, typically, pay serious attention to the political problems involved in trying to impose drastic and novel coercive devices upon private enterprise. The OAS Committee was neither so naive nor so irresponsible, however, and suggested that private capital formation should be induced through the existing mechanisms of Nacional Financiera and the Bank of Mexico. Government actions did, in fact, indicate that it meant to use its usual strategy of encouraging private investment by a combination of persuasion and exhortation and the granting of tax and other concessions.[56] These are procedures that seem unheroic to some critics unburdened with political responsibilities. In his annual message, September 1963, President López Mateos spoke of a "program" of "private industrial promotion" which had seen at least the beginnings of projects representing 38 per cent of the total investment of the program. He coupled this with the litany of all Mexican administrations of the last quarter-century: that he wanted to stimulate rather than interfere with private capital.[57]

b. Other comments on investment by the OAS Committee are of interest. It pointed out that the Plan's projects tended to be capital-intensive, and recommended government investigation of investment in labor-intensive activities, for both economic and social reasons. It found the investment projects of the organs and enterprises of the state generally sound. It recommended that irrigation investment be raised above the Plan levels. It judged that too many companies had been let into the new automotive industry, with resultant duplication of investment and creation of excess capacity.

3. The Plan stated a strategy of income redistribution, strengthening the consumption power of the "majority groups" of the population and creating a more vigorous internal market, while at the same time keeping up the incomes of higher-income groups and encouraging the latter to invest. This was to be done within a framework of effort to hold down popular consumption, especially in 1961–65, and to try to confine that consumption increases to the lower-income groups. Private consumption was to grow only 4.9 per cent and 4.7 per cent in the periods 1963–65 and 1966–70 respectively, while in those periods the projected growth of production was 5.4 per cent and 6.0 per cent. The Plan proposed to increase taxes considerably in 1966–70 in the highest-income groups, with the double objective of keeping down private consumption and getting funds for public investment.

The OAS Committee pointed out that the 1963–65 projection for private consumption was not unreasonable in view of the fact that in 1962–63 production grew 5.4 per cent and private consumption 4.6 per cent. On the other hand, it stated that it was important for Mexico to promote growth of the internal market by improving the purchasing power of low-income groups. In the long run, the OAS Committee asserted, this meant better distribution of income, partly through taxes. It also offered the view that personal income distribution could be improved "without diminishing the growth capacity of the economy." The OAS Committee defended the 12 per cent average growth of public consumption shown in the Global Projection for 1961–70 by pointing out that much of this would go for things that aided development: e.g., agricultural technology, better education, popular housing, public health, social security, industrial development, and better planning.

4. Although the Plan's attention to agriculture and the rural population is noticeable in what was said above about investment, income distribution, and the control of private consumption, it included considerably more on the subject. Even so, the OAS Committee thought it not enough, and made many suggestions: e.g., "a maximum increase" in extension services in 1963–65, and other technical measures in aid of "especially the small farmer and *ejidatario*," and declared:[58]

> The Committee wishes to state that, even though the short range increase in productivity may be small, it is indispensable to channel

a much larger volume of investment resources into small pastoral/agricultural enterprises. . . . Although the impression exists that the results that may be obtained in this field are limited, studies that have been done show very encouraging prospects.

5. The Plan included many of the propositions that had guided Mexican policy for years.

a. In the financial realm, the Plan declared itself dedicated to the improvement of credit facilities, the maintenance of price stability, and increases in taxes. The OAS Committee recommended that government subsidies be restricted and prices of government activities be raised, partly to increase public saving and permit higher levels of public investment.

b. Although displaying the strong interest in foreign trade that has marked Mexican policy for years, the Plan was founded on the premise that export demand would slow,[59] and that future economic development would depend more on internal growth, and on continued increase in tourist income. The Plan noted the importance of export diversification, long a well handled part of Mexican national economic strategy. In this connection, the Plan recognized the need for a great effort to promote exports of manufactures, which would require improved productivity to make Mexican industry more competitive in the international market. The Plan proposed to continue the long-time stress on import substitution.

c. The Plan proposed to promote industrial integration, especially by obtaining better use of installed capacity, and by promoting the modernization of certain industries with the idea of reducing costs of production. The OAS Committee agreed that a major problem for Mexico was increased production of capital goods, both for better industrial integration and to alleviate the balance of payments problem by cutting imports. They set the decentralization of industry as a desirable goal, thus repeating what many Mexicans had said in general terms, with no effect, for many years.

d. The commentary by the OAS Committee contained considerable discussion of the Mexican planning system, praising the work done, but clearly not considering the recent changes revolutionary. It made recommendations, especially for better coordination of planning between government agencies, and between the public and private sectors. Most of the OAS Committee's criticism and recommendations with regard to planning are incorporated in Chapter VIII, below.

VIII

Some Conclusions

A. Planning Agencies and Activities

1. *How Much Planning?*

Observers have had difficulty labeling and categorizing Mexico's post-Revolutionary institutions. The economic system—and planning therefore—is no exception. Popular tags have been "unplanned,"[1] "essentially unplanned,"[2] "without true planning."[3] As early as 1955, however, an analyst perceived that the then-current definitions of planning were at least as difficult to understand as the Mexican planning system, and found that it was "not accurate to say that there is a complete absence of government economic planning in Mexico," and in fact the country had a "close approximation of national economic planning."[4] Between the terms "essentially" and "approximation" in the mentioned tags was abundant room for descriptive variety. But by 1964 it seemed necessary to agree that Mexico had some sort of national planning system,[5] especially when the Organization of American States was advising the Mexican government how to improve it.[6]

The earlier descriptions were due in part to the fact that planning in Mexico was both weaker and less clearly labeled before the mid-1950's than thereafter. But the descriptions also were due at times to the following propositions: (1) that national planning means only an activity formalized, centrally quantified, clearly labeled, and comprehensive in terms of the entire national economy; (2) that there can be no true national planning in a market economy (such as Mexico's). No one now should take the second of these propositions seriously; Mexican planners do not, and only partly because they know of the French system. The other proposition now is increasingly considered by social scientists to be conceptually naive, almost to the point of confusing form with essence.[7]

2. *Sector Planning*

No one denies, but many commentators slight, the fact that there is considerable sector planning by the Mexican federal government, and some regional, state, and municipal planning.[8] Sector planning by federal agencies has a history of a third of a century, and through the years has grown notably in magnitude and sophistication. Responsibility for sector planning is distributed among a number of federal agencies. Although much of this sector activity is physical planning, attention is given to economic, financial, and social factors. The theory of regional planning is popular with Mexican intellectuals, and the implementation of regional plans is pleasing to politicians. There is reason to believe that sector planning by the government—especially irrigation, electric power, transportation, and petroleum—has played an important role in Mexico's good rate of economic growth.

3. *Intersectoral or Aggregate Planning*

In Mexico there are two ways—interrelated—in which intersectoral, aggregate, or integrative planning is done. One is through the policy coordinative, control, and regulatory agencies and activities that have existed for many years, and which some commentators decline to admit to any connection with planning. The other is through the agencies and activities clearly labeled for intersectoral planning.

a. For many years in Mexico various institutions and practices have set up a web of boundary conditions, expectations, and action systems that are in various ways intersectoral, aggregative, and integrative, and in part of their operation amount to a system of national planning of sorts. Even some years ago it was possible for a careful student to state that there was an approximation of planning in the government's economic policy directives, and in the directive actions of the presidency and some of the major government entities.[9] These factors included the striking policy continuity of the Mexican administrations, especially the determination to provide both agricultural and industrial development, and the concentration year after year of government investment in the same lines of socioeconomic infrastructure.[10] These factors have permitted a certain amount of coupling of goals to futurity, and created some boundary conditions that have functioned as a sort of coordination. But there was, in fact, more coordination than this, and it has increased in recent years, especially since 1958.[11] Before 1958 some coordination was accomplished by the presidency, either in the secretariat, or by means of the president's relations with government officials and the representatives of private interests. Since the presidency was poorly staffed for this function, and since we know little about the detail of its coordinative activities, it is painless—and quite common—to say that such coordination as existed was handled by the presidency, with the implication that it must have been insignificant. In addition to the presidency, we have adduced in earlier chapters some evidence of interdepartmental coordination at the working level, both in planning and in economic study in support of planning.[12] There certainly was and is coordination by the Bank of Mexico and Nacional Financiera, not only by way of their banking activity, but by way of their economic study and planning functions. Clearly, there was more interagency coordination than can be found in published records.[13]

b. The explicitly labeled national planning agencies for intersectoral activity during World War II had little more than political or public relations functions.[14] They may, however, signify increased interest in planning. At any rate, following the war there were increased efforts at broader-scale government planning in Mexico.[15] The investment coordination work of the Investment Commission of 1954–58 was the most ambitious and best executed effort at the coordination of planning in Mexico to that time.[16] This led on to even more ambitious efforts at coordination in the administration of López Mateos (1958–64).

A central planning office was created for the first time in 1958, in the Ministry of the Presidency. Its Bureau of Public Investments took over the public investment coordination functions of the Investment Commission of 1954–58, so this system now has been in operation for a decade. The new Ministry's Planning Bureau has been slowly developing the wide planning functions assigned to it by law. The slowness has been due to several factors: sector planning was left to many agencies by the 1958 law; the Ministry of the Presidency lacked adequate staff; and older agencies with coordinative and general planning functions (Ministry of Finance, Bank of Mexico, Nacional Financiera) resisted the growth of the new planning office. This has necessitated new laws and regulations to try to adjust the system to the facts of public administration and political power in Mexico. It led also to use of that common Mexican device for the resolution or obscuring of differences between government agencies, the interministerial group.

An Interministerial Planning Commission was created in 1962, with representatives of the Ministries of Finance and of the Presidency.[17] It has been dominated by the Ministry of Finance and its allied institutions, the Bank of Mexico and Nacional Financiera. Personnel of these institutions, rather than of the Ministry of the Presidency, drafted the Plan of Immediate Action for 1962–64. This was based on a Projection of Growth Goals, an Intersectoral Projection, and other studies for the 1961–70 period, prepared in 1961. The Plan of Immediate Action for 1962–64 was plucked out of these documents in response to the economic slowdown of 1961 and the planning requirements of the Alliance for Progress in the face of Mexico's increased need for long-term foreign public credits. The Plan of Immediate Action was submitted for review to technicians of the Organizations of American States and the World Bank.

The Plan included hoped-for growth rates for 1962–64 (later adjusted through 1965), and for 1966–70; figures and a strategy for both public and private investment, and a stated hope that the investment plans of the two sectors might be better coordinated; figures on the expected directions of public and private investment, including a higher percentage of public investment for social development than in recent years, and a rise in the proportion of public economic development investment devoted to agriculture. The system was continued into the administration of Gustavo Díaz Ordaz (December, 1964——), and elements of the plan for 1966–70 were to be ready for coordination in mid-1965.[18]

c. The Organization of American States' technicians found in 1964 that Mexico's intersectoral planning system still required improvement, a judgment that had been rendered frequently for some years.[19] The OAS group stated that although the governments of Mexico had made various efforts to organize planning and especially to improve the coordination of public sector planning, it had not functioned as well as it might. This certainly was a mild, highly generalized, and unarguable reproof. It judged the problem to be in part one of coordination. It recommended closer adjustment of the investments of state organs and enterprises to national plans. It asserted that the government had not clearly separated the work of technical formulation of the plan from the work inherent in the annual approval of the programs of investment and the control of their execution. It found insufficient correlation between investment programs and the corresponding policies of development. It recommended that the various dependencies of the federal government and some decentralized organs that were allowed to intervene in the planning process should have their activities coordinated, in a planning office

> whose principal function would be to coordinate, at the technical level, the diverse planning efforts until now dispersed, and to integrate them into plans, at short and long range, that may cover all the sectors of the national economy. This office should be attached to the Executive, so that the decisions and means adopted in rela-

tion to the annual programs of investment and the policies of development, especially the financial, may constitute an organic whole that will permit better use of resources.[20]

4. *Public and Private Sectors*

The publicity given the Plan, and its expected successor for 1966–70, and the explicit linkage of private investment with the nation's economic growth and social well-being, may have been helpful in exerting pressure for greater coordination.[21] This effort is potentially important in that it might lead to a more open, and more predictable, system of coordination between the public and private sectors of the economy. Some factors, however, militate against such a development. First, no inducement was offered in the Plan of Immediate Action for the hoped-for improvement of coordination,[22] and the formal and informal inducements offered later apparently were less than revolutionary. Second, the secretiveness of the Mexican government will make difficult a workable system of coordination, as the Organization of American States evaluation group seemed to believe in 1964.[23] Third, there is, of course, resistance from those elements of the business community that fear any government-promoted project as a scheme for the advancement of socialism. Fourth, the antibusiness tradition of the Mexican Revolution (and, to some extent, of Hispanic culture generally) opens such collaboration to complaint from the left, and observers wonder whether the political establishment has the courage to outface it.[24] Finally, no obviously applicable theory exists for such coordination in the Mexican social environment, so that both government and private initiative must grope for workable mechanisms and better understanding,[25] a process that the recent history of Mexico suggests will be directed with pragmatism and caution rather than with unbuttoned theory and zest.[26]

Commentators will disagree as to whether this last suggestion, if correct, is grounds for optimism or pessimism. Some other plausible reasons for optimism exist. First, the dominant leadership of PRI and government cherishes private enterprise, needs to keep the economy growing for political reasons, and has for several years indicated that improved coordination of the public and private sectors is one device on which it counts for preservation of the system it has created and wishes to preserve.[27] Although the government appreciates the necessity of proceeding cautiously in drawing private enterprise to activities for which the latter's enthusiasm is limited, it does possess many fiscal and other weapons that private enterprise would prefer not to face. Second, both the history and the present condition of the political establishment suggest that it can withstand leftist dissent from such a change if it wishes to make the effort. As a part of this, it is obvious that the *políticos* are less than craven and perfectly pliable in the face of the leftist yearnings of government *técnicos.* Third, France's planning system, oriented toward private enterprise, exists as one example of the possibility of working out a unique system of collaboration to suit the Mexican environment.[28] Fourth, it has been suggested that business might become willing to cooperate in a tighter system of coordination of planning for the two sectors, if the inducement were an increase in the predictability of government actions relative to business, secured by an increase in the formality and impersonality of government decision-making.[29]

5. *Some Other Characteristics of Planning in Mexico*

a. There is sufficient knowledge of planning concepts and techniques so that this cannot be considered a major barrier to adoption of an adequate planning system.[30] Furthermore, there is increasing aid in planning and programming activity available from international public and foreign private agencies.[31] There are shortages of skills, but not of ideas and concepts; the former can be bought, the latter must be sold to political leaders.

b. The number of federal (and state and municipal) agencies doing planning is large and increasing. More and more the governments give these offices the planning title and function, rather than leaving planning as a residual function of an economic study or statistical unit.[32] Creation of the Ministry of the Presidency added yet another factor to the adjustment system. It has not been able to control the demands of the various agencies engaging in planning, and they still display independence, recalcitrance, and a willingness to try for political rather than technical decisions. Nor has the Ministry of the Presidency managed to extinguish the coordinative roles of the Ministry of Finance, Bank of Mexico, and Nacional Financiera. This is because these last two agencies retain staffs more competent to perform national planning functions than those of other agencies, by reason of the fact that they are larger, more varied, have greater experience, and better facilities; and, by itself explanation enough, by reason of the fact that they continue to receive support from the President of Mexico.[33] Thus the dispersion of decision-making in the public sector remains a feature of the planning process.[34] It is this that has led us to suggest that "mutual adjustment" decision-making must be an important feature of the Mexican planning system, even though we know as yet little of the detail of the adjustment process. The suitability of application of this process to planning would seem to be demonstrated by the general use of the process—as students are increasingly aware—in Mexican public and public-private affairs, and by its seeming rationality in the environment—as attested by the sustained high rate of economic growth.

c. There have been important developments in connection with plan activation or implementation. The Ministries of National Properties and Administrative Inspection (1946–58) and its successor National Patrimony (1958——) have increased the government's ability to control the execution of development projects and plans.[35] Public discussion of planning has increased, although there continues to be pressure for improvement of such debate.[36] The Plan of Immediate Action for 1962–64 provided a new focus for such discussion, and for complaints about government secrecy. The Plan provided a focus for pressure on private enterprise to cooperate in national development or explain its refusal. The necessity of discussing the Plan with the Organization of American States and the World Bank put some additional pressure on the Mexican government to consider views other than its own.

6. *Intersectoral Focus of Criticism*

There are certain obvious criticisms that can be leveled at any planning system, with greater or lesser plausibility and justice—and safety from official punitive action. These are heard in Mexico, and many have been stated or implied above. One that has not been discussed here is the frequent plaint that Mexican planning is opportunistic and done only out of sheer immediate necessity, in the face of crises that might have been anticipated,[37] and thus scarcely is planning at all. The charge recently has been leveled at the Plan of Immediate Action for 1962–64, drafted under pressures from the economic downturn of 1961 and its effects in Mexican politics, and the demands of the Alliance for Progress. There is, of course, opportunism in the planning of all governments. Critics do not make it clear whether they consider Mexican opportunism to be unusually damaging (to say nothing of possibly being useful, on occasion, as a demonstration of prudent reaction to changing conditions), or whether it is beyond alteration or dilution. Such criticism is only mildly interesting. Much more important, and not well appreciated, is the fact that criticism of sector planning in Mexico is rather perfunctory. Appreciation of this helps explain why the clouds of criticism of intersectoral, or aggregate, or comprehensive, or true planning often seem to lack very solid connections with the earth.

a. The question often is asked whether the Mexican government carries out its sector development activity with sufficient "planning" to achieve optimum national growth, and whether private enterprise might have done this sector development and planning better. With regard to the government, there is much reiteration of the charges that there has been a tendency to plan for projects too much in isolation, and to concentrate too much on the more obvious physical aspects and to neglect ancillary developments that would enhance the value of works. This is a standard comment all over the world, nearly always in some measure justified and in some measure misleading.

Criticism of sector planning in Mexico is, in fact, so muted as to lead one to wonder whether such planning has not been so well done as to admit of little complaint. In fact, the high quality of government sector planning seems to be one reason for this situation, but there are others: (1) the fact that data are not readily available to permit good analysis of sector planning; (2) reluctance of government departments to criticize each other in detail, especially without encouragement from the presidency; (3) a surprising number of commentators scarcely seems to realize that sector planning has been done in Mexico for many years, since they think of planning only in the centralized and comprehensive sense mentioned above; and (4) demands for true or integrated planning apparently strike some commentators as more important or more plausible, and in any event are politically fashionable.

b. Thus, most criticism of Mexican planning is directed above the sector, at levels where decisions are made with regard to programs developed by sector planners, resources are allocated, integration is attempted, consistency with policy is debated or ignored, and efforts can be made or countered in relation to the coordination of public and private economic plans. Pleas for more of this comprehensive and integrative planning are bolstered with economic, public administration, and humanitarian reasoning. In its most exaggerated form the economic view simply assumes that cooperation will be forthcoming from private enterprise, or that it will "pay" to use whatever cajolery or coercion are thought necessary. On such a basis, it is easy to assert that Mexico "must" adopt integrated national planning, as Mosk did in 1950, stating that the country could not afford the luxury of planless development, which he judged to be her state at that time.[38] The public administration emphasis is on administrative barriers to broader and/or more effective economic planning. One may, indeed, hope for some useful results from better civil service tenure rules, higher pay for bureaucrats, expanded in-service training, reduction of secrecy, better publication and dissemination practices, tighter control of autonomous agencies, and the like.[39] The humanitarian belief in the necessity for centralized and comprehensive planning in Mexico rests on faith; it is not arguable.

It is not surprising that none of these views has been entirely persuasive with the political masters of Mexico. The political view of the lack of comprehensive planning in Mexico must concentrate on the problems of the PRI in maintaining control of a large population which contains many interest groups with immediately conflicting purposes and considerable determination to express them in word and deed. Not least of these groups are leaders of party and of private enterprise who share a determination to maintain the market economy. Surely, no foreigner can be so daft as to inform these leaders that it would be well-advised politically as well as economically to institute centralized and comprehensive national planning in a given form at a given time.[40]

B. Factors Affecting Mexican Planning

1. Mexican tradition accepts considerable state intervention in the economy, and confers upon the business community little popular influence as an interpreter of the national destiny. This tradition must be borne in mind when contemplating differences between Mexican government and private enterprise with regard to planning.[41]

2. The private sector in Mexico is large, vigorous, growing, and, on the whole, complements rather than competes with the public sector. Government and PRI long have indicated that they intend the private sector to retain these characteristics. Thus, an important bloc remains cool to government planning, especially if it is to involve the extension of detailed government planning from the sectors in which the government is the principal owner into those where private enterprise is predominant.[42]

3. The PRI tends so much to a policy of conciliating its conflicting elements that some grounds exist for doubting its willingness to rush precipitously to the support of innovation. This is, however, a far cry from the assertion that it simply will not take strong stands on issues. Its record in recent decades suggests a quite effective mix of policy continuity and flexibility.[43]

4. The conditions of public discussion in Mexico are important to an understanding of the conflict of views and competition for support there.

a. There are important conflicts of goals and values, some similar to those in other countries, some peculiar to Mexico.[44] The most effective expression of goals and values is through organized interest groups, which are numerous and powerful in Mexico.[45] Much of the population is illiterate or has had little schooling, and is apathetic toward public affairs. The value of planning is so widely accepted—if not understood

—in Mexico today that the terms *planeación* and *planificación* threaten to become shibboleths, like *revolución*. If few persons have clear ideas of what is required to *planear* or *planificar,* this lends magic to processes already somehow touched with science and justice. Another value that is widely accepted is social justice, so that official discussions of plans and planning at least feel obliged to use the phrase "social and economic planning" and to state its purpose as elevation of levels of living.

b. Although speech and publication are free enough in Mexico so that a great variety of views is available, the government does interfere sufficiently to weaken discussion by antigovernment groups.[46] The government has great advantages in the competition to influence public opinion.

c. Discussion is weakened by other factors also. The predominant position of the PRI renders unimportant the discussions in the national legislature. There is considerable government secrecy, which does not aid national debate. Professional study, publication, and public leadership by specialists in economics and public administration make less of a contribution to discussion than might be desirable.

d. There has been little sophisticated study of Mexican information networks, communications techniques, and methods of propaganda, bargaining, and pressure. There are reasons for believing—and research in other countries is one reason—that information systems are more complex in Mexico than has been assumed by most observers of political and social affairs. Much of the work that has been done on Mexico relates to the more obvious aspects of control of the media of communications and interferences with free speech. At least as important, however, are the numerous and varied public devices employed by government and private groups to advance their views, the essentially nonpublic and little-perceived relationships between individuals and groups that often are of prime importance in decision-making, and the tendencies of certain groups to follow leads given by others.

5. The federal government's structure and operating practices are an important part of the environment affecting actual or putative government planning. First, it is commonly asserted that the government is excessively compartmentalized, and that coordination between agencies could be improved.[47] Second, it is generally agreed that year after year the Mexican government handles fiscal affairs in a highly competent manner.[48] Third, some critics find an unusual amount of overlap in the responsibilities of Mexican departments and agencies. It is not possible to state how it compares with other nations in losses due to this cause, or to guess as to effects on planning, except in general terms. Fourth, it sometimes is said that the machinery of government in Mexico

has not been changed to meet changing conditions, and is therefore obsolescent. It is easy to overlook the fact, however, that the uses of governmental forms in Mexico often have changed even when the more obvious aspects of the forms themselves have not. Fifth, many excellent upper-echelon Mexican bureaucrats devote but part of their working energies and time to their government duties. This is so often pointed out that we are in some danger of forgetting that the government gains much from the time they do devote to official duties. Both the underuse of the best-trained public servants, and the poor training of the rank-and-file are in large measure the result of budgetary limitations.[49] Sixth, Mexican government statistics leave something to be desired. They are, however, sometimes criticized too indiscriminately.[50]

C. Concluding Observations

1. The luxuriant variety of views available on Mexican government intervention in the economy suggests the difficulty of saying anything on the subject that will suit all mixtures of emotionalism and rationality in contemplation of social problems. The difficulty stems partly from a "mixed" economy, with possibly even more built-in contradictions and confusions than in the United States; partly from the very profusion of government economic policies, agencies, and actions, which offer some support to almost any assertion; and, in a minor way, from the fact that so many intellectuals—within and without Mexico—have enriched the discussion with a humanity often splendidly divorced from the dismal science. At any rate, it would appear that conditions in Mexico are favorable to extension of planning activity if it is desired.[51]

2. We must be aware, also, that the misinterpretations that come so easily to the foreign observer are made the easier in this case by the fact that little literature exists on the operations of the numerous Mexican planning agencies. No inventory exists of these agencies, their personnel, activities, budgets, or publications; to say nothing of their relations with each other, and their influence on government policy and action. Although it is known that there is controversy within the government of Mexico over planning policies and mechanisms, information on the subject is difficult to locate or substantiate.

3. The important question is, of course, not how much or what sort of planning Mexico has had, but how much and what sort of economic development. Planning can be defined in many ways; and economic development can proceed satisfactorily in the presence or absence of various of its manifestations, or with a combination of its manifestations suitable for one country alone. Since the economic development experi-

ence of Mexico in the past quarter-century has been, on the whole, satisfactory, the planning mix there must be conceded some suitability.[52] Diffused or mutual adjustment decision-making may be best there.[53]

4. We feel justified in concluding as we began, with the assertion that Mexico's successes in economic development rest on a combination of will and technique. If the former does not falter, she may continue to adjust the latter to tomorrow's needs.

Appendixes

APPENDIX I. Mexican Balance of Payments, 1961–62

Components	(thousands of dollars) 1961	1962*
Exports of goods and services:		
Exports of goods and gold and silver production**	844,306	945,571
Foreign tourist expenditures and border trade	715,156	788,905
Remittances of Mexican labor in the United States	34,146	35,231
Other components	11,250	9,306
Total of exports of goods and services	1,604,858	1,779,013
Imports of goods and services:		
Imports of goods	1,138,633	1,143,000
National tourist and border trade	319,850	340,580
Other components	68,344	84,534
Total of imports of goods and services	1,526,827	1,568,114
Balance of commodities and services	78,031	210,899
Net movements of long-term capital:		
Long-term credits	357,337	385,619
Long-term credit amortization	–171,965	–236,958
Foreign debt amortization	–11,749	–14,511
Securities transactions (net)	–7,431	1,421
Total net movements of long-term capital	166,192	135,571
Net receipts or expenditures estimate monthly	244,223	346,470
Net receipts and expenditures not estimated monthly (interest and dividends on foreign investments, new investments, etc.) and errors and omissions	–266,592	–254,448
Balance (change in Mexico's new short-term international assets)	–22,369	92,022

* Preliminary data.

** Excluding gold and silver used domestically for industrial purposes.

Source: U.S. Dept. of Commerce, WTIS, "Basic Data on the Economy of Mexico," Feb. 1964, p. 18, based on Bank of Mexico figures.

APPENDIX. II. Mexican Federal Budget of Expenditures, 1960 and 1962–64

Item	1960	1962	1963	1964
	(millions of pesos)			
Legislative	53.9	56.6	66.1	66.4
Presidency	14.5	24.1	29.6	45.3
Judiciary	45.9	60.8	55.2	62.6
Interior	57.3	58.5	86.7	104.6
Foreign Affairs	115.9	134.5	149.9	165.6
Finance	413.0	446.7	540.4	571.8
Defense	751.5	821.6	958.0	1,062.1
Agriculture	224.1	273.3	270.8	324.9
Communications	648.4	797.9	881.5	999.2
Industry and Commerce	105.2	101.5	108.1	129.1
Education	1,884.7	2,577.9	3,012.3	4,062.0
Public Health	534.3	562.9	607.7	778.4
Marine	339.4	326.3	388.6	442.0
Labor	37.1	38.7	41.8	51.7
Agrarian Affairs	62.3	83.3	90.2	99.6
Hydraulic Resources	762.2	779.6	852.3	1,405.2
Attorney General	19.0	25.8	27.3	33.3
National Patrimony	64.4	96.6	150.5	161.6
Military Industries	58.6	69.7	71.5	77.2
Investments	748.2	802.0	1,240.4	768.3
Public Works	1,140.5	1,223.7	927.2	1,234.8
Tourism	22.4	35.7	49.6	65.7
Additional (subsidies and Social Security)	1,292.1	1,811.6	2,186.1	2,287.0
Public Debt	861.5	1,110.3	1,009.6	972.1
Total	10,256.4	12,319.6	13,801.4	15,953.5

Source: U.S. Dept. of Commerce, WTIS, "Basic Data on the Economy of Mexico," Feb. 1964, p. 18, and U.S. Embassy, Mexico City.

APPENDIX III. Mexican Budget Income by Categories, 1960 and 1962–63

Source of Income	1960	1962	1963
	(millions of pesos)		
Income Tax	3,100	4,234	4,960
Social Security	—	—	—
Tax on Natural Resources	230	272	230
Excise Taxes	1,387	1,561	1,887
Commercial Gross Receipts Tax	1,080	1,366	1,517
Stamp Tax	170	212	215
Immigration Tax	32	30	31
Insurance Tax	38	43	44
Health Taxes	—	—	—
Import Taxes	1,420	1,788	1,512
Export Taxes	890	850	698
Lottery Taxes	70	103	96
Capital Taxes	10	33	3
Fees	498	485	441
Exploration and Natural Properties	177	321	826
Arrears and Fines	500	373	692
Total Ordinary Receipts	9,602	11,671	13,152
Sales of Capital Assets	50	50	50
Loans	600	600	600
Gross Total	10,252	12,231	13,802

Source: U.S. Dept. of Commerce, WTIS, "Basic Data on the Economy of Mexico," Feb. 1964, p. 18.

APPENDIX IV. Reproductive National Investment in Mexico, 1950–1962

Year	At Current Prices (millions of pesos)	At 1950 Prices (millions of pesos)	Change in 1950 Prices (%)
1950	5,560	5,560	
1951	6,881	5,738	+ 3.2
1952	8,149	6,305	+ 9.9
1953	7,853	6,131	− 2.7
1954	9,765	8,679	+41.6
1955	12,260	7,687	−11.4
1956	13,992	8,201	+ 6.7
1957	16,070	8,823	+ 7.6
1958	17,287	8,998	+ 2.0
1959	17,796	8,902	− 1.1
1960	21,207	10,109	+13.5
1961	22,960	10,579	+ 4.6
1962*	23,649	10,616	+ 0.3

* Preliminary estimate.

Source: *ESEM,* Jan. 1964, p. 17.

APPENDIX V. Private Investment in Mexico, 1950–62

Year	At Current Prices (millions of pesos)	At 1950 Prices (millions of pesos)	Change in 1950 Prices (%)
1950	3,294	3,294	
1951	3,900	3,252	− 1.3
1952	4,732	3,661	+12.6
1953	4,600	3,591	− 1.9
1954	5,400	3,804	+ 5.9
1955	7,600	4,765	+25.3
1956	9,060	5,310	+11.4
1957	10,124	5,558	+ 4.7
1958	10,770	5,606	+ 0.9
1959	10,944	5,474	− 2.4
1960	12,435	5,927	+ 8.3
1961	12,500	5,803	− 2.1
1962*	12,500	5,803	

* Preliminary estimate.

Source: *ESEM,* Jan. 1964, p. 15.

APPENDIX VI. Mexican Federal Government Investment from Budgetary Funds, and Other Funds, 1950–62

	Government Investments from Budgetary Funds (millions of pesos)			Investments from Other Funds (millions of pesos)		
Year	At Current Prices	At 1950 Prices	Change in 1950 Prices (%)	At Current Prices	At 1950 Prices	Change in 1950 Prices (%)
1950	1,396	1,396		870	870	
1951	2,214	1,846	+32.3	767	640	− 26.4
1952	3,153	2,439	+32.1	264	205	− 68.0
1953	2,396	1,871	−23.3	857	669	+227.3
1954	2,597	1,829	− 2.2	1,768	1,246	+ 86.1
1955	3,002	1,882	+ 2.9	1,658	1,040	− 16.5
1956	3,258	1,910	+ 1.5	1,674	981	− 5.6
1957	3,742	2,055	+ 7.6	2,204	1,210	+ 23.3
1958	3,639	1,894	− 7.8	2,878	1,498	+ 23.8
1959	3,935	1,969	+ 3.9	2,917	1,459	− 2.6
1960	4,323	2,061	+ 4.7	4,449	2,121	+ 45.3
1961	5,192	2,411	+17.0	5,268	2,365	+ 11.5
1962*	5,530	2,482	+ 3.0	5,619	2,522	+ 6.6

* Preliminary estimate.

Source: *ESEM*, Jan. 1964, p. 16.

APPENDIX VII. Trend of Private Investment in Mexico, 1948–62

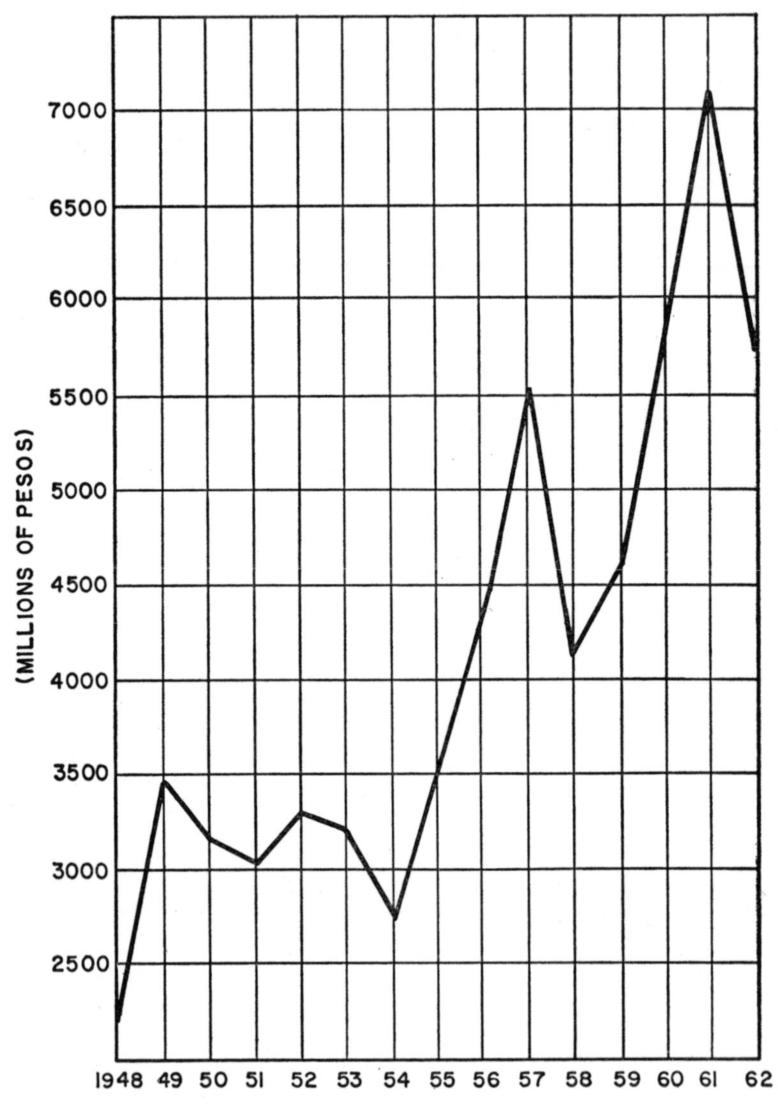

Source: *ESEM,* Jan. 1964, p. 20.

APPENDIX VIII. Trend of Private Investment by Sectors in Mexico, 1948–62

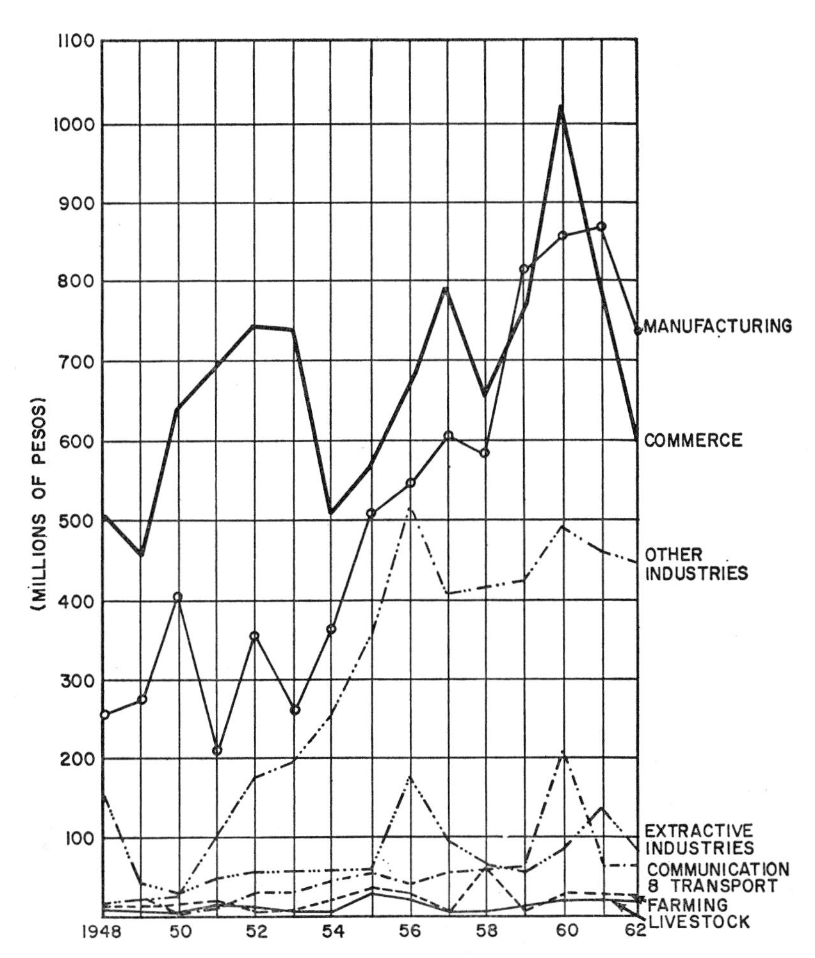

Source: *ESEM,* Jan. 1964, p. 21.

APPENDIX IX. Origin of International Credits through Nacional Financiera in 1942–54, 1958, and 1963

(thousands of dollars)

	1942–54	%	1958	%	1963*	%
TOTAL	360,698	100.0	125,790	100.0	221,598	100.0
United States	284,553	78.9	79,286	63.0	66,849	30.2
International Organs	67,685	18.8	19,183	15.8	57,775	26.1
France	3,163	0.9	2,327	1.8	29,481	13.3
Italy	1,594	0.4	7,901	6.3	10,379	4.7
England	——	——	2,742	2.2	14,960	6.8
Canada	2,988	0.8	675	0.5	23,782	10.7
Others	715	0.2	13,046	10.4	18,372	8.2

* To September.

Source: *MV,* Jan. 6, 1964, p. 1.

APPENDIX X. Foreign Investment in Mexico, 1959–62, as Percentage of Gross National Product

(millions of pesos)

Year	A GNP	B Direct Foreign Investment	C International Credits	D Total Foreign Participation	D/A %	B/A %
1959	136,200	1,014.4	2,762.3	3,776.7	2.77	0.74
1960	154,137	980.4	4,159.8	5,140.2	3.33	0.64
1961	163,757	1,490.8	4,466.7	5,957.5	3.64	0.91
1962	177,533	1,619.8	5,011.9	6,631.7	3.74	0.91

Source: *ESEM,* Nov. 1963, p. 6.

APPENDIX XI. Revised Figures on Mexican National Income 1950–62

	National Income (millions of pesos at current prices)			National Income *per capita* (pesos)	
Year	Previous Figure	Corrected Figure	Population (thousands)	Previous Figure	Corrected Figure
1950	37,500	36,630	25,791	1,454	1,420
1951	46,800	47,289	26,585	1,760	1,779
1952	52,000	52,967	27,403	1,898	1,933
1953	50,200	52,601	28,246	1,777	1,862
1954	59,180	64,432	29,115	2,033	2,213
1955	74,760	78,718	30,011	2,491	2,623
1956	84,000	89,743	30,935	2,715	2,901
1957	92,000	103,077	31,887	2,885	3,233
1958	101,800	114,688	32,868	3,097	3,489
1959	109,000	122,820	33,880	3,217	3,625
1960	120,100	139,084	34,923	3,439	3,983
1961	126,000	147,802	36,075	3,493	4,097
1962	n.d.	160,476	37,265	n.d.	4,306

N.B.: the corrected figures resulted from a reassessment of data by the Banco de México.

Source: *ESEM,* Nov. 1963, p. 5.

APPENDIX XII. Revised Figures on Rate of Economic Growth in Mexico, 1950–62

Year	Gross National Product (millions of pesos at 1950 prices) Previous Figure	Corrected Figure	Annual Growth of Production (%) Previous Figure	Corrected Figure	Population Growth (%)	Rate of Economic Growth (%) Previous Figure	Corrected Figure
1950	41,500	40,577	—	—	3.1	—	—
1951	44,500	43,621	7.2	7.5	3.1	4.1	4.4
1952	45,000	45,366	1.1	4.0	3.1	*	0.9
1953	44,400	45,618	−1.3	0.6	3.1	*	*
1954	47,800	50,391	7.7	10.5	3.1	4.6	7.4
1955	52,500	54,767	9.8	8.7	3.1	6.7	5.6
1956	56,000	58,214	6.7	6.3	3.1	3.6	3.2
1957	58,000	62,708	3.6	7.7	3.1	0.5	4.6
1958	60,600	66,177	4.5	5.5	3.1	1.4	2.4
1959	63,400	68,119	4.6	2.9	3.1	1.5	*
1960	67,000	73,482	5.7	7.9	3.1	2.6	4.8
1961	69,300	76,038	3.4	3.5	3.1	0.3	0.4
1962	n.d.	79,691	4.2	4.8	3.1	1.1	1.7

* No growth, by definition.

Source: *ESEM,* Nov. 1963, p. 4.

APPENDIX XIII. Mexican Gross Domestic Product by Sectors, 1950–62

(millions of pesos at 1950 prices)

Activities	1950	1951	1952	1953	1954	1955	1956	1957	1958	1959	1960	1961	1962
GROSS NATIONAL PRODUCT	40,577	43,621	45,366	45,618	50,391	54,767	58,214	62,708	66,177	68,119	73,482	76,038	79,801
Payments to external factors of production	—483	—596	—573	—411	—468	—545	—748	—723	—741	—733	—835	—889	—1,051
GROSS DOMESTIC PRODUCT	41,060	44,217	45,939	46,029	50,859	55,312	58,962	63,431	66,918	68,852	74,317	76,927	80,742
Agriculture	5,999	6,299	6,017	6,053	7,571	3,417	7,931	8,669	9,430	8,711	9,178	9,417	10,013
Stockraising	2,903	3,109	3,222	3,164	3,315	3,460	3,603	3,893	4,076	4,233	4,450	4,624	4,779
Forestry	263	267	209	208	226	256	255	243	225	254	254	228	236
Fishing	77	73	61	70	70	86	102	94	108	122	136	147	147
Mining	1,243	1,198	1,330	1,316	1,240	1,437	1,452	1,547	1,539	1,587	1,648	1,579	1,599
Petroleum	1,129	1,242	1,310	1,330	1,432	1,545	1,648	1,756	1,962	2,224	2,346	2,613	2,662
Manufactures	8,437	9,332	9,744	9,632	10,575	11,605	12,915	13,763	14,500	15,800	17,116	17,726	18,862
Construction	1,287	1,409	1,587	1,465	1,577	1,757	2,028	2,295	2,216	2,265	2,595	2,620	2,649
Electric Energy	370	411	447	477	526	586	655	707	761	818	898	983	1,047
Transportation & Communications	1,988	2,179	2,403	2,479	2,658	2,851	3,159	3,298	3,403	3,507	3,638	3,664	3,671
Commerce	10,750	11,793	12,147	12,427	13,169	14,233	15,157	16,318	17,157	17,608	19,167	19,780	20,769
Government	1,294	1,378	1,466	1,492	1,563	1,599	1,694	1,815	1,837	1,892	1,985	2,129	2,264
Other Activities	5,320	5,527	5,996	5,916	6,937	7,480	8,363	9,033	9,704	9,831	10,906	11,417	12,044

Source: *MV*, Nov. 18, 1963, p. 602.

APPENDIX XIV. Indices of Mexican Gross National Product, and of Gross Domestic Product by Sectors, 1950–62

Indices 1950 = 100

Activities	1951	1952	1953	1954	1955	1956	1957	1958	1959	1960	1961	1962
GROSS NATIONAL PRODUCT	107.5	111.8	112.4	124.2	135.0	143.5	154.5	163.1	167.9	181.1	187.4	198.4
GROSS DOMESTIC PRODUCT	107.7	111.9	112.1	123.9	134.7	143.6	154.5	163.0	167.7	181.0	187.3	196.6
Agriculture	105.0	100.3	100.9	126.2	140.3	132.2	144.5	157.2	145.2	153.0	157.0	166.9
Stockraising	107.1	111.0	109.0	114.2	119.2	124.1	134.1	140.4	145.8	153.3	159.3	164.7
Forestry	101.4	79.4	79.0	85.9	97.2	97.1	92.5	85.7	96.4	96.4	86.6	89.8
Fishing	94.6	78.8	90.9	90.4	111.3	132.7	122.0	139.8	158.6	177.1	190.9	190.9
Mining	96.4	107.0	105.9	99.8	115.6	116.8	124.5	123.8	127.7	132.6	127.0	128.6
Petroleum	110.0	116.0	117.8	126.8	136.8	146.0	155.5	173.8	197.0	207.8	231.4	235.8
Manufactures	110.6	115.5	114.2	125.3	137.5	153.1	163.1	171.9	187.3	202.9	210.1	223.6
Construction	109.5	123.3	113.8	122.5	136.5	157.6	178.3	172.2	176.0	201.6	203.6	205.8
Electric Energy	111.0	120.7	128.9	142.0	158.3	177.0	191.1	205.7	221.0	242.6	265.6	282.8
Transportation & Communications	109.6	120.9	124.7	133.7	143.4	158.9	165.9	171.2	176.4	183.0	184.3	184.7
Commerce	109.7	113.0	115.6	122.5	132.4	141.0	151.8	159.6	163.8	178.3	184.0	193.2
Government	106.5	113.3	115.3	120.8	123.6	130.9	140.3	142.0	146.4	153.4	164.5	175.0
Other Activities	103.9	112.7	111.2	130.4	140.6	157.2	169.8	182.4	184.8	205.0	214.6	226.4

Source: *MV*, Nov. 1963, p. 603.

APPENDIX XV. Volume of Production in Selected Manufacturing Industries, 1950–62

	units*	1956	1957	1958	1959	1960	1961	1962
Pig iron	000 tons	227	429	496	631	777	913	967
Steel ingots	000 tons	390	1,049	1,115	1,328	1,540	1,682	1,694
Cement	000 tons	1,388	2,519	2,496	2,638	3,086	2,984	3,266
Plate glass	000 sq. yards	6,047	9,144	6,355	8,236	8,705	10,169	13,778
Sulphuric acid	000 tons	43	186	200	243	249	276	339
Caustic soda	000 tons	8	34	39	52	66	72	83
Ammonium sulphate	000 tons	3	99	114	143	147	152	157
Ammonium superphosphate	000 tons	15	84	78	95	93	104	109
Nitrate of ammonium	000 tons	—	—	—	10	54	67	124
Synthetic fibers	000 tons	8	17	20	23	23	24	19
Cotton cloth	000 tons	66	82	93	100	102	99	96
Railway cars	units	—	1,507	1,791	1,761	1,686	2,165	787**
Trucks and buses	000 units	11	23	19	24	22	23	26
Passenger vehicles	000 units	10	18	20	27	28	39	40
Radio sets	000 units	67	274	327	390	450	530	608
Television sets	000 units	—	80	52	60	80	95	90
Refrigerators	000 units	n.d.	45	40	40	45	54	55
Stoves	000 units	n.d.	122	136	120	132	137	157

* Tons = metric tons.

** The reduction in part reflects a change in the type of vehicle manufactured.

Source: *MV*, July 29, 1963, p. 401.

APPENDIX XVI. Mexican Exports by Principal Commodity Groups, 1957–62

(millions of dollars)

	1957	1958	1959	1960	1961	1962	% of total 1962
Agriculture and stock	336.9	377.5	373.3	352.9	343.6	428.3	47.5%
Cotton	173.5	193.8	202.6	160.1	162.9	221.3	24.6
Coffee	108.8	79.2	62.6	71.7	71.7	71.3	7.9
Tomatoes	10.6	22.7	23.8	25.5	14.1	20.1	2.2
Livestock (on hoof & slaughtered)	22.9	53.6	47.9	42.8	57.9	74.9	8.3
Other	21.1	28.2	36.4	52.8	37.0	40.7	4.5
Fishing	23.7	33.9	41.0	36.3	46.1	47.4	5.2
Minerals	218.5	159.0	160.8	157.6	167.3	171.1	19.0
Lead (metal)	51.8	35.1	33.9	33.6	37.1	25.7	2.9
Sulphur	22.0	23.2	23.9	28.2	29.1	30.3	3.4
Zinc (metal & mineral)	41.6	19.9	24.9	29.5	27.2	28.7	3.2
Copper (metal & mineral)	37.2	29.9	29.8	25.8	19.0	24.4	2.7
Petroleum & natural gas	39.9	29.4	28.7	19.9	33.3	38.3	4.3
Other	26.1	21.5	19.6	20.7	21.5	23.7	2.6
Manufactured goods	72.7	82.2	86.2	134.8	168.8	149.5	16.6
Sugar	10.9	17.1	14.8	52.9	68.7	43.4	4.8
Other foodstuffs	12.3	13.3	14.7	18.3	22.2	22.8	2.5
Henequen fabrics	13.5	18.3	19.6	17.8	19.7	21.1	2.3
Other textiles	9.5	8.4	10.3	15.9	24.3	19.4	2.2
Chemical products	12.2	15.1	14.1	16.0	21.6	26.4	2.9
Other manufactures	14.4	10.1	12.7	13.8	12.3	16.5	1.8
Other Exports	54.3	56.5	61.8	57.2	77.8	104.6	11.6
Total exports*	706.1	709.1	723.0	738.7	803.5	901.0	100.0

* Including revaluation for some products.

Source: *MV*, July 29, 1963, p. 405.

APPENDIX XVII. Mexican Public and Private Investment Plan, 1962–65

Item	Millions of dollars	Total (%)
Public Investment Plan:		
Basic development investments	2,412	75.7
Agricultural-livestock development	566	17.8
Irrigation	541	17.0
Other agricultural investments	16	0.5
Forestry	10	0.3
Industrial development	914	28.7
Electricity	428	13.4
Petroleum	394	12.4
Iron and steel	37	1.2
Other investments	56	1.7
Communications and transport	911	28.6
Highways	375	11.8
Railways	410	12.9
Other investments	125	3.9
Other items	21	0.6
Social welfare works	746	23.4
Administration and defense works	30	0.9
TOTAL	3,187	100.0
Private Investment Plan:		
Agricultural-livestock activity	448	14.2
Manufacturing industry	1,280	40.6
Construction	1,040	33.0
Transportation	304	9.6
Other activities	80	2.6
TOTAL	3,152	100.0

Source: U.S. Dept. of Commerce, WTIS, "Basic Data on the Economy of Mexico," Feb. 1964, p. 22.

Notes to Chapters

ACKNOWLEDGMENTS: My thanks are due to several score employees and officials of the governments of the United States and of Mexico, and of the Organization of American States, and the United Nations, both in the United States and in Mexico, for their kind assistance.

KEY TO ABBREVIATIONS

CE	Banco Nacional de Comercio Exterior, *Comercio Exterior*
CEPAL	Comisión Económica para América Latina of United Nations; ECLA in English
HA	*Hispano Americano* (Mexico)
HAR	*Hispanic American Report* (Stanford University)
IAEA	*Inter-American Economic Affairs*
IBRD	International Bank for Reconstruction and Development
IDB	Inter-American Development Bank
MV	Nacional Financiera, *El Mercado de Valores*
OAS	Organization of American States
PAU	Pan-American Union
PRI	Institutional Revolutionary Party (Partido Revolucionario Institucional)
RAP	*Revista de la administración pública*
ESEM	Banco Nacional de México, *Examen de la Situación de México*
(*RESM*)	(*Review of the Economic Situation in Mexico*)
UNAM	Universidad Nacional Autónoma de México
WTIS	World Trade Information Service, U.S. Department of Commerce

I. WILL AND TECHNIQUE

1. Of course, Argentine development was more rapid than Mexican before 1940.
2. Miguel S. Wionczek, "Incomplete Formal Planning: Mexico," pp. 150–82, in Everett E. Hagen (ed.), *Planning Economic Development* (Homewood, Illinois, 1963). This is the best overview of Mexican planning, and excellent as far as it goes.
3. It would be an exciting enterprise to apply to Mexico, with appropriate modifications, the theses of Charles E. Lindblom, *The Intelligence of Democracy: Decision Making through Mutual Adjustment* (New York, The Free Press, 1965).

II. THE PLANNING ENVIRONMENT IN MEXICO: GOVERNMENT AND SOCIETY

1. Modern investigation in depth of Mexican politics and government has barely begun. Useful studies include: Robert Scott, *The Mexican Government in Transition* (University of Illinois Press, 1959), emphasizing organization and operation of the PRI; Frank Brandenburg, *The Making of Modern Mexico* (Englewood Cliffs, N.J., 1964), emphasizing the role of a small number of leaders, within and without the PRI, as opposed to the formal party apparatus; William Tucker, *The Mexican Government Today* (University of Minnesota Press, 1957), with much detail on government structure; Howard Cline, *Mexico: Revolution to Evolution 1940–1960* (Oxford University Press, 1962), Chaps. XIV–XVII, a balanced view of politics and government; William P. Glade, Jr., "Revolution and Economic Development, a Mexican Reprise," in William Glade and Charles Anderson, *The Political Economy of Mexico* (University of Wisconsin Press, 1963), emphasizing motivations, interaction of interest groups, and recent changes in decision-making; Raymond Vernon, *The Dilemma of Mexico's Development* (Harvard University Press, 1963), emphasizing the role of private enterprise in the decision-making of government and PRI; *México: Cincuenta Años de Revolución,* III, *La Política* (Mexico, 1963), Chap. XLV, "Partidos y Corrientes Políticas," a pro-government view.

2. The PRI resulted from a reorganization of the PRM in 1945, and the latter was created in 1937 as a reorganization of the PNR, itself created in 1929 to formalize the ruling coalition that had come out of the Revolution of 1910–17.

3. In 1962, for example, all twenty-nine state governors were members of PRI, as were all sixty federal senators, and 172 of the 178 members of the Chamber of Deputies.

4. In 1958 and 1964 the PRI candidates were elected president with about 89% of the total votes cast.

5. About the only commentators who can perceive such a threat are foreigners —including some in the United States—of two types: those who have somehow conceived the fantastic notion that there is a Communist problem in Mexico, and those of liberal persuasion who can find nothing good in the political and governmental structure of Mexico.

6. There is much disagreement on this. The opponents of the PRI assert, of course, that it is highly tyrannical. Much of the literature of Mexican politics is composed by domestic opponents and foreign romantics, and their laments regarding the asserted misdeeds of the party obscure the fact that as an organizer of political power the PRI has been brilliantly successful in a system of conciliation rather than of mobilization or coercion. Cf. Vernon, *Dilemma,* p. 133, for the flat judgment that Mexico is an "open society"; and for a somewhat conflicting view, Brandenburg, *Making Modern Mexico,* p. 163, that the security system is so extensive that the poor cannot revolt. Just before the presidential election of 1965 the government began moves to abolish many of the special police groups and the secret service. It may be doubted that the long-continued abuses of police power in Mexico can be much reduced soon.

7. Critics of the PRI understandably prefer not to deal with the question of alienation.

8. The PRI's own figures on membership fluctuate widely.

9. Of the other parties, only the minuscule Communist Party has an organization of any consequence.

10. Cf. Glade, "Revolution and Economic Development," p. 63, for a recent statement of this.

11. Daniel Cosío Villegas, "The Mexican Left," pp. 126–39, in Joseph Maier and Richard Weatherhead (eds.), *Politics of Change in Latin America* (New York, 1964), at p. 137.

12. The opposition, of course, prefers to claim that the PRI maintains its hold mainly by bribery and force. Judgments vary widely as to whether such acts are "excessive" in Mexico, and whether and to what extent violence has increased in the last few years. See Glade, "Revolution and Economic Development," pp. 95–96, for statement of the view that the system of "accommodation and consensus" helped Mexico escape the class divisions and conflicts found in much of Latin America, that the system helps all classes in Mexico, and that the relative absence of violence indicates this.

13. Cf. Brandenburg, *Making Modern Mexico,* 3ff., 141ff., *et passim,* for the thesis that Mexico is ruled by an elite he calls the "Revolutionary Family," whose affairs are conducted on three levels: (1) an inner council of about twenty, including the President of the Republic, former presidents, a few national and regional leaders which usually include the Minister of Government, the Minister of National Defense, and a few other outstanding cabinet members, and a few wealthy industrial and/or labor leaders; (2) the second level consists of about 200 spokesmen from finance, commerce, private industry, and agriculture; from various government agencies and enterprises; from educational, religious, professional, and social organizations; from the armed forces and veteran groups; from labor unions, cooperatives, communal agricultural groups, and civil-service federations, and from the judiciary, political groupings (the PRI and "opposition" parties), and the press; and (3) the formal political apparatus, the national bureaucracy, the armed forces, membership of the PRI, the captive opposition, and state and local public administrations. Understandably, the nature of the evidence available to support such a thesis will not be completely convincing to all.

14. Scott, *Mexican Government,* p. 290, states that "the political system forces all factors of political power either to discipline themselves in accord with the policies and programs of the presidency or to be prepared to pay the consequences." Cf. Brandenburg, *Making Modern Mexico,* pp. 141ff., *et passim,* for discussion of which presidents of Mexico have and which have not controlled the "Revolutionary Family"—i.e., the ruling elite.

15. I often heard this theory voiced in Mexico in early 1963.

16. Cf. R. A. Gómez, "Latin American Executives: Essence and Variations," *Journal of Inter-American Studies,* Jan. 1961, pp. 81–96, for rejection of the accusations of fraud and imposition against the PRI, describing it as "a very large confederation of political groups within which the ordinary differences of politics are fought through, similar to the Democratic Party in some United States southern states"; and for another recent analysis, taking much the same line, Ward Morton, "The Mexican Political 'Establishment' in Operation," in A. C. Wilgus (ed.), *The Caribbean: Mexico Today* (University of Florida Press, 1964), pp. 19–42.

17. Cf. Héctor Solís Quiroga, *Los partidos políticos en México* (Mexico, 1961), detailing what he considers the misdeeds of the PRI and the weaknesses of the other parties, and arguing that the PRI's opposition is so feeble that "political parties do not exist in Mexico."

18. In the July, 1961, elections the left not only won no Chamber seats, but received fewer votes than expected by those observers especially sensitive to the verbalisms rather than the organizational strength and popular support of the left. In the July, 1964, elections there was no leftist candidate for the presidency.

19. Cf. Charles W. Anderson, "Bankers as Revolutionaries; Politics and Development Banking in Mexico," in Glade and Anderson, *Political Economy of Mexico,* pp. 125, 129ff., for comment on the difficulty of determining the relative importance in decision-making of the operations of the PRI apparatus generally, as contrasted with the activities of the party inner circle, and possibly some non-PRI business elites, both concentrated in Mexico City.

20. Cf. Glade, "Revolution and Economic Development," p. 92, for the judgment that in Mexico intervention is not statism, and indeed aids private enterprise. See Chap. III, A, and Chap. V, E, above, for further comment on this.

21. No important measurement of the seriousness of these impediments is known to the author. Other impediments to planning, such as deficiencies of governmental statistical work, are discussed in subsequent chapters. It has been asserted that another impediment is the constitutional prohibition of presidential reelection, which forces planning into six-year molds, and that it is a factor contributing to projectitis—that is, decisions on individual projects without sufficient reference to others. One cannot imagine how to judge this proposition quantitatively.

22. It is almost unheard of to attack the president in the press. Members of the party elite do not campaign publicly for the nomination. The actual nominee is known as "el tapado" (the "bottled up," or hidden, candidate), and is not revealed by the president until late in the administration. No authoritative explanation of the method of selection ever has been made. Not even the press of Mexico is sure who makes the decision. Indeed, to speculate unduly and too early on the identity of the nominee is condemned by the party leadership as "futurismo," an undesirable form of prediction. (Cf. *Mañana,* Feb. 2, 1963.)

23. Cf. Paul Lamartine Yates, *El desarrollo regional de México* (2d ed., Mexico, Banco de México, 1962), pp. 204–05, on "Centralismo" in government relations with the economy as favoring the producers and consumers of central Mexico, leading to mistaken decisions on remote areas, and inhibiting private enterprise.

24. Scott, *Mexican Government,* pp. 255–56, *et passim,* makes the point that the extraconstitutional policy-deciding mechanism under the direct control of the president is necessary because Mexico lacks "the broadly based national political value system" that would "assure loyal and coordinate cooperation without" such a mechanism. He also judges that the mechanism adjusts easily to the changing needs of the country for political controls.

25. With regard to business and industrial associations, it must be remembered that in Mexico they have neither the general political and social influence of such organizations in the United States, nor as much hope of successful resistance if the president should decide to use his numerous powers to harass recalcitrants.

26. See Chaps. V and VII, above, for further discussion.

27. By a law of Dec. 1958, effective Jan. 1, 1959, the ministries and departments of state were rearranged. Among other changes, the Ministry of the Economy became Industry and Commerce, the office of the presidential secretary became the Ministry of the Presidency, the Ministry of National Patrimony was created and absorbed the Ministry of National Assets, the Ministry of Communications and Public Works became that of Communications and Transportation, and Public Works became a separate ministry; a Tourism Department was created,

and the Agrarian Department was renamed the Department of Agrarian Affairs and Colonization.

28. *CE*, Nov. 1960, put the number at 370.

29. Of total public sector imports in a recent year, 86.6% were by *organismos descentralizados* and *empresas de participación estatal* (of which 32.0% by Petróleos Mexicanos, 16.6% by the government railways, and 11.9% by the Comisión Federal de Electricidad), only 12.3% by the ministerial agencies of the federal government, and a mere 1.1% by state and local government (*MV*, Sept. 12, 1960, p. 453).

30. Cf. Lic. Sealtiel Alatriste, Jr., *La estructura del control externo de los organismos descentralizados* (Mexico: Secretaría del Patrimonio Nacional, 1962), for lists of 104 *organismos descentralizados*, dividing them into those created by law or decree (78) and those created by presidential order (24); also dividing those created by law or decree into six categories by function: (1) those engaged in the production and distribution of goods and services for the market—a list of seventeen, including the very important Pemex and Federal Electricity Commission; (2) those engaged in regional and local development; (3) those dealing in credit, securities, and finance; (4) those engaged in cultural development and scientific investigation; (5) those in social assistance; and (6) "others." Cf. William P. Glade, "The Role of Government Enterprise in the Economic Development of Underdeveloped Regions: Mexico, a Case Study" (unpublished Ph.D. dissertation, University of Texas, 1955), pp. 112ff., for discussion of the *organismos* and *empresas*; Anderson, "Bankers as Revolutionaries," pp. 134–36, for a good summary on these agencies; Tucker, *Mexican Government*, pp. 142ff.

31. There is no way of measuring "conflict of interest" problems in Mexico. Undoubtedly, some public officials use government data to personal advantage, and the particularistic nature of administration in Mexico facilitates this, as does the practice of multiple job holding (i.e., public officials retaining active private connections). There is no overpowering reason for believing, however, that this sort of activity is any more nearly "unbearable" economically in Mexico than in the United States.

32. In 1961–63 conservatives charged that the slowdown in economic growth and the flight of capital were due to government policies damaging to business confidence, especially a tendency toward socialization of the economy.

33. E.g., the Compañía de Subsistencias Populares (CONASUPO), by its purchasing and distribution activities, aids both small producers and low-income purchasers.

34. Other government policies include: industrialization, by means of subsidies of various sorts; broadening of domestic markets, partly through income distribution; greater domestic processing of export raw materials; expanding exports generally, and of manufactured goods especially in recent years.

35. Cf. *RESM* (Spanish-language edition *ESEM*), June, 1964, pp. 14–15, "National Economic Stability and the Federal Budget"; David Shelton, "The Banking System: Money and the Goal of Growth," pp. 111–89 in Vernon (ed.), *Public Policy and Private Enterprise in Mexico* (Harvard University Press, 1964), n. 20 to Chap. III, on Mexican deficits and surpluses in recent years.

36. Mexico's gold and dollar reserves reached an all-time high of $490.4 million in 1964 (*New York Times*, March 13, 1964). Declining trade deficits and increased tourist receipts since 1960 have sharply improved the balance of payments (Chase Manhattan Bank, *Latin American Business Highlights*, Fourth Quarter, 1963). According to the Minister of Finance, the monetary reserves of

Mexico rose from $29 million in 1934 to $465 million in June, 1963, and $525 million in June, 1964 (*New York Times,* Aug. 9, 1964). See Chap. III, B, 6, above, for comments on the balance of payments. See Appendix I for "Mexican Balance of Payments, 1961–62."

37. The public debt rose from $525 million in 1957 to $1.4 billion in mid-1963, by which time foreign indebtedness required about 15% of annual foreign exchange income for servicing alone (*New York Times,* Jan. 17, 1964). See *ESEM,* July 15, 1962, pp. 5–6, that amortization of foreign credits required $17.6 million in 1950, $44.2 million in 1955, $141.7 million in 1960, and $180 million in 1961.

38. Cf. *MV,* March, 1964, for a report by the Minister of Finance. In 1958, 24% of the external public debt pertained to the Federal Government, and 76% to the decentralized organs and state participation enterprises; at the end of 1963 the figures were 14% and 86%. In 1958, 41% of the external debt was due in five years or less; at the end of 1963 only 18% was in the same category. The annual service of the external debt represented 4.5% of fiscal income in 1958, but only 4.1% at the end of 1963.

39. On the investments of these agencies see Chap. III, C, below; on control of these agencies see Chap. V, C.

40. *International Commerce,* April 19, 1965, p. 27, that the 1965 budget consists of the regular budget of 17.9 billion pesos and 19.1 billion pesos for the more important of decentralized agencies, and that receipts and payments of the latter must be channeled through the Ministry of Finance.

41. "Economic Development in Mexico, 1961," WTIS, Nov. 1962; "Revised Basic Data on the Mexican Economy," *RESM,* Oct. 1960, pp. 15–17; *ESEM,* Dec. 1962, p. 23. Actual expenditures exceed the original budget figures: e.g., in 1961 by 17%. As adjusted for inflation of prices, with 1938 = 100, the 1947 expenditures were 377.8 and the 1958 were 1,777.5.

42. Cline, *Revolution,* p. 238.

43. Putting population increase at one million per year, and using original budget figures for expenditures. Cf. Ernesto Flores Zavala, *Elementos de finanzas públicas mexicanas. Los impuestos* (4a. ed., 1959), p. 389, for peso totals of government income in 1920–59.

44. *MV,* Dec. 16, 1963, pp. 645ff., "El presupuesto federal de egresos de la federación para 1964."

45. The 1952 and 1960 figures from Cline, *Revolution,* p. 239; 1961–63 from *ESEM,* Jan. 15, 1961, pp. 4–5, *ibid.,* Dec. 1962, pp. 22–23, *RESM,* Jan. 1961, p. 305; 1964 from an American Embassy, Mexico City, source. Of the 10,201 million pesos for economic and social development in 1963, "economic development" was allocated 5,381 million, and 4,820 million was for "investment and social protection."

46. Per capita terms for 1952 and 1960 from Cline, *Revolution,* p. 239; calculations for 1961–63 by the present author.

47. Cline, *Revolution,* p. 240. See Appendix II above for "Mexican Federal Budget of Expenditures, 1960, and 1962–64."

48. Cf. Tucker, *Mexican Government,* p. 161, that in 1939–51 the percentage of income going to all units of government increased from 11.5 to 13.7; p. 158, that about one-tenth of GNP was taken annually in taxes; and *ibid.,* p. 160, that Mexico is one of the least heavily taxed countries in Latin America. Cf. *Cincuenta años,* I, *La Economía,* p. 529: in 1939–59 the income of the Federal Government only represented an average annually of 8% of national product; it was 8.5% in 1935, and declined to 7.67% in 1959. The author observes that the

figures indicate a need for a change. Cf. OAS, Inter-American Economic and Social Council, *La marcha de la Alianza para el Progreso 1961/62. Primer Informe . . .*, Vol. II, p. 176, for Mexican comment that at the time of the 1961 tax reform the tax level in Mexico was "one of the lowest among developing countries."

49. The changes modernized collection procedures, eliminated the inheritance tax, increased rates on personal income, made the capital gains tax more progressive, and consolidated the income taxes that previously were levied under separate schedules, imposed a progressive surtax up to 30%, and provided for a new register of individual taxpayers that was expected greatly to expand the list of respondents. See *New York Times,* Jan. 17, 1964, for advertisement of Mexican Federal Government, for data to the effect that the number of tax subjects increased from 700,000 in 1961 to 4,000,000 by the end of 1963; and the expectation that soon 20% of the population would be paying taxes, compared with only 2.0% before 1961. See *ESEM,* Dec. 1963, on the increase in the tax rolls; *ESEM,* Oct. 1963, pp. 9–12, "El Consumo y los Impuestos," for speculation as to whether the new income taxes will cut middle class consumption expenditures; U.S. Dept. of Commerce, *International Commerce,* July 4, 1964, p. 13, that Mexican Federal income tax collections rose to $1.2 billion in 1963, an increase of 61.4% since the beginning of 1959.

50. Personal income taxes and income levies on industry and commerce accounted for the following shares of total federal revenues: 38.8% in 1955, 55.1% in 1960, 55.4% in 1961, 58.1% in 1962. The 1955 and 1960 figures from Cline, *Revolution,* p. 243; the 1961 and 1962 figures calculated by the present author on the basis of statistics of the Banco de Comercio Exterior, as cited in WTIS, "Economic Developments in Mexico, 1961."

51. Cline, *Revolution,* p. 243.

52. Cf. Appendix III for "Mexican Budget Income by Categories, 1960, and 1962–63."

53. Robert Scott, "Budget Making in Mexico," *IAEA,* (Autumn 1955), pp. 3–20, that in recent years about 90% of public spending has been by the federal government. Tucker, *Mexican Government,* pp. 285–86, about 81% in 1951, including expenditures of autonomous federal agencies; and p. 149, that in "recent years" nearly nine-tenths of all public spending has been by the federal government. Scott, *Mexican Government,* p. 47, that in 1956 federal government revenues were 79.7% of all government revenues. Henry J. Gumpel and Hugo B. Margáin, *Taxation in Mexico* (Boston, 1957), p. 49, on the relative unimportance of state and local taxation. Armando Servín, *Las finanzas públicas locales durante los últimos cincuenta años* (Mexico, 1956), p. 56, that in 1945 public revenues were 75.6% federal, 19% state, and 5.4% municipal. IDB, Social Progress Trust Fund, *Second Annual Report 1962,* p. 322, that in 1961 the Mexican Federal Government's net cash receipts represented about 8% of GNP, while total cash receipts of the entire governmental sector (federal, state, municipal) amounted to 11% of GNP.

54. Cf. Calvin P. Blair, "Nacional Financiera: Entrepreneurship in a Mixed Economy," pp. 191–240, in R. Vernon (ed.), *Public Policy.*

55. Other national credit institutions include: National Bank for Foreign Trade, National Bank for City Mortgages and Public Works, National Bank for Agricultural Credit, National Bank for Ejidal Credit, and others. Cf. Glade, "Role of Government Enterprise," *loc. cit.,* pp. 144–268, on government enterprises in the field of banking and finance; Gumpel and Margáin, *Taxation in Mexico,* pp. 20ff.,

on Mexican banks. For a brief summary of banking see WTIS, "Basic Data on the Economy of Mexico," Feb. 1964.

56. *ESEM,* Jan. 1963, p. 18, for dollar-peso exchange rates since 1920.

57. *Ibid.,* p. 19. This is Mexico City prices, from 1954–62. The table shows the rise separately for classes of commodities.

58. *Ibid.,* Feb. 15, 1961, pp. 4–5, for data on the purchasing power of the peso in 1950–59, emphasizing the importance of stability of purchasing power of the currency to economic development, and pointing out that the Mexican record is much superior to that of much of Latin America, including Argentina, Brazil, and Chile. Cf. *ibid.,* March 15, 1962, pp. 6–7, on prices in 1940–60.

59. Scott, "Budget Making in Mexico," pp. 8–11, but citing some weaknesses in performance data.

60. *Ibid.,* pp. 16–19.

61. *Ibid.,* for these judgments. Cf. Tucker, *Mexican Government,* pp. 149–57, on budgets and the budgetary system; Gumpel and Margáin, *Taxation in Mexico,* pp. 39–40.

62. A number of recent measures (including legislation in 1963) have been directed to this end. Apparently some new relationship between the ordinary budget and those of the decentralized agencies was set up in the budgeting process for 1965 (*New York Times,* Dec. 16, 1964). See Chap. V, C, 2, above on control of these agencies.

63. Cf. Albert Hirschman, *The Strategy of Economic Development* (Yale University Press, 1958), pp. 176–82, to the effect that such pressures stimulate rather than frustrate economic development; Cline, *Revolution,* pp. 85–86, for comments on strains put on Mexico by this increase.

64. In the 1920's the Mexican population increased 15.5%, in the 1930's it rose 18.8%, in the 1950's by 30.8%, from 1950 to 1960 by 34%. The population was 25.8 million in 1950, 34.6 million in 1960; at the rate of growth of the 1950's, it would reach 46.3 million in 1970, and 62 million in 1980. Cf. *ESEM,* Jan. 1963, p. 5.

65. Cline, *Revolution,* p. 337, Table V.

66. *Ibid.*

67. In his first annual message (1959) López Mateos had referred to the provision of jobs as the greatest economic problem he faced. In his message of 1962 he used the figure 350,000.

68. Cline, *Revolution,* pp. 101, 103; *ESEM,* Aug. 1963, p. 5.

69. See Oscar Lewis, "Mexico Since Cárdenas," in *Social Change in Latin America* (New York, 1960), p. 288, for acceptance of N. Whetten's figure of 10,000 as a more meaningful dividing line between the urban and rural environments in Mexico. Using this standard, in 1950 over 70% of the population was rural. There is, of course, no dividing line that is most useful for all purposes.

70. Lewis, "Mexico Since Cárdenas," p. 289.

71. Cf. Cline, *Revolution,* p. 105, for comment on this.

72. *Ibid.,* p. 104.

73. Cf. Oscar Lewis, *The Children of Sánchez* (New York, 1961), for a picture of the difficulties of penetrating this realm in detail.

74. Cline, *Revolution,* pp. 95–96; Lewis, "Mexico Since Cárdenas," p. 290.

75. Indianness is, in any event, disappearing under the impact of national education (formal and informal), and improved transportation and communications.

76. Many figures are published in Mexico that bear on attachment to the traditional or the modern societies. *La Prensa,* Jan. 27, 1963, printed Bank of Mexico

figures showing that from 1950 to 1960 the population that ate wheat bread went from 54.5% to 68.56% of total population, and shoe-wearers rose from 54.3% to 62.28%. *ESEM,* Aug. 15, 1962, p. 5, for similar figures, but also showing the great variation between states—i.e., the traditional society (by these measures) is clearly clustered. *ESEM,* Oct. 1963, pp. 17–20, "Comunidades Indígenas—Aspectos Económicos," pointing out the great differences in productive technology—i.e., in their integration into national life—among Indian groups. *ESEM,* Sept. 1963, pp. 18–19, for more figures on diet and dress.

77. Cline, *Revolution,* Chap. XI. He asserts that knowledgeable people consider that 300 pesos a month "is the minimum for a reasonably secure but marginal living in Mexico." He also offers figures to indicate that the upper and middle classes rose from 9.3% of total population in 1895, to 15.5% in 1940, to 27% in 1950, and possibly 40% in 1960.

78. Glade, "Revolution and Economic Development," pp. 47ff., accepts this view as clearly indicative of changing social classes. Cf. Lesley Byrd Simpson's review of Cline's *Revolution* (*Hispanic American Historical Review,* May 1963, pp. 295–97) for an example of reluctance to be cheery about statistics of economic growth in Mexico.

79. For comment on achievement motivation in Mexico, see Glade, "Revolution and Economic Development," pp. 33ff. See Scott, *Mexican Government,* pp. 89–91, for division of Mexican population into "six broad subcultural types": (1) the Indian; (2) the peasant, including *ejiditarios* and small farmers; (3) the small-town dweller; (4) the urban proletariat; (5) the metropolitan middle class; and (6) the metropolitan upper class. Cf. Lewis, "Mexico Since Cárdenas," pp. 334–39, on changing social classes.

80. Cf. *Cincuenta años,* II, Chap. XXI, "Clases y Estratos Sociales." It states (p. 58) that the distribution of "social classes" in the distribution of income in 1956 was: popular class, 83.3% of Mexican families and 54.3% of national income; middle class, 13.8% of families and 30.3% of national income; upper class, 2.3% of families, and 15.4% of national income. This source also states (p. 66) that in 1956 the popular class had 47.9% of its workers engaged in agriculture, and that they constituted 89.5% of all workers in agriculture; that 21.3% of the popular class was in manufacturing, and that this constituted 92.2% of all manufacturing employees; and that the middle class was 51.1% in commerce, and 28.6% in services. As will be seen below, commerce gobbles up a large share of national income in terms of number of persons engaged in it. This chapter in the useful series of government apologia rests the case for PRI and government, by concluding (pp. 76–77) that social change continues at a great pace, that a large middle class has been created, though it admits that the popular classes should have more income. Cf. *ESEM,* March 1965, p. 8, on occupational groups.

81. Cf. Cline, *Revolution,* pp. 99–100, on the Oscar Lewis view that poverty is more important than "Indianhood."

82. In 1962 Mexico's per capita income (current prices) was 4,258 pesos (355 pesos a month), or $342 a year.

83. Cf. WTIS, "Basic Data on the Economy of Mexico," Feb. 1964, p. 5, citing a UN study that Mexico's per capita income in 1962 was above that in Guatemala, Ecuador, or Brazil; but only 73% of that in Argentina and 79% of that in Costa Rica. Such comparisons are of limited use without extensive analyses of exchange rates, price levels, and other factors. See Appendix XI for Mexican national income per capita in 1950–62.

84. Cf. Scott, *Mexican Government,* pp. 90–91, on the dangers of using cash in-

come figures. See *Siempre,* Feb. 6, 1963, p. 12, for a ludicrous example of the use of statistics to "refute" government claims of rising incomes. This opposition magazine in effect claimed that national income was less per capita in 1957 than in 1939, and tried to pretend that this fact (!) showed that the average man's position had worsened.

85. For the form, and much of the material, in these suggestions, I am indebted to David Pickett, an anthropologist with considerable experience in Mexico. Pickett founds his formulation both upon observation and upon a large number of documentary sources. Cf. Vernon, *Dilemma,* p. 207, n. 4, for the judgment that Mexican cost-of-living indexes and nominal wage measures are riddled with pitfalls—e.g., ignoring fringe benefits, and taking no account of the differences between official ceiling prices and actual prices.

86. Cline, *Revolution,* Chap. XI; Ifigenia M. de Navarrete, *La distribución del ingreso y el desarrollo económico de México* (Mexico, 1960), pp. 74–75.

87. Cf. *ESEM,* Oct. 1963, pp. 9–12, "El Consumo y los Impuestos," that the lower class in terms of income averages less than 900 pesos a month; United Nations, *Monthly Bulletin of Statistics,* Sept. 1963, Table 49, that the average earnings in pesos in manufacturing in Mexico are 964 a month. See *ESEM,* March 1965, p. 9, for monthly income figures in 1960 of 7.19 million persons.

88. *HAR,* March 1964, p. 18. At 21.5 pesos daily, and assuming 25 days' work in the month. The secretary-general of the Mexican Workers Confederation asserted in criticism that a minimum of 36.04 pesos daily was required to satisfy the material, cultural, and social needs of a give-member worker family. Obviously, the specification of "needs" is what is lacking.

89. Cf. OAS, Committee of Nine, "Evaluation of the Plan of Immediate Action," pp. 50–60, commencing with the statement that no precise data exist that permit analysis of the distribution of income and wealth in Mexico, finding disequilibrium of distribution of income, noting evidence of some improvement over the years, rather hinting that conditions are disquieting, but concluding that rapid change cannot be expected.

90. Cline, *Revolution,* Chap. XI, claims a striking income rise for the general population in 1950–56, and asserts that a process of "up-grading" has been going on for many years, to some extent since the Revolution, but especially since 1940. He puts the "popular class" as a percentage of the total economically active population at 90.7 in 1895, down to 78 in 1940, and to 50 in 1950; and finds that the "poor became less poor, nor were they so numerous." Glade, "Revolution and Economic Development," p. 21 and n. 125, supports the thesis that in 1950–57 the real income of the bottom 20%, and of the top 2.4%, declined, while all other income sectors enjoyed at least some absolute increase, and while many had a real increase also. Adolf Sturmthal, "Economic Development, Income Distribution, and Capital Formation in Mexico," *The Journal of Political Economy,* LXIII, No. 3 (June, 1955), pp. 183–201, that wages increased in real terms in 1939–50, perhaps by 10–12%, but at any rate appreciably. Vernon, *Dilemma,* pp. 93–94, accepts the view that in 1940–60 a considerable part of the population seemed to increase its living levels, and asserts that the evidence is poor for the notion that Mexican growth is characterized chiefly by the rich becoming richer and the poor becoming poorer. But see Scott, *Mexican Government,* pp. 91–92, that in 1939–50 income fell for the 86% of the population in the lower class that earned its living from rural and urban labor and services, while it rose for the 14% not in the lower class who got income from capital, salaries, etc., but he

admits that there are some difficulties with the evidence. For comment on the shift after 1939 away from wages and salaries and toward profits, accomplished in part through inflation, see Cline, *Revolution,* pp. 123, 258; Scott, *Mexican Government,* p. 90; Sturmthal, "Economic Development," pp. 186ff., 190, 193; H. G. Aubrey, "Structure and Balance in Rapid Economic Growth: The Example of Mexico," *Political Science Quarterly,* LXIX, No. 4 (Dec. 1954), pp. 517–40, at pp. 521–24.

91. I. Navarrete, *Distribución del ingreso,* p. 75, states that 700 pesos per family per month was attained by 67% of families in the Federal District and North Pacific states, by 40% in states in the North and on the Gulf of Mexico, and only 20% of families in the Pacific and Central states. All her figures are based on a small (5,000 families) questionnaire of 1956.

92. Cf. *ESEM,* Sept. 15, 1962, pp. 9–11, for data that suggest more pessimism; and Inter-American Committee for Agricultural Development, *Inventory of Information Basic to the Planning of Agricultural Development in Latin America: Mexico* (Washington, PAU, 1964), p. 4, accepting the figures of Ana M. Flores, *La magnitud del hambre en México* (Mexico, 1961). Cf. *ESEM,* March 15, 1962, p. 14, Mexican caloric intake compared with other countries.

93. Cf. *ESEM,* July 1963, pp. 3–4, on the distribution of income between consumption and savings, with conclusion that in 1959–60 population and production increased faster than consumption.

94. Cf. I. Navarrete, *Distribución del ingreso,* that distribution of income in Mexico is excessively unequal, both from the point of view of a sound social condition, and for optimum economic development, though neither point is much developed. *CE,* Feb. 1961, pp. 86–90, comments on Navarrete's book to the effect that she states, but does not prove, that unequal income distribution does not permit enough capital accumulation, and that she does not say whether Mexico's distribution is normal for an underdeveloped country. Glade, "Revolution and Economic Development," p. 63 and n. 107, on the consumption and savings-investment chain, and on consumption increments as part of an end-means continuum of activity; and n. 125, agreeing with Navarrete that in 1957 there was too much concentration of income, with 4.9% of families receiving 36.6% of national income; but see *ibid.,* n. 152, that the great increases in the demand for consumer goods in Mexico at least indicate an increase in purchasing power that surprised some entrepreneurs. IBRD, *The Economic Development of Mexico* (Baltimore, 1953), p. 10, that although per capita consumption increased 55% in 1939–50, it probably was concentrated in a small part of the population, due to the shift in the distribution of income in favor of profits and against wages and salaries, so that although the exact number of persons who got about half of the national income from profits, rents, and interest is unknown, it must have been small. Brandenburg, *Making Modern Mexico,* p. 344, states that for a time "factory workers and peasants simply must pay the price of rapid industrialization and commercialization of the Mexican economy."

95. I. Navarrete, *Distribución del ingreso,* p. 48.

96. Cf. Brandenburg, *Making Modern Mexico,* pp. 237–38, on difficulties of determining the size of the labor force; *ESEM,* Sept. 1963, pp. 17–18; and cf. *ibid.,* Nov. 1963, pp. 8–10, "La desocupación en México."

97. Nacional Financiera figure in WTIS, "Basic Data on the Economy of Mexico," Feb. 1964. The full data on the economically active population of Mexico (Dec. 31, 1960) are as follows:

Economic Sector	Thousands of persons	Per cent of total
Agriculture (includes livestock, forestry and fishing)	6,342	52.8
Industry (includes mining, petroleum, construction, electric power, etc.)	2,008	16.7
Commerce and finance	1,092	9.1
Transportation and communications	423	3.5
Services, including governmental	1,550	12.9
Not specified	458	3.8
Temporarily unemployed	141	1.2
Total economically active	12,014	100.0
Total economically inactive	23,218	
TOTAL POPULATION	35,232	

98. Cf. Lewis, *Children of Sánchez,* pp. xxx–xxxi, that the political stability of Mexico shows the capacity for misery of the ordinary Mexican, but hints that they may not put up with much more. He also informs us that "it is common knowledge that the Mexican economy cannot give jobs to all of its people" (p. xxix), without informing us that the same is true of the United States, and that the Mexican economy provides many more and better jobs than ever before in its history. He also points out that the poor are paying the cost of the industrial progress of the nation, whereas he might better have said paying a disproportionate share, and have noted that they always do. He does agree that production has increased and that there is "apparent prosperity"; however, the "culture of poverty includes at least the lower third of the rural and urban population" (p. xxvi), which may be a good enough statistic for so loosely defined a group.

99. The press in 1962–64 carried many indications of PRI and government sensitivity to this issue.

100. Cf. I. Navarrete, *Distribución del ingreso,* p. 96, for argument that excessive inequality of income distribution hurts economic development by restricting demand for products, limiting occupational mobility, and in other ways. Demands for increases in popular purchasing power on both technical and moral grounds are very numerous in Mexico. An interesting recent example is Horacio Flores de la Peña, "Reflexiones sobre el Plan General de Desarrollo Económico," *Ciencias Políticas y Sociales,* año 9, no. 32 (April-June, 1963), pp. 127–42, tracing almost all shortcomings in the economic and social orders to the fact that "the diminution of income of the popular sectors [through government inflationary and other policies] reduces drastically the rate of growth of internal demand and thus of general growth."

101. *RESM,* March, 1961, pp. 16–17, states that the rural population deserves a larger share of the national income and that "if this is not accomplished, their purchasing power will decline still further, to the detriment of Mexican industry." This neatly combines the moral and technical reasons for income redistribution.

102. For example, those of I. Navarrete, *Distribución del ingreso,* pp. 97–99, recommending large government expenditures to raise the incomes and level of living of the poor.

103. Cline, *Revolution,* p. 208, for an optimistic summary; also Lewis, "Mexico Since Cárdenas," pp. 329ff.; *Cincuenta años,* IV, *La Cultura, passim.*

104. Cf. *HAR,* July, 1964, p. 399, for a Mexican charge that the school system is meeting only 17% of industry's annual demand for professional, technical, and

supervisory personnel; and that the loss of productivity suffered each year is far in excess of the cost of adequate training.

105. Cf. Cline, *Revolution,* pp. 195–96, on purposes of education. The conservative PAN, backed by the Church, has recently been agitating against the restrictions put on educational activities by religious groups. Lewis, "Mexico Since Cárdenas," p. 352, states that the new aim is more conventional than previously when the school was thought of as a means of advancing the Revolution. On purposes, see J. Torres Bodet, pp. 4–26 in *Cincuenta años,* IV; *ibid.,* pp. 73–78, on educational philosophy, especially as it relates to primary education.

106. Cf. Marjorie Johnson, *Education in Mexico* (Washington, 1956), pp. 54ff. A *secundaria* student may transfer to a two-year *preparatoria* course. The National Polytechnic Institute, on the vocational "path," includes degree programs in engineering and social sciences as well as for the preparation of technicians.

107. Cf. Johnson, *Education,* pp. 27ff., *et passim,* on federal control and influence. Some of the mechanisms of federal control and influence in education are: (1) technical direction of all state (which includes municipal) schools; (2) building and/or direction of federal schools in the states, which remain "federalized" as contrasted with the "coordinated" schools supported only by the state (but supervised by the federal government); (3) licensing the establishment and the programs of all private institutions offering elementary, secondary, or normal school training for workers; (4) a Director of Federal Education residing at each state capital; (5) a federal Minister of Education not only having great powers but a prestige enhanced by the propaganda apparatus of party and government, and by the fact that truly distinguished men sometimes are appointed to the post; (6) the UNAM approving the institutions of higher education, except the technical; (7) the National Preparatory School (administered by UNAM) setting standards for preparatory schools throughout the country; (8) the Federal District schools are under the Education Ministry, and absorb about 20% of the entire education budget. By these and other devices the federal government exercises a predominant influence in the educational institutions of the country.

108. Cline, *Revolution,* p. 194: 12.3 million pesos (4.9% of budget) in 1921, 75.3 million (11.9%) in 1940, 314 million (9.1%) in 1950, 1,900 million (18.6%) in 1960. It was 19% of the 1961 budget, 20% in 1962, 22% in 1963, 25% in 1964. Cf. *Cincuenta años,* IV, for cost of all education (federal, state, private) in 1910–60.

109. *Cincuenta años,* IV, pp. 69–70. In 1960, 5.02 million received instruction of the total of 7.66 million school age children. In 1962 about 8 million persons were enrolled in educational institutions, or more than 20% of the population.

110. Cf. Cline, *Revolution,* pp. 199ff. The census of 1950 showed that only 10% of adults had more than six years' schooling.

111. *Cincuenta años,* IV, p. 131. There is much difficulty in interpreting Mexican figures in terminology meaningful to citizens of the United States, where the school system is quite differently arranged and named. Cf. Cline, *Revolution,* p. 203, that in 1958 the total post-primary enrollment was some 332,000, perhaps 6% of the total 14–29 age group potentially eligible. For example, "vocational" students (e.g., at the National Polytechnic Institute) can be listed as "nonuniversity" when in fact their studies would be labeled college or university in the United States. Cf. Johnson, *Education,* pp. 55ff., on the secondary and preparatory systems.

112. *Cincuenta años,* IV, p. 133. UNAM, in the Federal District, with 43,188 students (excluding its preparatory courses) in 1961, had a third of the total national enrollment in higher education. The National Polytechnic Institute, a dependency of the Education Ministry, is not autonomous, and thus lacks one of the distinguishing marks of Latin American universities. The Institute of Technology at Monterrey is a private institution in a community dominated by a conservative, business-oriented group that has deep reservations about the PRI. The offerings of the institutions of higher learning in the states are more limited than those of three mentioned above, and their prestige is much less. (Cf. Johnson, *Education,* pp. 87ff.)

113. Johnson, *Education,* pp. 49–50, 50–53, 72–73.

114. Cline, *Revolution,* p. 204, that in 1948–57 degrees in commerce outranked any other group, and accounted for nearly one-half the total (of both degrees and "titles," not entirely comparable certificates). The commerce group included preparation for many of the common positions in business and government bureaucracies: e.g., auditors, accountants, bookkeepers, secretaries. Cf. *Novedades* (Mexico), Feb. 8, 1963, for article on commerce and economics as the most popular subjects at the UNAM.

115. Related to this is the provision of free textbooks. The federal government distributed an annual average of 20 million free texts in 1960–62. The Church and conservative business groups have been bitterly objecting to this program. Such tactics by the opposition strengthen the impression that no group in Mexico is likely soon to challenge seriously the influence of the PRI.

116. *Cincuenta años,* IV, p. 135, on the need for national planning for expansion of higher education. Cf. John Galbraith, *Economic Development in Perspective* (Harvard University Press, 1962), p. 55, for criticism of excessive "democracy" in Latin American universities if they are properly to serve the development process.

III. THE PLANNING ENVIRONMENT: ECONOMY

1. This is the predominant view among foreign observers. For a good recent summary in this vein, see Cline, *Revolution,* pp. 231–36, finding it a "mixed system" of partnership between government and private enterprise. A typical judgment is Glade, "Role of Government Enterprise," p. 564, that "one of the prime functions of the government sector of the economy is to strengthen and stimulate the private." Cf. Tucker, *Mexican Government,* pp. 215–22, on Mexican government regulation philosophy and mechanisms.

2. For a typical statement, see Mexico, Secretaría de la Economía, *Memoria 1958,* p. 14, that Mexico is a private enterprise country, and that intervention by government in the economy takes these forms: (1) measure for promotion or development (e.g., aid to "new and necessary" industries, controls on foreign trade, tariff protection, credit); (2) public investments to promote development; and (3) protection of the weakest sectors of the population.

3. And see above, Chap. II, A, 4, on government fiscal operations. Cf. A. Manero, *La revolución bancaria* (Mexico, 1957), pp. 306–07, that President Ruíz Cortines (1952–58) stated that the government would adopt "a prudent and coordinated monetary, credit, financial, and investment policy." This might be the motto of all the administrations since 1940.

4. For a recent summary of accepted government activity in economic development, see *Cincuenta años,* I, pp. 168–70. Cf. Vernon, *Dilemma,* p. 188, on the

importance of the government in economic development; Vernon (ed.), *Public Policy,* p. 11 of introduction, on role of the Mexican President in the regulation of business.

5. Cf. Glade, "Role of Government Enterprise," pp. 112ff., 557–65, for an administrative division of Mexican government enterprises in the economy: (1) those organized as part of the ministries; (2) those organized as autonomous public corporations, the capital stock being owned by the federal government or other autonomous public corporations, mainly the government banks; and (3) mixed corporations, notably industrial enterprises promoted and financed by Nacional Financiera, most of these being originally conceived as only temporarily under government ownership and operation. Cf. Eduardo Bustamante (Minister of National Patrimony), "Discurso el día 5 de mayo en la ciudad de Puebla," *Revista Patrimonio de México,* No. 8 (1962), for extensive comment on government contributions to national production, and the key sectors in which much of it occurs; Glade, "Revolution and Economic Development," pp. 91ff., on government intervention in the economy; Brandenburg, *Making Modern Mexico,* pp. 225ff.; Blair, "Nacional Financiera," pp. 193ff.

6. Frank Brandenburg, *The Development of Latin American Private Enterprise* (Washington, National Planning Association, 1964), p. 68, that the Mexican government seldom relinquishes ownership; Glade, "Role of Government Enterprise," pp. 588–90, for similar doubts. See *HAR,* July 1964, p. 400, that the government has purchased the Yucatán rope-making industry in order to "liberate" the *ejidatarios* who grow the henequen, and that private enterprise spokesmen are protesting the action.

7. Cf. OAS Committee of Nine, "Evaluation of the Plan of Immediate Action," pp. 17, 239, *et passim,* for recent comment on pricing policies.

8. Glade, "Role of Government Enterprise," pp. 565–78, for an effort to determine the impact of government on national income, and giving a history of Mexican attempts, beginning in 1938, to arrive at figures on the question. Glade, although somewhat dubious about the statistics, estimates that the government accounted for at least 10–15% of national income and GNP. Vernon, *Dilemma,* p. 23, that the private sector accounts for more than 90% of output. For the same general view, but considerably different figures, see *Conferencia . . . Bustamante . . . Secretaría del Patrimonio Nacional* (Mexico, 1959), that the activities of the government generate only 15% of national product in Mexico, compared with 25% in the United States.

9. Brandenburg, *Development of Private Enterprise,* pp. 61–63, for this analysis. He is aware of its limitations. The eleven largest enterprises descending in order of size, are: Ferrocarriles Nacionales de México (railroad), Comisión Federal de Electricidad, Petróleos Mexicanos, Cia. Mexicana de Luz y Fuerza (electricity), Banco Nacional de Crédito Ejidal, CONASUPO (consumer goods distribution), Ferrocarril del Pacífico, Banco Nacional de Crédito Agrícola, Industria Eléctrica Mexicana, Nacional Financiera, Ferrocarril Chihuahua al Pacífico.

10. Cf. Shelton, "The Banking System," pp. 121–22, on government support of private banking; Blair, "Nacional Financiera," p. 234, on "accords" and official price fixing which prevent Nacional Financiera activity from hurting private competitors.

11. *Cincuenta años,* I, p. 618, for figures that Mexican economic growth has been more rapid in recent years than that of any other Latin American country, and than a large list of well-developed countries; *ibid.,* p. 579; *ESEM,* Oct. 1962, pp. 8–11, "México y paises subdesarrollados," on some comparisons with other

countries; Erik Baklanoff, "Argentina, Chile, and Mexico: Contrasts in Economic Policy and Performance," *IAEA,* Oct. 1961, pp. 497–508.

12. *Cincuenta años,* I, p. 600. See OAS, Committee of Nine, "Evaluation of the Plan of Immediate Action for Mexico. Commentary Presented to the Government of Mexico by the Committee *ad hoc,* August 1964" (263 pp. mimeographed), p. 28, for table of growth and structure of internal gross product, 1940–63.

13. *MV,* March 10, 1965, pp. 125–26, with growth figures by sector, showing the highest growth in construction (17%), electric energy (14.9%), manufacturing (13.5%), and commerce (10.6%).

14. For production by sectors in 1950–62, see Appendixes XIII–XIV, above. For other data on the growth of production: Cline, *Revolution,* pp. 254–58, 260, Appendix Table XIV; *Cincuenta años,* I, pp. 523–28, 576, 579, 587–89; Sept. 5, 1960, Jan. 9, Feb. 27, 1961; *ESEM,* July 1963, May 1964; *RESM,* July 1960, March, April, 1961, June 1964; *CE,* Jan. 1963; WTIS, "Economic Developments in Mexico, 1960, 1961"; *Noticias* (Mexico), XVII, Nos. 3, 10; *International Commerce,* Jan. 18, April 5, 1965; OAS Committee of Nine, "Evaluation of the Plan of Immediate Action," pp. 6ff., on growth in recent decades, and on the recent slowdown and government measures to combat it; Shelton, "The Banking System," pp. 170–73, on efforts to meet the slowdown after 1961.

The pages cited in *Cincuenta años* give detailed data on the history of economic growth. GNP in 1895–1910 rose 2.9% annually, or 1.6% per capita. In 1910–21 it went up only 7.7%, or 0.7% a year, but the per capita rate rose, due to population decline during the Revolution. In 1922–29 production rose 1.7% annually. In 1932 production was lower than in 1910. It recovered in 1933–34, and in 1934–45 there was increasing development, due especially to the recovery of the industrial nations, which increased demand for Mexican products; the policies of agrarian reform and of public works construction; and the necessity of building industrial plant during World War II. In those years manufacturing increased the most—161%. By 1945 manufacturing represented 18% of national product, agriculture and stock 16%, and mining and petroleum 5% each. In 1945–59 agricultural and stock production increased 123%, manufacturing 121%, petroleum 272%, electric energy 218%.

15. Robert Shafer, "Mexican Mining and Manufacturing," in Wilgus (ed.), *Mexico Today,* pp. 85–99.

16. *Cincuenta años,* I, p. 101: there are 196 million hectares (1 hectare = 2.47 acres) in Mexico, of which 55 million have slopes over 25%, and are little cultivated; *ibid.,* pp. 103–05, on land use, and 132–33, showing a huge area devoted to grazing; cf. Cline, *Revolution,* pp. 142–45, on climate and rainfall, and 45–48, on land use potential.

17. *Cincuenta años,* I, p. 102: arid lands are over 102 million hectares, or 52.13% of total land area; semi-arid land is estimated at 60 million hectares (30.56% of total area).

18. *Ibid.,* p. 610, the cultivated area increased from 5.33 million hectares in 1930 to 12.04 million in 1959; cf. Baklanoff, "Argentina, Chile, and Mexico," citing a Mexican economist, that the growth of agricultural production may be ascribed to new lands brought into cultivation (40% of the increment), shifts to more productive crops (about 35%), and increased yields (25%).

19. Cf. *ESEM,* May 15, 1962, pp. 3–8, ascribing the growth of agricultural production more to extensions of acreage than to increases in productivity.

20. *MV,* March 21, 1964.

21. *Cincuenta años,* I, p. 611.

22. L. B. Simpson, "Unplanned Effects of Mexico's Planned Economy," *Virginia Quarterly Review,* XXIX, No. 29 (1953), pp. 514–32, that the Ministry of Agriculture estimated in 1950 that independent farmers were producing 70% of all crops, against 30% for *ejidos* (individual and collective types). Cf. Glade, "Revolution and Economic Development," p. 59, for emphasis on the achievement represented by the producers of the 70%.

23. President López Mateos, in his September, 1962, message to the congress, made the point that he had distributed 10.04 million hectares since 1958, and that states had distributed another 0.5 million during that period.

24. Cf. Cline, *Revolution,* p. 221, on productivity on different types of land holdings; Armando González Santos, *La agricultura. Estructura y utilización de los recursos* (Mexico, 1957), pp. 114–15, for the view that transformation of the agricultural population is made difficult by the fact that three-quarters of the rural population is concentrated in central Mexico, and lives in an "indocolonial" condition, and that progressive elements are "lost in the immensity of the hostile population and territory," so that only "vigorous public action" can bring about radical change.

25. González Santos, *La agricultura,* pp. 228–47, on the sharp increase of private credit for agriculture after 1949. It became greater than public credit by 1955. Relatively little, however, flowed to *ejidal* agriculture.

26. *Cincuenta años,* I, pp. 108–09, figures on irrigated land and the potential for more irrigation; Cline, *Revolution,* Chap. VII, is excellent on irrigation, taking the view that it has been necessary and valuable; IBRD, *Economic Development of Mexico,* pp. 22–27; Chase Manhattan Bank, *Latin American Business Highlights, Fourth Quarter,* 1961, that irrigated land is calculated at 8.3 million hectares, of which 2.7 million are being tilled.

27. *Cincuenta años,* I, p. 113: in 1950 there were 4,823,901 economically active agriculturalists, which was 58.3% of the total active population. This was down from 65% in 1940, 70.2% in 1930, and 78% in 1910; *ibid.,* p. 169, that it was about 50% in 1960.

28. Official figures set agricultural and grazing operations as accounting for 20.4% of GNP in 1961; it was down to 19% in 1962 (including stock, forestry, and fishing) according to some figures. Cf. Sturmthal, "Economic Development," p. 197, on the possible understatement of Mexican agricultural figures; *RESM,* March 1961, pp. 16–17.

29. *Cincuenta años,* I, pp. 611–12, for figures.

30. This is one of the few economic or social improvements affecting the common man that defenders and critics of government policies tend to agree has occurred. They agree, however, only in the sense that the former cite nutritional gains as one improvement among many, but the latter consider it almost the only improvement.

31. *Cincuenta años,* I, pp. 611–12.

32. *Ibid.,* pp. 121ff., for other discussion of agriculture; Cline, *Revolution,* pp. 268–69; Brandenburg, *Making Modern Mexico, passim*; OAS Committee of Nine, "Evaluation of Plan of Immediate Action," Chap. I, section C, Chap. IX, section B; *MV,* July 29, 1963, on the volume of agricultural production in 1950–62.

33. *Cincuenta años,* I, p. 616, that total industrial capital in 1930 was 956 million pesos, with 313,153 persons employed in industry, or 3,650 pesos per worker; in 1955, at 1930 prices, total industrial capital was 10.49 billion, with 2.17 million

employed, or 4,820 pesos of capital (1930 value) per worker; *ibid.,* for table showing industrial capitalization in 24 classes of industry.

34. *Ibid.,* p. 197, with 1939 as the base year, a high for the pre-Revolutionary period was reached at 43.0 in 1910; during the Revolution it went down to a low of 27.2 in 1918; up to 78.0 in 1931; down in 1932–33; up to 171.2 in 1945; to 228.2 in 1950; 305.6 in 1955; 370.2 in 1959. See Appendix XV on volume of production in selected manufacturing industries, 1950–62.

35. Shafer, "Mexican Mining and Manufacturing"; *Cincuenta años,* I, p. 197.

36. Glade, "Revolution and Economic Development," p. 8, that in 1950–59, output of consumer goods rose 60%, of producer goods some 152%. *Cincuenta años,* I, p. 202: in 1950–58 the structure of industrial production by value underwent the following changes, among others—food manufacture was down from 38.55% of the total to 29.32%, textiles from 15.62% to 10.2%, chemicals up from 9.01% to 13.3%, steel and steel products up from 6.4% to 9.02%, machinery manufactures from 2.70% to 11.89% of the total of all manufactures. *Ibid.,* p. 614, for table of growth in volume of production for 14 items in 1930–59. Cf. Robert Shafer, "Mexico," *The Americana Annual 1963,* for growth in various industrial sectors in 1961.

37. *Cincuenta años,* I, pp. 209–10; *ESEM,* Feb. 15, 1962, pp. 3–8, on concentration of corporate capital in 1960–61; *ESEM,* March 15, 1962, on concentration of manufacturing, showing that the Federal District and the states of Nuevo León and Mexico in 1950–60 increased their share of the value of manufacturing production from 39% to 51% of the national total, and their share of industrial employment from 40.7% to 54.8%.

38. Cf. *ESEM,* Feb. 15, 1961, pp. 6–7, "Agricultura e industrialización," celebrating the growth of both agriculture and industry, though concentrating on the latter. This is a common tactic of Mexican government publications.

39. *ESEM,* April, 1964, pp. 3–6, "Proyectos y oportunidades de inversión"; *New York Times,* Jan. 17, 1964.

40. Cf. Glade, "Revolution and Economic Development," pp. 87ff., *et passim.*

41. On mining see: *Cincuenta años,* I, Chap. II, "Los recursos no renovables"; Shafer, "Mexican Mining and Manufacturing"; *ESEM,* April 1963, pp. 15–16; *ESEM,* Oct. 1962, pp. 15ff., on nonmetallic minerals; WTIS, "Basic Data on the Economy of Mexico, February, 1964"; Cline, *Revolution,* Chap. XIX; *MV,* March 16, 1964, that the value of mining production increased 3.3% in 1963, its best gain in years. The following table from *MV,* July 29, 1963, p. 403, shows the volume of production of principal mineral products:

(Tons)

	1950	1957	1958	1959	1960	1961	1962
Silver	1,528	1,467	1,481	1,371	1,385	1,255	1,282
Gold (1)	12,695	10,772	10,335	9,756	9,339	8,357	7,365
Sulphur	13,194	1,068,691	1,270,965	1,362,149	1,328,546	1,244,347	1,453,433
Lead	238,078	214,878	201,923	190,680	190,670	181,326	193,298
Zinc	223,520	243,029	224,105	263,935	262,425	268,973	250,683
Copper	61,698	60,600	64,963	57,274	60,330	49,314	47,125
Manganese	14,460	79,668	78,650	76,935	71,856	68,704	62,869
Coal	911,732	1,420,794	1,470,705	1,585,898	1,775,649	1,817,646	1,893,422
Iron	297,794	634,063	657,637	753,352	895,737	1,029,918	1,089,270

(1) Kilograms.

42. *ESEM,* March 15, 1962, pp. 4–5, for figures on commerce.
43. *Ibid.*
44. *Ibid.*
45. Cf. *ESEM,* July 15, 1962, pp. 11–17, on the approximately 1.5 billion pesos spent annually for advertising in all media.
46. Cline, *Revolution,* p. 64, on highway construction; p. 65, motor vehicles. The following table, from *MV,* July 29, 1963, p. 404, shows transport growth in 1950–61:

STATISTICS OF TRANSPORT OPERATIONS

	Highway			Railway	
Year	Registered autos (thousands)	Registered trucks & buses (thousands)	Gasoline consumption (millions of gallons)	Ton-kilometers (millions)	Passenger-kilometers (millions)
1950	173	130	590	9,390	3,023
1957	366	295	1,044	12,983	3,837
1958	379	296	1,113	12,810	3,491
1959	438	327	1,164	12,231	3,725
1960	483	320	1,195	14,004	4,128
1961	550	352	1,207	13,485	4,290

STATISTICS OF TRANSPORT OPERATIONS (Continued)

	Aviation		Shipping	
Year	National passenger-kilometers (millions)	International passenger-kilometers (millions)	Coastal (million tons)	International (million tons)
1950	n.d.	n.d.	3,104	6,254
1957	853	909	5,036	5,953
1958	711	1,105	4,906	4,733
1959	648	1,284	5,814	5,137
1960	679	1,531	8,248	6,031
1961	632	1,920	9,602	6,809

47. *Cincuenta años,* I, p. 292, and with figures on income from tourism. Cf. *ESEM,* Sept. 15, 1961, pp. 2–24, "El turismo en México y en el mundo." Tourists to the interior (i.e., not border town visitors) totaled 949,093 in 1962, in which year net income from tourism and border transactions was $445 million. Cf. *New York Times,* Aug. 9, 1964, that Mexican income from tourism rose from $30 million in 1934 to $655 million in 1963; *International Commerce,* July 6, 1964, p. 13, that Mexico had 1.04 million tourists in 1963.
48. Cline, *Revolution,* p. 291; WTIS, "Economic Development in Mexico, 1961"; WTIS, "Basic Data on the Economy of Mexico, February, 1964"; Shafer, "Mexico," *The Americana Annual 1963, 1964.* The increase in tonnage in 1940–58 was from 4.92 million to 13.35 million metric tons.

49. Chase Bank, *Latin American Business Highlights,* Second Quarter 1964, pp. 14–15.

50. Mexico also engages in some commodity barter activity.

51. Mexico's recent international trade in commodities:

(billion pesos)

Year	Imports	Exports	Deficit
1961	14.12	10.55	3.57
1962	14.23	12.15	2.08
1963	15.5	11.63	3.90

The drop in imports in 1962 was partly due to a cut in authorized public sector imports, from 4.78 billion pesos in 1961 to 3.67 billion in 1962 (not all spent in either year). This was due to the completion of major equipment programs by PEMEX and the Federal Electricity Commission. (Cf. *El Nacional,* Jan. 26, 1963, for comment on this.) In 1882–1940 Mexico always had export surpluses; since then there usually has been an import balance.

52. *RESM,* June 1961, pp. 6–8. The decline is continuing: the same group (but excluding lead) accounted for 41% of commodity exports in 1962 and 35% in 1963 (*New York Times,* Aug. 9, 1964). See Appendix XVI for exports by commodity groups, 1957–62.

53. Exports of manufactures increased from a value of $48 million in 1951 to $168 million in 1961. In 1963 about 16% of total exports were finished and semifinished products.

54. The existence of industrial production capacity in excess of domestic demand has been well known in Mexico for many years, and the subject of considerable debate. Cf. *Excelsior,* Jan. 29, 1963, for comment on Mexico's "usual negative commercial balance," the excess of installed industrial capacity, and the overproduction of some articles, all of which, this conservative and pro-government paper said, argued the need for more merchandise exports. Only 5% of Mexican exports went to LAFTA countries in 1963.

55. In 1950 exports were 55.4% agricultural (including stock products), 35% mineral, 10% manufactures (Cline, *Revolution,* pp. 292–93); in 1961 agricultural and stock exports accounted for 55%, mining was down to 25.5%, and manufacturing up to about 20% (Shafer, "Mexico"); in 1963 manufactures constituted about 20% of total exported goods (*RESM,* June 1964, p. 5).

56. Cline, *Revolution,* pp. 291ff., that they now run more than 40% of annual total imports.

57. See above, Chap. II, A, 4, on government fiscal policy.

58. This source of income is declining, due to pressures in both Mexico and the United States. From a record of 444,418 Mexican hands in the United States in 1959, the number fell to 194,978 in 1962, with threats of a complete cessation of legal migration of seasonal workers.

59. A recent profit-sharing law provides that a company must distribute a maximum of 20% of its profits among workers. As might be expected, this led the business community to intensify its charges of a drift toward socialism. But up to 30% of profits can be reinvested and deducted, on a sliding scale, from the amount that must be shared. Probably this will be a strong incentive to reinvestment.

60. IBRD, *Economic Development of Mexico,* pp. 148ff., in 1953 pointed out that this would occur; Aubrey, "Structure and Balance," p. 526, for comment.

61. Cf. *Cincuenta años,* I, pp. 533–35, for summary of Mexican development financing, contrasting Porfirian and Revolutionary principles, and especially the intent of the latter to use investment to raise popular living levels; *ibid.,* p. 608, emphasizing that private investment has grown equally with public, and that the government intends to increase its role in planning private investment. The government since 1941 has used the device of declaring industries "saturated," and investment therein is discouraged by the Ministry of Industry and Commerce. (Cf. *ESEM,* Sept. 15, 1962, pp. 7–9.)

62. Cf. Glade, "Revolution and Economic Development," p. 17, for the further point that since the Revolution the decline of foreign investment relative to domestic, and the decline of export-oriented investment relative to that oriented to internal growth, are indicative of the decreased dependence of domestic expansion on the international market mechanism. Other points might be made: e.g., private investment in mining (mostly foreign-owned) has been discouraged, and has declined drastically; increases in foreign private investment in manufacturing and in retailing point to confidence in the growth of the national market. *Ibid.,* p. 71, on the government and capital formation.

63. *Cincuenta años,* I, p. 523, states that these periods are due to the beginning of public works about 1925, the modernization of agriculture about 10 years later, and the development of industry about 1940. IBRD, *Economic Development of Mexico,* p. 150, *et passim,* ascribed the greatly increased savings of 1945–50 to deficit financing and credit expansion, the unequal distribution of incomes, import restrictions on consumer goods, and devaluation; and found domestic savings near their upper possible limit. On total pesos investment in 1939–61, see *Cincuenta años,* I, p. 524; *RESM,* April 1961; WTIS, "Economic Developments in Mexico, 1961."

64. *Cincuenta años,* I, p. 523.

65. *Ibid.,* p. 528, noting that since both growth of GNP and of investment slowed in 1950–59, as compared with 1939–50, it is common to ascribe the former to the latter. For similar analysis, see *ESEM,* May 1963, p. 4.

66. *ESEM,* Jan. 1964, p. 17, for a table showing that in the 12 years, 1951–62, investment increased an average of 6.18%, with three years of decline. See Appendix 4 for this table. *ESEM,* July 1963, states that investment increased 795% in nominal terms in 1939–50, and only 252% in 1951–62, ascribing the slower growth largely to a worsening of the terms of trade. Cf. *CE,* Jan. 1963, pp. 2–3, "La economía mexicana en 1962."

67. *MV,* March 2, 1964.

68. *Cincuenta años,* I, p. 523.

69. *Ibid.,* p. 528.

70. *MV,* Nov. 20, 1961.

71. *Ibid.* On investment in relation to national product and national income, also see *Cincuenta años,* I, pp. 576, 591 (with tables showing GNP, investment, and investment as % of GNP), 608. But an official of Nacional Financiera in 1964 put capital formation at about 14% of GNP, Oct. 12, 1964).

72. *RESM,* Nov. 1962, p. 25, "Destino de los créditos." The figure in *RESM,* June 1961, p. 19, show industry with much the same proportion.

73. *New York Times,* Aug. 9, 1964.

74. *Cincuenta años,* I, p. 531, showing the accumulated total of direct foreign investment at the end of 1959 valued at 17.4 billion pesos.

75. *Ibid.,* pp. 523–24.

76. *MV*, Jan. 15, 1962: credits totaled $249 million, with the Export-Import Bank the largest provider (39.7%); 26.7% of the total of foreign loans went to electric energy, 18.5% to public works, 12.5% to transportation, smaller amounts to other destination. Amortization and interest payments in 1961 are stated as $115, but there seems to be a discrepancy in the figures. The total of foreign credits was $36.5 million less than in 1960, and the net intake $48.4 million less. Cf. *RESM*, Nov. 1960, pp. 7–9, that in 1955–59 the amounts Mexico actually drew from international credits surpassed the amounts of direct foreign investment. The direct foreign investments, plus the yearly international credits actually drawn upon, increased from 2.67 billion pesos in 1955 to 4.52 billion in 1959, a rise of almost 70%. See *HAR*, April 1963, that foreign credits in 1962 totaled 6.56 billion pesos.

77. In 1963 Mexico made its first public dollar bond offerings ($40 million) in the United States since 1910. It was to finance electric power equipment. Cf. *New York Times*, May 31, 1964, on the increasing flow of foreign private capital to Mexico because of high returns on private industry guaranteed by the government; *ESEM*, Sept. 1963, pp. 3–5, "Posición de nuestro crédito en el exterior"; *ibid.*, Nov. 1963, p. 6.

78. Cf. Wionczek, "Incomplete Formal Planning," pp. 171, 175, for comments on foreign public credits, and the increasing share of foreign exchange earnings devoted to servicing them; Appendix IX for origin of international credits through Nacional Financiera in 1942–54, 1958, and 1963; Appendix X on foreign investment in Mexico in 1959–62 as percentage of GNP.

79. See Appendix IX. But U.S. investment in Mexico increased considerably in 1964 (*New York Herald Tribune*, May 22, 1965).

80. *Cincuenta años*, I, p. 605, tables of investment in pesos and dollars for 1939–59, showing private investment growing at about the same rate as public.

81. Cf. *New York World Telegram and Sun*, March 24, 1962, for interview of F. H. Bartholomew, President of United Press International, with President López Mateos, in which the latter stated that private business should provide 60% of Mexico's annual investment requirements.

82. *Cincuenta años*, I, p. 523.

83. *Ibid.*, p. 529: Expenses of the Federal Government went up from 5.3% of national product in 1955 to 6% in 1958, due in part to higher salaries and to subsidies for articles of popular consumption; *ibid.*, p. 528, that the decline of total annual investment growth in real terms was from 10.5% in 1939–50 to 5.6% in 1950–59, due more to a decline in the growth of public investment (from 12.3% annual growth in the former to only 4.0% in the latter period) than to the decline of private investment growth (from 9.2% to 6.0% average annual increase); *ibid.*, p. 507, public investment in unadjusted pesos went from 85 million in 1925 to 8 billion in 1960, or, adjusted to 1950 prices, from 356 million to 4 billion; *ibid.*, p. 529, that the total deficit in the public sector in 1950–59 was 13.2 billion pesos, one-half of which occurred in 1957–59, whereas in 1939–50 the deficit was only 2 billion pesos.

84. *RESM*, April 1961.

85. WTIS, "Economic Developments in Mexico, 1961"; *ESEM*, Sept. 15, 1962, p. 23, public and private investment totals in pesos for each year, 1950–60; Hugo B. Margáin, "Intervención estatal en la economía," *CE*, April 1961, pp. 209–11, for comments on continued large private investment. Recent developments are reflected in credit figures for May, 1962, and Feb., 1961, published in *RESM*,

Nov. 1962, Jan. 1961, showing for the latter date 57% of total credits ascribable to the public sector ("public institutions 45%, Banco de México 12%), and for the earlier date 52% ("public institutions" 41%, Banco de México 11%). Cf. IDB, Social Progress Trust Fund, *Second Annual Report 1962,* p. 322.

86. *ESEM,* Jan. 1964, pp. 15–16; and see Appendixes IV–VII, above. Total private investment (at 1950 prices), in the ten years 1951–60, increased at an annual average of 6.35% (with three years decline); in 1961 it declined 2.1%, and in 1962 it was at the same level as in 1961. This recent slowdown looks even worse when one considers that private investment in 1953–57 rose an average of 9.1% annually, and in 1958–62 rose less than an average of 1% a year.

87. *Cincuenta años,* I, pp. 524, 529.

88. *ESEM,* Jan. 1964, p. 16; Bustamante, "Discurso el día 5 de mayo"; *MV,* Nov. 20, 1961, showing that in 1960 the investment of the Federal Electricity Commission went up 96%, railway investment rose 42.5%, PEMEX investment rose 22.4%, and investment of other *organismos* and *empresas* rose 75.5%; *HA,* April 9, 1962, for report of Minister of Finance that in 1951–61, of total public investment 30–35% was financed with the current revenues of the *organismos* and *empresas,* more than one-third with current fiscal income, and the final third depended on internal and external credit in equal amounts; Glade, "Revolution and Economic Development," n. 37, for much the same figures; *Boletín Oficial de la Secretaría de Hacienda y Crédito Público,* March 1961, for chart showing public sector investment in 1950–60—federal, state, territorial, and municipal, and the shares of the *organismos* and *empresas;* R. Alfredo Navarrete, "El crédito a las empresas del estado," pp. 31–41 in *Nuevos Aspectos . . . Conferencias de Invierno 1960,* that in 1939 the investment of the *organismos* and *empresas* was 40% of total public investment, and rose to 55% in 1959; Secretaría del Patrimonio Nacional, *Memoria 1961* (Mexico, 1961); Wionczek, "Incomplete Formal Planning," pp. 155, 181, for comments on public sector investment; *MV,* Sept. 7, 1959, showing public sector investment in 1958 totaling 5.51 billion pesos (2.64 billion Federal Government and Federal District, 2.16 billion state enterprises, 0.24 billion decentralized organs, and 0.46 billion state and municipal government).

89. Cf. *ESEM,* Nov. 1962, p. 25, showing credits from private institutions as of May, 1962, totaling 15.2 billion pesos, of which 46% went to industry, 41% to commerce, 12% to agriculture and livestock; *MV,* Aug. 15, 1960, showing direct private investment in the first half of 1960, with a total initial authorized capital of 1.03 billion pesos, of which 77% was in manufacturing industries, commerce, banks, and real estate, with the next largest construction, and all others (agriculture, fishing, mining, electricity, transportation, and communications) very small; *ESEM,* June 15, 1962, pp. 3–7, on the insufficiency of private bank financing of industry, with table showing private bank credits to commerce, industry, and nonindustrial production, for each year, 1942–61; Glade, "Revolution and Economic Development," n. 37, on private investment in residential construction; see Appendix VIII, above.

90. *MV,* Aug. 15, 1960, that of the 1.03 billion pesos of direct private investment in the first half of 1960, the Federal District received 766 million, and Nuevo León (Monterrey) received 93 million.

91. *Cincuenta años,* I, p. 606, for emphasis on this.

92. *Ibid.,* and p. 607 for table showing the destination of public investment in pesos for each year from 1939–59 for agriculture and hydraulic resources, trans-

portation and communications, electricity, petroleum, and "others"; *CE,* May 1961, for figures showing that of the record 10 billion pesos of public investment for 1961, economic development would receive 83% and social benefit work would get 17% (the more specific distributions being 4.2 billion pesos for industrial development, and especially electrification, petroleum, and petrochemicals; 2.7 billion for communications and transportation; 1.7 billion for social benefits, which included drinking water, housing, schools, etc.; and 1.5 billion for agricultural development, which included irrigation, forestry, grazing, etc.); cf., on Nacional Financiera investments, *Cincuenta años,* I, p. 192, and Glade, "Revolution and Economic Development," n. 167. Cf. OAS Committee of Nine, "Evaluation of Plan of Immediate Action," pp. 14, 24, *et passim,* for extensive analysis of investment.

IV. HISTORY OF MEXICAN PLANNING

1. For the flavor of present judgments on the Díaz economy see D. López Rosado, "La experiencia mexicana en materia de intervención estatal," in Escuela Nacional de Economía, *La intervención del estado en la economía* (Mexico, 1955), p. 46, that in the Díaz years economic development occurred "without a national plan, and with a policy of laissez faire," which in fact impeded development to improve the general level of living. Cf. Vernon, *Dilemma,* pp. 40ff., that the Díaz government was the first with "a strategy directed toward economic development," the chief instrument being a greatly expanded use of foreign capital. Vernon points out that the *hacendados* opposed economic development because they depended on an immobile labor force. In a few places labor mobility was notably increased by the industry and modern agriculture developed under Díaz. For statistics on economic development during the late Porfiriato, see *Cincuenta años,* I, pp. 171–76, 512ff., and for the Porfirian concept of development, *ibid.,* pp. 596–97, 604. Cf. I. Navarrete, *Distribución del ingreso,* p. 11, that there is reason to believe that there was little per capita production growth from 1803 (*sic*) to 1935.

2. Cf. Glade, "Revolution and Economic Development," pp. 9–40, 98–101, for analysis of the views of scholars on the much-disputed question of the role of the Revolution in later Mexican economic development. Glade's position is that the Revolution constituted a real discontinuity, and that the new basic patterns and orientation could not have evolved out of the rigidities of the Díaz system. The new elements to which he refers in this argument include: domestic rather than foreign capital investment; redirection of public expenditures toward basic development; change in institutional framework making for a widening range of production; and the elevation of social and technical innovation to a position of centrality in national activity.

3. The usual judgment (e.g., Howard Cline, *The United States and Mexico,* Harvard University Press, 1953, p. 57; Glade, "Role of Government Enterprise," p. 75), although some students of Mexico prefer to imply something more by listing efforts rather than assessing their immediate material effects.

4. *Ibid.,* p. 586.

5. *Ibid.*

6. See Chap. II, A, 1, above, for comment on the changing roles of government and party; Glade, "Role of Government Enterprise," p. 586, for criticism of Mosk for over-reliance on the annual policy statements of the executive branch

as a dependable indicator of decisive policy breaks in administrations, and "ignoring the deeper continuity of economic development and policy."

7. *Ibid.*, pp. 198ff.; Glade, "Revolution and Economic Development," pp. 71–72, on government banks to 1932.

8. Margáin, "Intervención estatal," pp. 209–11.

9. Cf. *MV,* Sept. 19, 1955, pp. 448–49, that "programming," at any rate, dates to the activities of the 1920's of the Banco de México and the Irrigation Commission.

10. Quoted in Javier Icaza y Conrey, *Principios para el establecimiento de un organismo planificador* (thesis, UNAM, 1956), p. 48, and declaring, without citing evidence, that these words inspired the First Six-Year Plan of 1933. Also quoted, in slightly different form, in Antonio Luna Arroyo, *¿Qué hará mi país en seis años?: el plan sexenal al alcance de todos* (Partido Nacional Revolucionario, 1935), pp. 7–8.

11. L. Solís Vicartta, *El instituto de administración pública* (thesis, UNAM, 1956), p. 74, states that it was constituted by *acuerdo* of June 14, 1928 (*Diario Oficial,* June 15, 1928), but gives almost no information on it.

12. Mexico, Laws, Statutes, etc., *National Planning Law for Mexico, July 12, 1930.* Solís Vicartta, *Instituto de administración,* Chap. III, gives a fairly detailed account of national planning institutions, but does not mention this law of 1930.

13. Icaza y Conrey, *Principios,* p. 41, on the law of July 31, 1933, and its *reglamento* of Dec. 14, 1933, and his statement that it was intended to meet before 1934, but it did not; Glade, "Role of Government Enterprise," p. 98.

14. Efforts at rigid periodization of the history of government planning and intervention in Mexico are not too persuasive. Cf. *MV,* Oct. 12, 1959, for an attempt by the Subsecretary of National Patrimony to periodize government intervention in the economy in terms of the 70 greatest state enterprises created to 1959: only four created before 1925; seven in 1925–34; two in 1935–44; 29 in 1945–54; and five in 1955–59. It may be said that this is suggestive rather than conclusive, and that the suggestions may be misleading.

15. Luna Arroyo, *¿Qué hará mi país?,* p. 8, on drafting of the Plan by the Government of the Republic, the Comité Ejecutivo Nacional of the PNR, and the Segunda Convención Ordinaria of the party. This PNR publication of 1935 calls the Plan a "compromise of the Government and the PNR," to convert into reality the promises of the Revolution.

16. Text of Plan in Gilberto Bosques, *The National Revolutionary Party of Mexico and the Six-Year Plan* (Mexico, 1937), pp. 129–214.

17. Cf. Scott, *Mexican Government,* pp. 136–37, for amusing examples of the identification or confusion of party and government functions.

18. Cf. Wendell Schaeffer, "National Administration in Mexico: Its Development and Present Status" (dissertation, University of California, 1949), pp. 202–08, 209, 212, on this point. For a contemporary PNR view, see Bosques, *National Revolutionary Party,* pp. 29–30, a paragraph titled "Integrating Mexico," in which it is asserted that the PNR is going to promote economic independence, so that Mexico could "become a thoroughly integrated nation by means of: a well-coordinated nation-wide economic structure; systems of communications . . .; a system of education . . .; and a sense of national wholeness within which any effort . . . to better any one region or any one population group shall be felt as bettering the entire country."

19. Bosques, *National Revolutionary Party,* p. 41. Cf. a much later view, Daniel

Cosío Villegas, "Programmed Economic Development and Political Organization," pp. 243–59, at p. 253, in UNESCO, *Social Aspects of Economic Development in Latin America,* Vol. I (1963), for contemptuous dismissal of the plans of 1934 and 1940 as containing "not very much to be proud of," and "mere ideological outpouring," and containing no targets.

20. *Realización del plan sexenal, 1935–36.* This was published by the Secretaría Particular de la Presidencia.

21. Cf. Bosques, *National Revolutionary Party,* pp. 3ff., for 1937 statement by PNR official regarding achievements to date under the Plan. Bosques contains much information on PNR efforts in support of the Plan. Cf. Luna Arroyo, *¿Qué hará mi país?,* the initial pamphlet (published 1935, in an edition of 150,000 copies) in the PNR series called "La Biblioteca de Cultura Social y Política," which was to promote "el estado revolucionario." It was a primer of the Six-Year Plan for the populace.

22. *Realización del plan sexenal, 1935–36,* p. 44, stating that no "Supervising Board" was required, as some critics claimed, because the "Executive Power, vested in the President and through him in the Secretaries of States . . . is such a Board."

23. That is, by coordination in the office of the Secretary to the Presidency. (See Chap. II, B, above, on this office.)

24. Cf. Tucker, *Mexican Government,* p. 212, that planning was "insufficiently developed" to contribute much to the solution of problems at that time.

25. *Ibid.*

26. Cf. Glade, "Revolution and Economic Development," p. 75, on the controversy as to Cárdenas' "socialism."

27. Anderson, "Bankers as Revolutionaries," p. 20, asserts that the new banks were due to the impact of Keynesian thought and Cárdenas' leadership.

28. Successor to the Depto. de la Estadística Nacional, created by law in 1923.

29. The Ministry of Finance in 1936 had, in its Dept. of Control of Federal Disbursements, a Preparation of the Budget Section, and in its Dept. of Fiscal Studies, a Section for Compilation of Statistics, and another Section of Economic Investigations. See José Mijares Palencia and Charles de Haven, *The Mexican Government* (Mexico, 1937), pp. 37–49. This guide contains only the most indirect suggestions that planning might be a function of any government agency.

30. There was some planning in the Federal District and in Monterrey in the 1920's, and more in the 1930's (Tucker, *Mexican Government,* pp. 214, 403, 413–14). Cf. Comisión de Planificación de Nuevo Laredo, Tamaulipas, *Planificación de Nuevo Laredo* (Mexico, 1938), for its "Program of Works 1937 to 1938," which lists twenty items, with cost of each. The Commission was formed in 1936, and included representatives of the Federal Ministry of Finance and of the Urban Bank of Mexico.

31. The First Six-Year Plan's education section (printed in Bosques, *National Revolutionary Party,* pp. 183ff.) had a subsection on "Scientific Research," which stated that there was no need for an increase in the number of liberal professionals (physicians, lawyers, engineers, etc.), but that more scientists were needed. On the other hand, the PNR had an Institute of Social, Political, and Economic Studies (*ibid.,* p. 43).

32. R. V. Austin, "The Development of Economic Policy in Mexico with Special Reference to Economic Doctrines" (dissertation, Univ. of Iowa, 1958), p. 74.

33. *Cincuenta años,* I, pp. 587ff., for national product figures.

34. *Ibid.,* p. 605, for investment.

35. Cf. Glade, "Role of Government Enterprise," pp. 76–77, for comments on Cárdenas' aid to industry; Sanford Mosk, *Industrial Revolution in Mexico* (University of California Press, 1950), pp. 57–59, on Cárdenas' stimulation of modern industry, despite his major interest in agriculture, and his preference for rural handicrafts; Cline, *Revolution,* p. 231; Glade, "Revolution and Economic Development," pp. 52ff., on the increasing prevalence of the view that land reform probably affected other things more importantly than agriculture.

36. Vernon, *Dilemma,* p. 75.

37. Cf. Pedro Teichert, "Economic Policy Revolution in Latin America," *IAEA,* Winter 1956, pp. 82–83, for insistence that "real policy revolution" in Mexico came in 1933 with the Six-Year Plan.

38. Cf. Glade, "Revolution and Economic Development," pp. 19–20, 85.

39. E.g., see Fernando Rivera Arnáiz, "Planeación administrativa para el desarrollo económico," *Revista de Economía,* Aug. 1952, pp. 243–46, on the growing amount of, and appreciation of, planning.

40. Although Mosk's *Industrial Revolution in Mexico* (1950) was none of these, and not unsophisticated, Glade, "Role of Government Enterprise," p. 85, effectively rejects "as not an independent variable" the industrial "New Group" influence which Mosk implied came out of nowhere to influence the government; cf. Mosk, *Industrial Revolution,* pp. 1–6, 21–23, *et passim;* Glade, "Revolution and Economic Development," p. 4, that most Mexican analysts emphasize continuity after the revolutionary discontinuity as paramount. A well-known example of emotional criticism is Jesús Silva Herzog, *Un ensayo sobre la revolución mejicana* (Mexico, 1946), finding that there had been many valuable developments since 1917, but lamenting the "insufficient formation of a collective revolutionary spirit," and decrying the fact that a revolutionary mystique had not been created, which he defined as a fervent passion and ardent desire to serve with love and distinterestedness a cause beneficial to the country. In short, this is the intellectual and visionary crying out against the practical party politician and governmental manager.

41. Cf. Simpson, "Unplanned Effects of Mexico's Planned Economy," that in 1941 the country "swung away from the Messianic and isolationist extremists of the Revolution," and that it was made "inevitable" by food deficits, some of them ascribable to weaknesses of small *ejidos,* and that the new agricultural policies after Cárdenas were a great success in terms of production.

42. Pedro Teichert, *Economic Policy Revolution and Industrialization in Latin America* (University of Mississippi Press, 1959), pp. 153–54, for this view, but stating that the period after 1940 is of greater interest for the development economist.

43. Cf. *Cincuenta años,* I, pp. 190ff., on aid to industry via protective tariffs, tax exemptions, etc.; Glade, "Role of Government Enterprise," pp. 178ff., on revision of Organic Law of Bank of Mexico in 1941 which helped it to promote industry. During the war the country's reduced import payments freed funds for domestic investment, good prices were received for exports, and the United States gave technical aid to industry.

44. Partido Revolucionario Mexicano, *Segundo Plan Sexenal, 1941–1946* (Mexico? 1939?); also published in English. Cf. Schaeffer, "National Administration," pp. 209–10, that the first plan carried over into another administration because "no work had been done to provide a detailed program for the next

six-year period." Schaeffer's point is supported to some extent by the provision in Chap. XIV of the Plan that the National Council of the PRM adapt the Plan to the data of the first Plan and, especially, with the census of 1940. We must remember, of course, that serious barriers then existed both to planning and to the execution of plans, and the party's purpose was to turn out a political document. On the political function of the Second Plan, see the campaign pamphlet put out in 1939 in Mexico, in Spanish and English versions, under the authorship of General Jara, President of the Central Executive Committee of PRM, and titled *The Second Six-Year Plan and Avila Camacho.* A good part of the pamphlet was on the accomplishments of the Cárdenas administration, claiming that it exceeded the goals of the First Plan. It claimed that the First Plan represented "the first time a nation of America began to plan her economical [*sic*] life, began to organize her institutions according to a program."

45. Cf. Miguel Alemán, *Program of Government* (San Antonio, 1946); he included a large section on "Economic Development," but did not call it a plan.

46. Mosk, *Industrial Revolution,* p. 60, on Avila Camacho's initial lack of conviction on development policy.

47. PRM, *Segundo Plan Sexenal,* "Preámbulo." Cf. Wionczek, "Incomplete Formal Planning," p. 152, for the judgment that the preamble to the Second Plan shows at least some modest improvement in planning concepts, but that the Plan itself is much as the first, prepared without knowledge of planning methods.

48. *Ibid.,* that Avila's administration had even less use for the Second Plan than had Cárdenas' for the first, but for different reasons: i.e., wartime growth and government revenues were so high that national planning seemed unnecessary.

49. Schaeffer, "National Administration," p. 213, citing William Ebenstein, "Public Administration in Mexico," *Public Administration Review,* Spring 1945, pp. 106–07, that there was little understanding among government officials of the "close relationship between the gathering and use of information and planning." Cf. Stephen S. Goodspeed, "The Role of the Chief Executive in Mexico: Policies, Powers, and Administration" (dissertation, University of California, 1947), that in Avila Camacho's administration his personal secretary maintained a department of studies, of approximately twenty-five persons, which was the only planning agency for the government, that many legislative proposals originated in this department, and that largely as a result of its activities Mexico enjoyed a somewhat more coordinated administrative policy. He offers no evidence. Tucker, *Mexican Government,* p. 212, found that under Avila Camacho little broad-scale planning was attempted, but important long-range sectoral plans were carried out—e.g., under the Federal Electricity Commission and the National Irrigation Commission.

50. See Chap. VI, above, for more information on sector planning.

51. See Chap. V, A, above, for such assistance after World War II.

52. Solís Vicartta, *Instituto,* p. 91, for this judgment.

53. *Ibid.,* p. 76.

54. Icaza y Conrey, *Principios,* pp. 41–42, stating the other study projects to include the wheat shortage, the railway system, agricultural production, rural credit, industrial investment, and food prices.

55. The members included representatives from five ministries and from semiofficial and private agencies (e.g., National Railways, the National Cooperative Federation). The decree abolishing it in June, 1942, stated that the diverse membership of the National Economic Council had rendered it unsuitable for dealing

with the emergency problems of the war ("Mexican Federal Commission on Economic Planning," *International Labour Review,* Sept. 1942, pp. 314–15).

56. The others: Chief of the Department of the Federal District, and Under-Secretaries of Finance, Agriculture, Communications and Public Works, Labor and Social Welfare, and Marine.

57. National Confederation of Workers, National Federation of Employers, Mexican National Railways, Petroleum Administration.

58. *Planificación Económica,* a monthly, published by the Secretaría de la Economía, beginning with March 1943. It was successively under the control of the Comisión Federal de Planificación Económica, the Coordinación y Fomento de la Producción, and the Comisión de Coordinación Económica Nacional. The issues were short and simple, with considerable information on economic and governmental questions, and little of interest on planning.

59. Cf. on the Federal Commission, Icaza y Conrey, *Principios,* p. 42; "Mexican Federal Commission," *International Labour Review.*

60. Icaza y Conrey, *Principios,* p. 42; Solís Vicartta, *Instituto,* pp. 80–82. These authors pronounced the Coordinación a failure, possibly because too much of the work was done by the Coordinator, this in turn being possibly because no member was paid. Cf. Solís Vicartta, *Instituto,* pp. 87–89, on the Mixed Councils mentioned above. A decree in September, 1941, authorized creation of Consejos Mixtos de Fomento Agropecuario, to function in each state, to turn out programs for the states. A decree in June, 1942, restructured them into Consejos Mixtos de Economía Regional, a name said to be better in accordance with their new functions. They were now consultative bodies that were expected to coordinate the efforts of federal and local government. A decree of September, 1943, reorganized them, and created the Comisión de Coordinación Económica Nacional, as we have indicated, which was to coordinate the programs and proposals of the Consejos Mixtos.

61. Solís Vicartta, *Instituto,* pp. 86–87. The decree of June, 1944, creating this Federal Commission, abrogated a law of March 24, 1942, that had created the Fondo de Fomento de la Industria y de Valores Mobiliarios. The law of December 28, 1953, which abolished the Federal Commission for Industrial Development, also created the Fondo de Fomento de la Industria Mediana y Pequeña, which Solís Vicartta says "cannot remotely be considered a planning organization." The members of the Federal Commission were: the Director of Nacional Financiera, as representative of the Finance Ministry; a member named by the Ministry of the Economy; and a chairman named by the President of the Republic.

62. According to Tucker, *Mexican Government,* p. 212, citing Patch and Mosk, and stating that business feared it as leading to government ownership; Glade, "Role of Government Enterprise," p. 99–100, that it failed completely, and produced no national industrial plan.

63. Tucker, *Mexican Government,* p. 213. Most important was the Mexican-American Commission for Economic Cooperation, established in 1943, through which the United States provided aid to Mexico. Other emergency agencies dealt with price controls, regulation of commodity markets, etc. One of the few successful ones, according to Tucker, was the National Distributing and Regulating Agency, for control of the prices of basic foods, which was succeeded in 1949 by CEIMSA (Mexican Exporting and Importing Company).

64. Comisión nacional de planeación para la paz, *Temario* (Mexico, 1945).

65. See Chap. III, C, above.

66. See Chap. III, C, above.

67. See Chap. V, B, C, above; cf. Vernon, *Dilemma,* pp. 115–16, that following World War II the improvement of technical work among other things improved government information on the private sector and permitted controls over it to become more particularistic.

68. See Chap. V, D, above.

69. See Chap. V, D, above.

70. Cf. Wionczek, "Incomplete Formal Planning," p. 154, for Alemán's campaign effort in 1946 to involve much larger numbers of persons than ever before in formulation of economic policy; and for a similar effort in the campaign of 1958, involving Consejos de Planeación Económica y Social, see *ESEM,* Feb. 1963, pp. 6–9, "Planeación Económica en Mexico," as well as Reuniones Regionales and round tables discussing economic questions in 1946–52.

71. IBRD, *Economic Development of Mexico,* pp. 151–52, one of its chief conclusions being that, in the past, circumstances had favored the selection of projects with high returns from low outlays, and a "project approach"; but the uncoordinated selection of projects no longer was likely to bring the same results; so Mexico might now want to abandon the project-to-project approach to economic development and look at the organic whole.

72. Agencies with some relationship to planning included the National Commission of Prices, set up in 1951 by the Ministry of the Economy, as a consultative organ; and the Council for the Development and Coordination of National Production, created in June, 1954. Scott, *Mexican Government,* p. 289, describes the latter as not primarily a staff agency for the study of planning problems, but a mechanism for bringing together representatives of the two major economic interests to discuss common problems, and to make recommendations; so it was not a part of the policy-making machinery of the presidency, but an auxiliary to it.

73. Raúl Salinas Lozano, "Comisión de Inversiones," *Revista de Administración Pública,* No. 5 (Jan.-Mar., 1957), pp. 7–17, for the assertion that this was the first. Salinas was Director of the Comisión de Inversiones. This was the Ley para el Control de los Organismos Descentralizados y Empresas de Participación Estatal. Cf. Glade, "Role of Government Enterprise," pp. 124ff., on factors that led to passage of this law.

74. Salinas, "Comisión de Inversiones."

75. *Ibid.*

76. *Ibid.*; and cf. Margáin, "Intervención estatal," that friction between the Ministry of Finance and the National Investment Commission led to abolition of the latter. Cf. Icaza y Conrey, *Principios,* p. 44, that the twelve Commission members were: Minister of Finance, Director of Credit, two representatives of Ministry of Finance, Director of Bank of Mexico, Director of Nacional Financiera, two representatives of Ministry of National Assets, and one each named by Ministries of the Economy, Agriculture, Communications, Marine, and National Defense. Cf. Glade, "Role of Government Enterprise," p. 129, that the law creating the Investment Commission also gave the Ministry of National Assets powers over contracts let by government enterprises, and over their purchases of supplies and equipment, and gave it the duty of making inspections and investigations at the request of the Ministry of Finance. See Chap. V, C, above, on the later development of this function in the Ministry of National Patrimony.

77. In its Sección de Inversiones del Departamento de Bancos, Moneda e Inversiones, Oficina de Control y Vigilancia de las Empresas descentralizadas y de Participación Estatal (Icaza y Conrey, *Principios,* p. 44).

78. No evidence is available on the date it began; it finished in August, 1948.

79. Schaeffer, "National Administration," pp. 219–21, citing Banco de México, Departamento de Estudios Económicos, *Proyecto de inversiones del gobierno federal y dependencies descentralizados—período 1947–52.*

80. *Ibid.,* pp. 221–22. He asserts that much of the work, however, was merely compilation, some of it poorly done. Each agency in charge of development programs had, on request, submitted a list of necessary and desirable projects. One Mexican economist involved informed Schaeffer that everyone put down his pet schemes. There was too little attention to necessity or feasibility; the assignment of priorities often was arbitrary; many of the expense figures were rough estimates; the integration and coordination of programs was poor. And Schaeffer concludes: "At worst, the plan represents a compilation of all the dreams of the ablest dreamers. At best, it is a work of doubtful value, representing much honest effort expended under enormous handicaps." Schaeffer does not really support these strong criticisms with evidence.

81. Rafael Mancera Ortiz, *Mexico's Attitude toward Development Programs* (Mexico, 1953). All data on Nacional Financiera's 1952 study are taken from this source.

82. *Ibid.,* claiming that it brought to the government's attention the desirability of a permanent organization to make such studies, "but with even greater accuracy, so that the government could have some very definite guides to policy and some clearly discernible goals in its investment decisions"; and he goes on to imply that this is what led to creation of the Investment Committee in 1953.

83. Salinas, "Comisión de Inversiones," and asserting that the Investment Committee did good work; Margáin, "Intervención estatal." Cf. *MV,* May 3, 1954, for speech of Minister of Finance that the Comisión de Inversiones (presumably meaning the Comité) was at work "to arrange and rank government projects, and it is the firm decision of the Government that this Commission shall be a constantly more vigorous and responsible organ." Wionczek, "Incomplete Formal Planning," states that the Comité operated so vigorously that it ran into political difficulties, so that it was transferred to the president's office (citing *Diario Oficial,* Oct. 29, 1954).

84. For extended discussion of the Investment Commission, see Chap. VII, above.

85. Cf. *MV,* Jan. 5, 1959, for speech by the Minister of National Patrimony, celebrating this centralization.

86. Its name remained the same (Secretaría de la Presidencia), but it was in fact elevated from a secretariat to a ministry.

87. See above, Chap. V, C, and VII, B, for discussion of this process.

88. OAS, Committee of Nine, "Evaluation of Plan of Immediate Action," p. 206.

89. *Ibid.,* p. 84.

90. *Ibid.,* pp. 9, 84.

91. *Ibid.,* p. 86.

92. *Ibid.,* p. 1.

93. *Ibid.,* pp. 1–5.

94. "Iniciativa de la ley federal de planeación de México," printed in *TE,* XXXI, Jan.-March, 1964, pp. 107–25; "Proyecto modificado de ley federal de planeación," *TE,* XXXI, April-June, 1964, pp. 285–89; *ESEM,* Dec. 1963, pp. 27–28; *El Universal,* April 13, 1963.

95. See Chap. V, E, above, for more on these *juntas.*

V. THE FRAMEWORK OF PLANNING

1. Evidences of this are abundant. The government periodicals *ESEM* and *MV* frequently discuss planning in other countries. Pedro Múñoz Amato, *Introducción a la administración pública* (Mexico, 1954), p. 125, on planning in other Latin American countries, and pp. 135–36 on national planning structures in Puerto Rico and the U.S.S.R. For another type of foreign influence, see Manero, *Revolución bancaria en México,* pp. 274–75, that a debate on the theory of productive inflation was touched off in 1951 by the publication of Mosk's book on the industrial revolution in Mexico.

2. To name only a few of those in the present author's files, with dates of publication in Mexico: Carl Landauer, *Teoría de la planificación económica* (1945); Barbara Wootton, *Libertad con planificación* (1946); Arthur Lewis, *La planeación económica* (1952); Karl Mannheim, *Libertad, poder y planificación democrática* (1953); Jan Tinbergen, *La planeación del desarrollo* (1959); A. O. Hirschman, *La estrategia del desarrollo económico* (1961); W. W. Rostow, *Las estapas del crecimiento económico* (1961); Preston P. Le Breton, *Teoría del planeamiento* (1962).

3. The briefest acquaintance with Mexican public officials makes this apparent.

4. Cf. Fernando Zamora, *La planeación económica en México* (Mexico, 1962), pp. 12, 65, on his experience with CEPAL training in 1961, and his use in 1957 of the ideas of the Dutch planner Tinbergen.

5. Benjamin Rogge, "Economic Development in Latin America: The Prebisch Thesis," *IAEA,* IX, No. 4 (Spring 1956), pp. 24–49, for criticism of some of the Prebisch animus against the industrial nations. Walter Krause, *Economic Development: The Underdeveloped World and the American Interest* (San Francisco, 1961), p. 191, for comment on Prebisch's statement in ECLA's *The Economic Development of Latin America* (1950), that "one of the most conspicuous deficiencies of general economic theory, from the point of view of the periphery, is its false sense of universality." See Pedro Teichert, *Economic Policy Revolution,* Chap. XVII, on the influence of the Prebisch theories in Latin America.

6. CEPAL in 1955 published *An Introduction to the Technique of Programming*; and in 1958 a *Manual on Economic Development Projects,* designed to give guidance on assigning priorities in resource allocation; CEPAL, *Economic Development Planning and International Cooperation* (1961), pp. 44–53, for good summary of pragmatic approach of CEPAL to planning, and statement that "the technique of planning in a system of private enterprise is in its infancy." Cf. *MV,* Aug. 29, 1955, on a new CEPAL study of programming; *ibid.,* Sept. 19, 1955, for Mexican delegation statements at the 5th annual meeting of CEPAL, on economic programming; *CE,* June, 1960, pp. 327–30, and July, 1960, pp. 376–79, on CEPAL action in the budgetary planning field.

7. *CE,* June, 1960, pp. 297–98, and Oct. 1960, p. 553, on the twelve-week course on "Problems of Economic Development and the Evaluation of Projects," given by UN and Mexican economists. The course had theoretical and applied components. It was designed for economists, engineers, and agronomists from both public and private agencies. Cf. CEPAL, *Annual Report May 1961-February 1962, Supplement 4,* pp. 8, 11, on Central American Seminar on Techniques of Programming, Mexico City, Oct. 31–Dec. 15, 1961; UN, *The United Nations and Latin America. A Collection of Basic Information* (New York, 1961), pp. 14–17, on programming work.

8. Cf. CEPAL's "Special Report to the Economic and Social Council on the Creation of the Latin American Institute for Economic and Social Planning, February 20, 1962"; "Activities of the Latin American Institute for Economic and Social Planning, Report of the Governing Council for 1963–1964," *Economic Bulletin for Latin America,* IX, No. 1 (March 1964), pp. 143–52. President López Mateos considered the Institute of sufficient importance for mention in his annual message to Congress, September, 1962 (*HA,* Sept. 3, 1962). The first training course of the Institute included 62 participants from 19 countries of Latin America, with financial support from the UN, BID, OAS, and Latin American governments.

9. *El Día,* Jan. 28, 1963. The delegation carried nearly fifty reports prepared by Mexican government agencies.

10. *HA,* Oct. 5, 1964.

11. See *Acción de las Naciones Unidas en México 1962* (n.p., 1962, 77 pp.), for summary of all UN activities in Mexico; Centro de Educación para el Desarrollo de la Comunidad en América Latina, *Informe de actividades Julio-Diciembre 1962* (Pátzcuaro, 1963), p. 30. Cf. Herbert Emmerich, "Administrative Roadblocks to Coordinated Development," pp. 345–60, in UNESCO, *Social Aspects of Economic Development in Latin America,* Vol. 1 (1963).

12. Cf. *Compilación de resoluciones sobre planeamiento, vivienda y edificación* (Washington, PAU, 1958), for summary of this activity since 1890.

13. Cf. its No. 24 (1957) for a wide range of news of operations in Latin America, foreign doctrine, and activities of the Inter-American Planning Society of Santurce, Puerto Rico.

14. *Informe de la Secretaría del Consejo Interamericano Económico y Social sobre la Primera Reunión Técnica Interamericana en Vivienda y Planeamiento* (Washington, PAU, 1958). The Mexicans included observers from the Cámara Nacional de la Industria de Construcción, the Cámara Nacional de la Industria de Transformación, and the Sociedad de Arquitectos Mexicanos.

15. *Programa Interamericana de Planeamiento Urbano y Regional* (Washington, PAU, 1962). The Program functions in collaboration with the Planning Institute of Lima, Peru. On this Institute, see PAU, *Revista Interamericana de Ciencias Sociales,* Nov. 1963.

16. E.g., A Delorenzo Neto, "Fundamentos sociológicos de la planificación—Aspectos regionales y locales," was republished from a Brazilian journal in the *Revista Interamericana de Ciencias Sociales,* Segunda Epoca, I, No. 3 (1962), pp. 415ff.

17. Cf. *Economic and Social Survey of Latin America 1961* (2 vols., Provisional Edition, Washington, PAU, 1962), for one evidence of this drift, possibly unconnected with the Alliance. The survey continues CEPAL's annual economic surveys, but now they are prepared jointly by the secretariats of OAS and CEPAL, but "under the direction" of the former.

18. *Alliance for Progress. Official Documents Emanating from the Special Meeting of the Inter-American Economic and Social Council at the Ministerial Level, Held in Punta del Este, Uruguay, from August 5 to 17, 1961* (Washington, PAU, 1961).

19. President López Mateos, in his address to Congress, September 1, 1962, stated this necessity under the Charter of Punta del Este (*HA,* Sept. 3, 1962). See Chap. VII, C, above, on the Plan.

20. PAU, Consultation on Economic and Social Development Planning, Feb.-March 1962, Santiago de Chile, *Report of the Meeting* (Washington, PAU, 1962), for extensive indications of the technical interests of the attending experts.

21. OAS, IA-ECOSOC, *Marcha de la Alianza 1961/62,* II, pp. 171–77. See *ibid.*, I, 31, for more on Mexican planning.

22. *Ibid.*, 21–35, for general statements on planning, and a survey of planning in the American republics. *Ibid.*, 119–21, on technical aid in the planning process by CEPAL, including the new Latin American Economic and Social Planning Institute.

23. *Final Report of the First Annual Meeting of the Inter-American Economic and Social Council at the Ministerial Level* (Washington, PAU, Provisional Version), p. 27 for resolution to establish the committee on "planning and project formulation," to operate between the annual meetings of the Economic and Social Council; and p. 47 on a resolution to hold a seminar on transportation planning and programming; cf. *Revista Interamericana de Ciencias Sociales,* Feb. 1963, on tentative agenda for the committee at Buenos Aires in Feb. 1963.

24. See bibliography to this study, below.

25. See Chap. V, E, above.

26. Some of this (e.g., in *TE*) is sophisticated, but much of it is sketchy (e.g., the numerous short pieces on planning the *Revista de Economía*).

27. E.g., *ESEM* and *MV*. Cf., *MV,* July 8, 1963, pp. 357–69, "El modelo de México de desarrollo industrial, 1960–1970, elaborado en Nacional Financiera," presented by the latter's subdirector, to a regional development seminar. The use to which the model was put by Nacional Financiera is not indicated. The study includes a large econometric element; and it emphasizes that planning should include fiscal, administrative, social, economic, and other elements.

28. E.g., Múñoz Amato, *Introducción a la administración pública,* pp. 101–44, on "Planificación," has more than the other treatments of public administration; Víctor Urquidi, *Viabilidad económica de América Latina* (Mexico, 1962), by a well known official of the Bank of Mexico, economist, and planner, has considerable information on government intervention in the economy, programming, and planning.

29. As early and recent examples we may cite: Manuel Bravo Jiménez, *Planeación industrial en México* (Mexico, 1949), by a Bank official who has remained in the economic study field; and *La Planeación económica en México* (Mexico, 1962), by Fernando Zamora, who had earlier (1950) published *Industrialización y Planeación regional de México.*

30. One of the offices doing input-output analysis today is Estudios Económicos Regionales of the Bank of Mexico.

31. Or consists of such scattered assertions as in *ESEM,* Jan. 15, 1962, pp. 11, 14, "Técnica, Productividad y Desarrollo Económico," pointing out that although it is impossible to get all the economic factors developing in equilibrium, something can be done to promote harmony between such things as industrial growth and personal income.

32. Cf. Sergio de la Peña, "Hacia la planeación del desarrollo en México," *CE,* Nov. 1960, pp. 610–13, as an example, although it is interesting as advocating more planning in Mexico; *MV,* May 25, 1953, pp. 174, 179, reporting a speech by the Minister of the Economy, outlining government economic principles in such generalities as improvement of productivity and of living conditions.

33. Carlos Novoa, *Planeación económica de México* (Mexico, 1952), which deals mostly with methods of studying economics and geography in order to provide data for planning, little about the planning function, and nothing about actual Mexican planning; Francisco López Alvarez, *La administración pública y la vida económica de México* (2d ed., Mexico, 1956), pp. 73ff.

34. Cf. Daniel Cosío Villegas, "Programmed Economic Development and Political Organization," pp. 243–59, in UNESCO, *Social Aspects of Economic Development in Latin America,* Vol. I (1963), at p. 245, for this line of reasoning, asserting that Latin America must be "intelligent and foresighted."

35. Cf. A. Hirschman, "Ideologies of Development in Latin American," in Hirschman (ed.), *Latin American Issues* (Twentieth Century Fund, 1961), at pp. 29–30, for the judgment that in Latin America only Mexico and Brazil have made a significant effort to come to grips with the phenomenon of growth, with attention by intellectuals, novelists, and "even by economists." See *ESEM,* Feb. 1963, pp. 6–9, "Planeación económica en México," which gives the history of planning in Mexico, and states that the country must resolve the following problems in connection with planning: (1) scarcity of capital, which requires a higher rate of internal formation; (2) lack of technically trained personnel, both to increase productivity and to coordinate activities, due to insufficient educational facilities; (3) deficient statistics; (4) lack of inducements for obtaining the voluntary cooperation of the private sector.

36. This is implicit in many of the frequent criticisms that there has been too little coordination of projects: e.g., Sergio de la Peña, "Introducción a la planeación regional," in Banco de México, *La planeación económica regional* (2d ed., Mexico, 1960), pp. 126–32.

37. Vernon, *Dilemma,* for this suggestion.

38. There is considerable material published in Mexico on regional planning. See Zamora, *Planeación económica,* which is chiefly on regional planning; Yates, *Desarrollo regional,* for an extensive treatment of the importance of regional planning for Mexico.

39. There is much complaint about this in Mexico. Cf. Schaeffer, "National Administration," pp. 210–11; Yates, *Desarrollo regional,* p. 133, that it is odd how little attention has been paid in Mexico to consumer expenditures.

40. *ESEM,* Jan. 1963, pp. 7–11, "Planeación económica en Francia," pointing out that one of the most interesting features is the role of the private sector; *ibid.,* Oct. 1962, pp. 6–8, "Notas sobre planeación," insisting that "to plan in no way means to force," and explaining the importance of the private sector in collaborating in French planning, and the importance of expanding such planning in Mexico; *ibid.,* June 1963, pp. 8–9, "Programación industrial e iniciativa privada"; the government-sponsored *Cincuenta años,* I, p. 608, that the government intends to play "an ever more preponderant role in the planning and expansion of private investment"; *MV,* March 20, 1961, for a speech by the Director General of Nacional Financiera, celebrating that institution as a link between public and private investment; Fernando Zamora, *El estado en la economía* (Mexico, 1958), p. 107, on the importance of encouraging coordination of public investment with private investment projects; *ESEM,* Sept. 15, 1962, p. 9, that "the great responsibility of the private sector is that its new investments truly contribute to the industrialization of the country and to the creation of permanent employment and the productive use of resources."

41. Vernon, *Dilemma,* pp. 140–47. *Cincuenta años,* I, is rich in the economic beliefs of Mexican *técnicos*; the same is true of the publications of the Mexican government—e.g., *ESEM,* Sept. 1963, pp. 5–8, "Industrias dinámicas."

42. Cf. Albert Lepawsky, "Mexican Facilities for Training other Latin Americans, with Special Reference to the Field of Public Administration," Sept. 30, 1962, typescript study for USAID, Mexico.

43. *Ibid.,* for 35 pages on the subject, with possibly the largest concentrations

in hospitals and in the field of geology. Cf. Antonio García Valencia, *Las relaciones humanas en la administración pública mexicana* (Mexico, 1958), Chap. IX, for public administration instruction.

44. Schaeffer, "National Administration," pp. 227–29, for a judgment, as of 1949, on the poverty of public administration study in Mexico; Catalina Sierra Casaus, "Estudios sobre administración pública en México," *RAP,* No. 1 (Jan.-March, 1956), pp. 63–67, for a judgment in the initial issue of the new Public Administration Institute's *Revista,* that such studies have been poor, and better ones are much needed in Mexico.

45. William Ebenstein, "Public Administration in Mexico," *Public Administration Review,* Spring, 1945, pp. 102–13, found it "remarkable" that Mexicans gave so little attention to planning as a management tool in public administration; Rafael Mancera Ortiz, "La administración pública en los planes de desarrollo económico," *MV,* April 13, 1953, a speech by the Undersecretary of the Treasury to the School of Economics of UNAM, pointing out some deficiencies in Mexico's organization for planning.

46. Cf. Public Administration Clearing House, *Public Administration in Latin America* (Washington, 1955), pp. 66–67, on public administration missions in Mexico.

47. As the Mexican section of the International Institute of Administrative Sciences.

48. Cf. Solís Vicartta, *El instituto,* pp. 107–08, for an early reaction to the organization. A number of people, including some members of the Board of Directors of the Institute, voiced this disappointment to me.

49. The author saw two examples in Mexico. The one in the library of Nacional Financiera is stamped 1960—apparently an acquisition date.

50. Brandenburg, *Making Modern Mexico,* p. 241, states that there were 416,000 in the federal government in 1960, excluding employees in state-owned enterprises. As for the latter, there are over 100,000 employees of Pemex (46,158) and Ferrocarriles Nacionales de México (55,430) alone.

51. Cf. Goodspeed, "Role of the Chief Executive," pp. 437, *et passim,* on the lack of coordination and the amount of duplicative effort.

52. Cf. Edward Schten, "Study of the Problems of Public Administration in Latin America, 1945–56" (thesis, University of Wisconsin, 1957), p. 121, and ascribing it in part to the fact that "the traditional values attached to humanism have far outweighed the importance attached to the empiricism of non-Latin American students of public administration." There are, of course, even more obvious practical political reasons for this reluctance; Wionczek, "Sustained Growth," pp. 179–80.

53. Cline, *Revolution,* p. 142, on the lack of a merit system in the civil service; Schaeffer, "National Administration," pp. 190ff., listing many deficiencies in the public service, and the reasons for them.

54. Tucker, *Mexican Government,* Chap. X, "Administration and Its Improvement," that little done in administrative or management planning; García Valencia, *Las relaciones humanas en la administración pública,* especially Chap. VIII, "El personal de la administración pública mexicana y las relaciones humanas"; *Directorio del poder ejecutivo 1963,* for the Comisión de Planeación Administrativo in the Secretaría de Salubridad y Asistencia, and an Oficina de Planeación Administrativa in Pemex; *Cincuenta años,* III, Chap. XXXVI, "La administración pública," by Lucio Mendieta y Núñez; *MV,* July 8, 1963, for comment by the

Subdirector of Nacional Financiera; R. Alfredo Navarrete, that the study of the administrative aspects of planning is fundamental, as indicated by the recent experience of Latin America, where administrative and political problems are an important reason why "in some countries of our continent there are plans, but planning is scarcely to be found."

55. Glade, "Revolution and Economic Development," p. 27, in a recent study finds that the bureaucracy has considerable independence, is creative, and although leftist is essentially pragmatic and nondoctrinaire.

56. Vernon, *Dilemma,* pp. 136–37, finds only a limited amount of the easy interchange between *técnicos* and agency heads that is found in the United Kingdom, U.S., and Canada.

57. Often noted by Mexican students: e.g., Rafael Mancera Ortiz, *La administración pública en planes de desarrollo económico* (Mexico, 1953; 22 pp.).

58. Two who thought it worked well: Rivera Arnáiz, "Planeación administrativa," pp. 243–46; Tucker, *Mexican Government,* pp. 37, 144, 156–57. Cf. *MV,* Oct. 12, 1959, for speech of Subsecretary of Patrimonio Nacional, on "El Control de las Empresas del Estado," for a review of the problem from the 1920's, with emphasis on recent activities of Patrimonio Nacional.

59. Horacio Castellanos, "Comentarios a la Ley de Secretarías . . .," *RAP,* No. 10 (Oct.-Dec., 1958), pp. 23–40, approving the change.

60. César Augusto Izaguirre Rojo, "La nueva ley de secretarías y departamentos de estado," *RAP,* no. 10, for text of the law. Cf. Castellanos, "Comentarios a la ley," for approval of the fact that National Patrimony, together with the Ministry of the Presidency, now appeared to have effective control of all agencies handling property or resources; and speculating that this meant centralized supervision, not control. Cf. *CE,* Nov. 1960, for Patrimonio Nacional estimate of public assets at 110 billion pesos.

61. Chap. VII, A.

62. Alatriste, *La estructura del control,* for an excellent essay on the subject, dealing with the period from 1947, noting that control is not yet adequate; Secretaría del Patrimonio Nacional, *Intervención de la Secretaría . . . en las Obras Públicas* (1962), for considerable data on the budgets and contracts for works registered with the Ministry, and on related subjects, such as lists of contractors, classified by government agencies, and by type of work and amount of money involved; *El Nacional,* Jan. 26, 1963, for an account of the activity of the Bureau of Inspection of Purchases of Patrimonio Nacional.

63. In a limited number of interviews in Mexico in early 1963, I was unable to discover anyone who considered that there had been a dramatic improvement in this regard since the creation of Patrimonio Nacional; Wionczek, "Incomplete Formal Planning," pp. 156, 180, considers that more control is necessary, although he may have investments primarily in mind; Anderson, "Bankers as Revolutionaries," p. 136, that this remains a serious problem; OAS, Committee of Nine, "Evaluation of the Plan of Immediate Action," p. 160, found it weak.

64. *MV,* March 15, 1965.

65. The law and later orders removed some agencies (e.g., national institutions of credit and insurance, these coming under the National Banking and the Insurance Commissions) from National Patrimony's control (cf. *CE,* April 1959, and noting that the executive could exclude others, also); *El Universal,* April 7, 1959, on statement by the Minister of National Patrimony on the newly created Junta de Gobierno (an interministerial body) that was to control the financing and

administration of the *organismos descentralizados* and *empresas de participación estatal,* and to make studies to determine which of these could be eliminated—one possible ground being goods offered at lower or equal prices by private suppliers.

66. Izaguirre Rojo, "La nueva ley de secretarías," p. 22. As usual, congressional objection to legislation prepared by the executive was ineffectual, and the Chamber of Deputies approved the law by 114–3.

67. Alatriste, *La estructura del control.*

68. Secretaría de Industria y Comercio, *Memoria 1959,* pp. 22–23, shows its Dirección General de Estadística with the following Departamentos: Estadísticas Económicas, Estadísticas Sociales, de Censos, de Recolección y Coordinación, de Agrupamientos Mecánicos, Técnico.

69. Cf. Secretaría de Industria y Comercio, Dirección General de Estadística, *Indice del Catálogo General de las Estadísticas Nacionales* (1960), pp. 7–8, for the names of government offices issuing statistics. The General Statistical Bureau dates from 1933.

70. Cf. Glade, "Role of Private Enterprise," p. 571, for an account of the development of improved national income figures by the Bank of Mexico in the 1940's; Secretaría de Industria y Comercio, *Memoria de Labores 1961,* p. 60, for an improved system of industrial statistics, worked out by the Ministry in consultation with the Ministry of Finance, the Bank of Mexico, Nacional Financiera, and private industrial associations. Cf. Peña, "Introducción a la planeación regional," pp. 130ff., on recommendations of (about) 1956 by Dr. Oomens, a Dutch consultant, on reform of statistical methods in Mexico.

71. For comment on this, see Wionczek, "Sustained Growth," p. 179.

72. Cf. Mosk, *Industrial Revolution,* pp. 110–11, on government and business statistics in Mexico in the 1940's. IBRD's *Economic Development of Mexico,* p. x, in 1953 found official statistics often incomplete or inaccurate, and the statistical work of government agencies insufficiently coordinated. In 1963 official statistics still were inadequate enough to cause the US-AID office in Mexico City to consider a sizable grant to improve them. OAS Committee of Nine, "Evaluation of the Plan of Immediate Action," pp. 209–10, 223, in 1964 called for better Mexican official statistics, an integral system of national accounts as soon as possible, and adequate coordination to ensure comparability of data published by different agencies.

73. Yates, *Desarrollo regional,* p. 32, on this question.

74. Secretaría de la Economía Nacional, *Memoria 1957.* The 361 investigations included: 138 on foreign commerce, 8 on credit, 60 on promotion and organization, 41 on prices, 80 on publicity, 34 on technical aid to the states. Categorized differently, by the study office, they included: 49 on primary activities; 193 on secondary activities; 86 on tertiary activities; and 33 on planning activities (subdivided thus: 8 on physical aspects, 4 on demographic, 14 on economic, 9 on international, and the other two on what was called "revenue, investment, etc., aspects"). The *Memoria 1959* and the *Memoria de Labores 1961* of the Secretaría de Industria y Comercio (successor to Economía in 1958) gave some data on the Bureau of Economic Studies, but not the type of statistics on studies quoted from the *Memoria 1957.* For earlier years, see the following reports of the Secretaría de la Economía: *Memoria septiembre de 1945-agosto de 1946,* for office of Barómetros Económicos before the Dirección de Estudios Económicos was created; *Memorias . . . 1954,* pp. 395–400, for 380 investigations undertaken during the

for "an institute of economic, social, and political planning for Mexico; *El Universal,* March 4, 1959, article by Lucio Mendieta y Núñez, wondering whether the new Ministry of the Presidency would manage to change Mexican planning practices, and complaining that projects were improperly ranked according to social value under the current system; discussions of planning at conferences at the University in *El Universal,* Jan. 28, 1963, and in the Feb. 9, 1963 issues of *Excelsior, La Prensa,* and *El Universal.*

105. *HA,* Sept. 3, 1963.

106. E.g., *Nosotros,* Jan. 31, 1963, carried accounts of plans by the governments of Campeche, Tlaxcala, and Guanajuato.

107. Wionczek, "Sustained Growth," p. 180.

108. "Iniciativa de la ley federal de planeación."

VI. SECTOR AND REGIONAL PLANNING

1. R. Alfredo Navarrete, "La planeación y la administración financiera del estado," *MV,* Aug. 3, 1964, pp. 458–65.

2. OAS Committee of Nine, "Evaluation of Plan of Immediate Action," never deals with sectoral planning except by implication in generally approving of sector goals in the Plan for Immediate Action (p. 12).

3. *MV,* July 20, 1959, for text of the law.

4. R. Alfredo Navarrete, "Planeación y la administración financiera."

5. E.g., *MV,* Jan. 5, 1953, p. 2, for the "Plan Agrícola para 1953," of the Secretaría de Agricultura, a listing of general goals on acreage, credit, combating disease, etc.; *MV,* Oct. 19, 1953, on the "plan agrícola de invierno," that is, the Ministry of Agriculture's winter acreage allotments for certain crops. Various plans are developed for the long-term development of single crops (cotton, sugar, coffee, etc.), both to increase exports and to reduce imports, subject to frequent revision in the light of shifting conditions. In the case of sugar, in Feb., 1962, a contract between the Unión Nacional de Productores de Azúcar, S.A., and the Financiera Nacional Azucarera, S.A., provided for the operation of the Fondo de Planeación de la Industria Azucarera, to study the sugar industry in all its aspects; a government plan for 1964–70 provides for a 70% increase in sugar production; and a government order published June 10, 1964, created a Comité Intersecretarial, of representatives of the Ministries of Industry and Commerce, Finance, and of Agriculture and Stock, to examine the situation of the sugar industry, to tie the credit available to mills to their registered capacity, and to annually review the situation of the industry (*MV,* June 15, 1964).

6. Cf. Simpson, "Unplanned Effects of Mexico's Planned Economy," for the great increase in Mexican agricultural production in 1945–50, as the result of government policies and actions, which Simpson says resulted in unemployment which "the planners had not foreseen." Simpson is saying, of course, that there was no integrated national planning. On agricultural credit see Glade, "Role of Government Enterprise," pp. 198–220; Lewis, "Mexico Since Cárdenas," pp. 318–19; González Santos, *La agricultura,* pp. 230–31, that the government would prefer more private and less public investment; and see *MV,* Feb. 9, 1953, p. 42, on the "program" for the year of the Bank of Agricultural Credit, with the principles followed.

7. Cf. *El Universal,* April 9, 1959, on an announcement by the Minister of Agriculture of a Consejo Nacional de Agricultura, to make up great national pro-

grams or plans for agriculture; *ibid.*, Jan. 15, 1963, on the government's "Plan Agricultura Integral"; Ramón Fernández y Fernández and Ricardo Acosta, *Política agrícola. Ensayo sobre normas para México* (Mexico, 1961), p. 100, on Consejo Nacional de la Investigación Agrícola, to coordinate work of government agencies, and tie them to private institutions; *RESM*, April, 1961, pp. 8–9, for a recent statement by the Bank of Mexico that "an integral plan should be adopted in favor of agriculture, both by private and public sectors"; *MV*, June 15, 1964, pp. 343–44, on what is called the Programa de Reforma Agraria Integral.

8. Cf. *Siempre,* Feb. 6, 1963, on "Un Plan Nacional para la Agricultura," an antiadministration demand for nationalization, that cried: "While there does not exist a program for the reform of national agricultural production, anarchy will continue"; *La Prensa,* Feb. 9, 1963, for CNC attack on what was declared to be the fact "that Mexico does not have long-term agrarian plans." Some of these political attacks clearly either ignore or do not understand the many coordinative and continuing elements in government agricultural policies in recent decades. Other attacks tend to concentrate on government credit policies as they affect agriculture: e.g., Flores de la Peña, "Reflexiones sobre el plan general," p. 128.

9. *ESEM,* April 1965, pp. 6–8, "Desarrollo agrícola y planeación," that more than ten agencies deal with agriculture, that lack of coordinated action is a big fault, noting that recent government declarations of increased interest in agriculture offer some hope of improvement, some achievement of which may be seen in provision for coordination by the Ministry of Agriculture of regional agricultural plans. Under the law of 1958 and its implementing regulations the Department of Agrarian Affairs was ordered "to plan, organize, and promote the agricultural and pastoral production of the *ejidos* and communities, with the technical cooperation of the Ministry of Agriculture" (*MV,* July 20, 1959; *RESM,* Aug. 1959). Cf. Departamento de Asuntos Agrarios y Colonización, *Memoria de labores 1960–1961* (Mexico, 1961, unpaginated), which states that the Department is to "plan, organize, and promote" ejidal production, and produce "general and concrete plans for colonization."

10. Inter-American Committee for Agricultural Development, *Inventory for Agricultural Planning in Mexico,* pp. 55ff., 105, 106–08, noting that Mexico has no single agricultural plan, but some general objectives which touch most aspects of agriculture and require cooperation among a number of agencies, although the objectives

> cannot be said to indicate variations in the relative support that will be given to different fields. This may be a virtue rather than a weakness. All of the fields named need support and attention, and a well conceived program requires breadth.

It is interesting that González Santos, *La agricultura,* put out by Nacional Financiera, and possibly the best study of Mexican agriculture, says little about planning or coordination of policy. Cf. Fernández and Acosta, *Política agrícola,* for an excellent discussion, without a strong view that more centralization of planning is necessary, though (p. 100) welcoming the recent creation of a Consejo Nacional de Investigación Agrícola, to better coordinate agricultural study and policy. Mosk, *Industrial Revolution,* Chap. XI, advocated careful planning by the government to make the most effective use of funds for agriculture, but the amount of "integration" of planning he wanted was not clear. See Marco Antonio Durán, "El desarrollo de la agricultura mexicana," *Journal of Inter-American Studies,* Jan., 1961, pp. 1–26, for a generally optimistic account, pointing out that investment is the main need in each of the various lines of technical improvement (transportation, seeds, fertilizer, etc.) in the agricultural realm; nothing on planning as such, simply dealing with efforts in various of the fields that affect agricultural production.

11. González Santos, *La agricultura,* pp. 127, 128–29, 144, *et passim.* CIDA, *Inventory for Agricultural Planning in Mexico,* was prepared in 1964 as a guide to data for planning.

12. Cf. IBRD, *Economic Development of Mexico,* p. 151, that relatively small expenditures of organizational improvements might produce substantial gains, for example in the use of fertilizer, improved seed, or crop rotation.

13. Cf. *Cincuenta años,* I, pp. 156ff., "Los Servicios Técnicos en la Agricultura."

14. *ESEM,* March 15, 1962, pp. 8–11, "Política Industrial," that there is no overall industrial planning, and that this is one reason for the geographic concentration of manufacturing; Secretaría del Patrimonio Nacional, *Conferencia . . . Congreso . . . Gerentes* (1959), for a statement by the Minister of National Patrimony that the state does not program for industry or commerce.

15. *Industrial Revolution,* pp. 307–08, and also stating that although the government aided investors (e.g., through tax exemptions), "it has not given direction to the industrialization process." This last statement certainly is somewhat misleading.

16. *Ibid.,* p. 157, that during World War II Mexico achieved a fourfold increase in cement production capacity, and that it was planned by the government to ensure the location of new plants so as to be of optimum benefit to the national economy.

17. *HA,* Sept. 3, 1962.

18. See Chap. VI, above, pp. 92ff., for electric power and chemicals. There are others. Cf. *MV,* Jan. 11, 1962, on a Presidential Reglamento, issued Oct. 4, 1961, on "Planeamiento de la Industria Azucarera"; *Excelsior,* Jan. 30, 1963, on a "program of development for the textile and clothing industries," prepared by the Ministries of Finance, Industry and Commerce, and Labor, and presented to interested private enterprise.

19. Mexicanization by way of forcing 51% of Mexican ownership of companies goes back to a decree of 1944, and has had only limited application (Glade, "Revolution and Development," p. 89).

20. Secretaría de Industria y Comercio, *Memoria de labores 1961,* p. 14. Cf. López Alvarez, *Administración pública* (1956 ed.), pp. 189–200, "La política industrial."

21. OAS Committee of Nine, "Evaluation of the Plan of Immediate Action," p. 23.

22. Scott, *Mexican Government,* pp. 386–87, on regulation by consultation between government and private enterprise.

23. A decree of 1962 required that by 1964 the use of locally produced parts and components must represent at least 60% of the direct cost of vehicles. This resulted in a rapid development of new manufacturing facilities in Mexico, many of them operating as subsidiaries of foreign firms.

24. *Chemical Week,* April 4, 1964, that auto makers and their suppliers expect to invest some $120 million in the Mexican market in the next few years—with 75% from the United States.

25. R. Alfredo Navarrete, "El crédito a las empresas del estado," pp. 31–41 in

Nuevos Aspectos . . . Conferencia de Invierno 1960 (UNAM, 1961). But see Blair, "Nacional Financiera," pp. 225–26, on Nafin's "complex of overlapping motives" investment in heavy industry: import replacement, investment in industries where the size of the initial capital requirement discouraged private action, increased direct participation of the public sector in what it considers "basic" industries, strengthening of the power position of Nafin, to pursue "linkage" effects, promoting enterprise that can be integrated into existing ones.

26. Cline, *United States and Mexico,* pp. 343–44, for several reasons for so considering it. See *MV,* July 8, 1963, pp. 357–69, "El modelo de México de desarrollo industrial 1960–1970, elaborado en Nacional Financiera," on planning industrial development, including projections of production to 1970 of steel ingots, autos and trucks, railway cars, agricultural tractors, and other items.

27. Cf. *Cincuenta años,* I, p. 190, on the many fields in which the Bank of Mexico has done studies affecting manufacturing. At present, studies of manufacturing industries are being done by a committee that includes representatives of the Bank of Mexico, Nacional Financiera, and the Ministries of Finance and of Industry and Commerce. Cf. *ESEM,* Sept. 1963, pp. 5–8, "Industrias Dinámicas," for exposition of government views toward development of manufacturing in terms of national effects of specific "dynamic" manufactures.

28. *MV,* June 3, 1963, pp. 298–303, on data furnished by the Cámara Nacional de la Industria del Hierro y el Acero to the Survey and Research Corporation of Washington, D.C., for a report to the Export-Import on the demand for steel in Mexico in 1963–70.

29. Cf. *Noticias,* XVII, No. 29 (1963), that the government was considering such action; Brandenburg, *Development of Latin American Private Enterprise,* p. 41, for doubts as to the wisdom of such decentralization.

30. Glade, "Role of Government Enterprise," pp. 510ff.; Tucker, *Mexican Government,* p. 286, that Alemán put almost as much land under irrigation in six years as the governments had in the preceding twenty-one; Cline, *Revolution,* pp. 68–77; *Cincuenta años,* I, Chap. X, "Las Obras de Irrigación," for an extensive discussion.

31. Brandenburg, *Making Modern Mexico,* p. 260.

32. *Economic Development of Mexico,* pp. 23–27.

33. Cf. González Santos, *La agricultura,* pp. 27–37, on irrigation works, and for indication that Mexican information on such subjects as rainfall has much improved in recent years.

34. Cf. *New York Times,* Nov. 17, 1963, for a United Nations estimate that over $500 million in construction cost for irrigation facilities in Mexico since 1945 had resulted in an annual production valued at $400 million.

35. Secretaría de Recursos Hidráulicos, *Informe 1956–1957* (1958?), pp. 597, 601–03, 659–60. The ministry does more in irrigation than in any other field, but it does have other functions—mostly related to irrigation and community development. It may be noted that Mosk, *Industrial Revolution,* who found little government planning in Mexico, conceded (p. 308) that long-range planning was done for irrigation.

36. There are many such Irrigation Districts (Distrito de Riego) in Mexico. These were apparently physical plans, involving distribution and drainage networks.

37. The following are abundant evidence of interest in planning and programming in the Ministry: *MV,* Jan. 14, 1952, pp. 3–4, "Programa de Irrigación para 1952," announcement by Recursos Hidráulicos, called a plan, but in fact a listing

of construction projects and investments; *MV,* Nov. 1, 1953, p. 370, on "Plan agrícola e industrial para la Laguna," for Recursos Hidráulicos development project; *Excelsior,* Feb. 2, 1963, on lectures on "Modern Methods of Planning, Programming, and Control of Works," for personnel of Recursos Hidráulicos; Inter-American Committee for Agricultural Development, *Inventory for Agricultural Planning in Mexico,* pp. 65–70, on irrigation.

38. *Ibid.,* p. 108, citing *Los recursos hidráulicos de México y su relación con los problemas agrícolas y económicos del país. Primera Parte: Proposiciones para establecer las bases de su desarrollo y planeación futura* (Mexico, 1962); and *idem. Tercera Parte: Proposición para establecer las bases de su planeación y desarrollo futuros* (Mexico, 1963).

39. Cf. IBRD, Bank Press Release No. 62/21, June 20, 1962, for reference to criticisms of Mexican highway planning, which the IBRD finds on the whole sound. On the other hand, the IBRD report of 1953 (*Economic Development in Mexico,* pp. 97–98), asserted that it was "difficult to detect any clear over-all policy in the field of transportation. Nor has any real attempt been made to attain a reasonable level of coordination among the ministries and agencies concerned." See also Tucker, *Mexican Government,* pp. 228ff., for mild criticism of transportation development; *Cincuenta años,* I, 494–95, "Política de Caminos"; *ibid.,* II, 447–60, on roads, and 461–76 on railways, for useful accounts of expansion and administration, but no discussion of planning; Cline, *Revolution,* pp. 60ff., noting that critics advocate consolidation of agencies, and noting the apparent need for closer integration between planning of main roads and railways; Glade, "Role of Government Enterprise," Chap. VIII, for developments to 1955; *El Día,* Jan. 28, 1963, for report of the Ministry of Public Works that in 1958–62 the government spent 1.9 billion pesos on federal highways, nearly as much as was spent on highways in 1934–58.

40. Cf. Secretaría de Obras Públicas, *Informe de labores 10 de septiembre de 1961 a 31 de agosto de 1962* (1962), pp. 2, 9, *et passim,* on transportation planning, with an account of many studies, including an inventory of the national road net, traffic on new and projected roads, evaluation methods used that permit quantification of the benefits to be obtained from the building of penetration roads in new zones, studies on 50 proposals for new highways and 268 proposals for feeder roads, etc. See Carlos Villafuerte, *Ferrocarriles* (Mexico, 1959), pp. 73, 93, 152, 153–54, 239, 240 247–49, *et passim,* on railway policy and planning; *HA,* Sept. 13, 1962, for a statement by President López Mateos on the role of the Ministry of the Presidency in railway planning; Carlos Villafuerte, "Perspectiva a los Ferrocarriles—La Coordinación," *Comunicaciones y Transportes,* Jan.-Feb., 1961, pp. 62–75, by an economic analyst in the Bureau of Investments of the Ministry of the Presidency; *El Universal,* Jan. 15, 1959, for announcement of its 1959 program, noting the work of its Departamento de Planeación; Tucker, *Mexican Government,* p. 238, on transportation planning; Glade, "Revolution and Economic Development," pp. 76–77, on the goals of railway policy; Glade, "Role of Government Enterprise," Chap. VIII; *ESEM,* Aug. 15, 1962, "Integración Vial," on goals of highway planning in Mexico.

41. Miguel Wionczek, "Electric Power. The Uneasy Partnership," pp. 19–110, in Vernon (ed.), *Public Policy.*

42. *Ibid.,* an excellent study, does not really grapple with this point.

43. See Chap. III, B, above, on the growth of the industry.

44. Cf. Comisión Federal de Electricidad, *Comisión Federal de Electricidad*

1937–1948 (1948), for organization chart showing Departamento de Planeación y Coordinación.

45. United Nations, ECLA, *Annual Report, May 1961–February 1962,* Supplement 4, pp. 53–58, listing principal documents issued by ECLA in connection with the Latin American Electric Power Seminar, including a number of Mexican contributions, on construction projects, electric power and regional development, expansion for 1961–70, statistics as a planning tool, methodology for forecasting power demand, and a study of planning by the Department of Planning and Studies of CFE for development of the Sonora-Sinaloa system.

46. Tucker, *Mexican Government,* Chap. 17. Cf. Glade, "Revolution and Economic Development," pp. 80–82, on CFE policy; Glade, "Role of Government Enterprise," Chap. VIII, for some planning activity of CFE.

47. *HA,* Jan. 29, 1962. Cf. *El Universal,* Feb. 10, 1963, for praise of planning activities in electric power.

48. E.g., in 1962 CFE got an IBRD loan for $120 million for a four-year expansion program.

49. See Chap. III, B, above.

50. *Economic Development of Mexico,* Chap. IV. Cf. Glade, "Role of Government Enterprise," Chap. VI, for review of the history of Pemex, the judgment that it had been successful in developing the national market for petroleum, and that it had on the whole used resources to national advantage; Antonio Bermúdez, *The Mexican National Petroleum Industry* (Stanford University Press, 1963), for detailed criticism of pricing, investment, and tax burdens imposed upon Pemex; J. R. Powell, *The Mexican Petroleum Industry 1938–1950* (University of California Press, 1956).

51. Bermúdez, *Mexican National Petroleum,* pp. 39–43, 147, *et passim.* Cf. Tucker, *Mexican Government,* Chap. 18; Cline, *Revolution,* pp. 277–78; Glade, "Role of Government Enterprise," Chap. VI; Glade, "Revolution and Economic Development," n. 6; *MV,* March 30, 1964, pp. 177ff., account by the Director General of Pemex of its operations during the López Mateos administration, including reference to the principles of development followed.

52. *Economic Development of Mexico,* pp. 38–45.

53. See Shafer, "Mexican Mining and Manufacturing." The law of 1960 prescribed that future mining concessions be granted only to Mexican government enterprises, or to private or mixed corporations controlled by Mexican capital. It also provided incentives for the Mexicanizing of existing foreign-controlled companies.

54. Including the Consejo de Recursos no Renovables, the Bank of Mexico, the Ministry of Finance and Public Credit, the Comisión de Fomento Minero, and the Nuclear Energy Commission.

55. See Chap. III, B, above.

56. *Directorio del Poder ejecutivo federal 1961* (Mexico, 1961), p. 129; *HA,* Sept. 3, 1962, reporting the president's annual message; *El Universal,* Feb. 10, 1963; *ESEM,* Nov. 1962, pp. 9–11, "Turismo."

57. On chemical technology and planning, cf. Ing. César O. Baptista, "The Mexican Chemical Industry," presented to the 56th Annual Meeting of the American Institute of Chemical Engineers, Houston, Texas, Dec. 4, 1963 (mimeo.).

58. Cf. Cline, *Revolution,* p. 277, on a five-year plan for petrochemicals.

59. Secretaría de Educación Pública, *A Panorama of Education Today* (1961).

60. E.g., see *MV,* July 29, 1963, p. 404, for education figures provided by the

Mexican government in the midst of information prepared for the guidance of investors in Mexican Bonds for Economic Development.

61. Cf. Glade, "Role of Government Enterprise," pp. 510ff.

62. Zamora, *Planeación económica en Mexico,* pp. 129–31.

63. *Ibid.,* pp. 131–33.

64. *Ibid.,* pp. 134–37.

65. *Ibid.,* pp. 19–27, for summary of his ideas.

66. Cf. Peña, *Introducción a la planeación regional* (2d ed.), pp. 134ff., recommending division of the country into "regiones de carácter unificado" (whatever that may mean), and regional planning commissions with wide powers, to support national planning institutions; Zamora, *Industrialización y planeación regional,* pp. 95–108, a section titled "Planeación Económica," for a short discussion of the theory of planning, including brief reference to TVA; Guillermo Armas Arias, *Planificación económica regional, su proyección a paises no industrializados* (thesis, UNAM, 1950), for reference to foreign planning theory, TVA experience, and criticizing the control of the Papaloapan and Tepalcatepec Commissions by the Ministry of Hydraulic Resources; Luis Cosío Silva and Fernando Rosenzweig Hernández, "Los desequilibrios regionales en la economía de México y la política de fomento del desarrollo," *CE,* Nov. 1961, pp. 665–69, that Yates' *Desarrollo Regional en México* is only a preliminary attack on the subject, as must be true of all studies in the current state of knowledge of the subject.

67. Cf. *MV,* July 8, 1963, pp. 357–69, paper of R. Alfredo Navarrete of Nacional Financiera to a regional development seminar, in which Navarrete emphasized that the debate over the relative importance of national or of regional planning is passé, that both are needed.

68. OAS Committee of Nine, "Evaluation of the Plan of Immediate Action," p. 209.

69. E.g., Río Fuerte, Río Balsas, Valley of Mexico, and the El Limón project in Tabasco, a 14-year plan, which in 1963 received IBRD financing.

70. See Chap. VII, above.

71. Cf. Peña, *Planeación económica regional* (2d ed.), pp. 120ff., for summary of the chief interests of the regional authorities, including the statement that they have done little in economic planning, mainly concentrating instead on physical planning.

72. *Ibid.,* pp. 130–32, complaining that their construction methods do not always do the maximum to aid unemployment. The policy question involved here is, of course, debated in many countries. Glade, "Role of Government Enterprise," pp. 530ff., found Papaloapan valuable, but did not try to indicate why the work was handled better by a regional authority than directly by the Ministry of Hydraulic Resources. Cline, *Revolution,* pp. 74–76, after detailing some of the accomplishments of the Papaloapan Commission, obviously useful, calls it "a successful experiment," but without suggesting what the regional authority principle contributed. Tucker, *Mexican Government,* pp. 261ff., mentions the Bureau of Planning of the Papaloapan Commission, stating that it studies all matters dealing with planning of the works to be built, seeking a balanced development of program and conservation of the river basin's resources, and maintaining liaison with other agencies. Cf. also Cline, *The United States and Mexico,* pp. 282, 374ff.; Armas Arias, *Planificación económica regional,* pp. 130–36.

73. *The Papaloapan Project; Agricultural Development in the Mexican Tropics* (Stanford University Press, 1964), pp. 98, 99–100, 116, 153–54, *et passim.*

74. Comisión del Papaloapan, *Economía del Papaloapan. Primera Parte. Evaluación de las inversiones y sus efectos* (Secretaría de Recursos Hidráulicos, 1958; 386 pp.).

75. *RESM,* June, 1961, pp. 8–13, "Economic Influence of Mexican Townships Bordering with the U.S.A."; WTIS, "Economic Developments in Mexico 1961"; *HAR,* May, 1964, p. 211. The exchange of goods and services between this area and the U.S. is quite large by Mexican standard; some $76.6 million in 1959–60, with a balance in Mexico's favor of some $16.2 million, all the balance resulting from foreign tourist expenditures in Mexico and from the earnings of Mexicans in the United States, with the commodity balance being unfavorable to Mexico.

76. Yates, *Desarrollo regional,* Chap. XXIII.

77. Cf. *El Nacional,* Jan. 26, 1963, and *Nosotros,* Jan. 31, 1963, for accounts of the "Plan Guanajuato," and the activities in its connection of that state's Secretaría de Fomento Económico and Oficina de Planeación del Estado. See Peña, *Planeación económica regional* (2d ed.), p. 132, on regional and municipal planning.

78. The first was *Proyecto de programa de gobierno del Estado de Sonora* (1957). This publication asserts that states and municipalities are growing ever more interested in planning; that this is the first time an agency of the federal government has given technical aid on economic planning to a state; gives recommendations, projects, data, projected costs, suggested sources of revenues, etc. Similar studies were done for the states of Michoacán and Mexico in 1958; an earlier, somewhat similar plan was done for Jalisco, in 1957 apparently; others were projected for later years. Cf. Secretaría de la Economía, *Memoria 1957,* p. 397, on planning studies on the states.

79. Cf. Yates, *Desarrollo regional,* pp. 196–97.

80. Cf. its publication *Nuevo Laredo, Ciudad Alemán, Reynosa, Matamoros, Tampico* (Mexico? 1961?), which consists of zoning plans for these cities. It declares that a Plano Regulador is "an instrument that facilitates the harmonious development of the total modern city," and requires federal, state, municipal, and private cooperation.

81. Cf. *El Universal,* Jan. 4, 1959, on "Urbanismo," dealing with planning, and including a section on experience in the United States.

VII. APPROACHES TO INTEGRATED AND COMPREHENSIVE PLANNING

1. See Chap. V, C, 2, above, on this function of the Ministry of National Patrimony.

2. Gustavo Romero Kolbeck, in *Cincuenta años,* I, 498.

3. From Salinas, "Comisión de Inversiones." Slightly different charts are shown in PAU, *Organismos de planificación y planes de desarrollo en la América Latina* (Washington, 1961), p. 113; UN, Technical Assistance Programme, *Introduction to Public Administration in Development Policy* (1957), p. 69.

4. PAU, *Organismos de planificación,* p. 59; cf. *ibid.,* pp. 58–59, for eleven "objectives" of the Commission.

5. All the foregoing based on Salinas, "Comisión de Inversiones." UN, *Introduction to Public Administration in Development Policy,* p. 8, summarizes this process.

6. Salinas, "Comisión de Inversiones," for this outline of the system. Salinas remarks that although it was often difficult to fix the economic value of "social" projects, it was convenient to fix priorities fundamentally on such a basis. Cf.

Cincuenta años, I, 502, that the Commission chose between different types of projects that simultaneously fulfilled the investment criteria on the basis of the economic bottlenecks that would be created if the projects were not carried out.

7. Wionczek, "Incomplete Formal Planning," p. 162, gives the estimate that over three-fourths of federal funds available each year for investment went to projects in progress. He points out that the Commission could do something to speed some projects and to slow others.

8. *Ibid.* states that the result of this well known fact was that all agencies competing for federal funds knew from experience what they might expect and what demands would be considered unreasonable by the Investment Commission and the President of the Republic. He states that from 1939 through 1959 in each year more than three-fourths of gross public investment went to the indicated three fields. Cf. Gustavo Romero Kolbeck, "La inversión del sector público," pp. 21–31 in *Nuevos aspectos—conferencias de invierno 1960* (UNAM, 1960).

9. Salinas, "Comisión de Inversiones." Wionczek, "Incomplete Formal Planning," p. 161, points out that delays in the execution of projects due to poor planning by an agency would affect its position with the Commission when submitting its program for the next year.

10. Salinas, "Comisión de Inversiones." Cf. PAU, *Organismos de planificación,* p. 57, for emphasis on the Commission's relations with these institutions.

11. Wionczek, "Incomplete Formal Planning," p. 164, cites IBRD opinions on this in 1957, approving movement toward longer-range planning, and praising the improvement of the performance of the Investment Commission generally. Cf. PAU, *Organismos de planificación,* pp. 61–62, for comment on the World Bank view. The earlier (1953) IBRD report on *Economic Development in Mexico* (p. 151) had noted that long-range planning was the more necessary in Mexico in that it apparently was faced with a need for more foreign public investment.

12. Wionczek, "Incomplete Formal Planning," p. 161.

13. *Ibid.,* pp. 164–65, ascribing this to: (1) access to the President; (2) because of its technical nature, it remained aloof from the worst of the executive branch conflicts; (3) it became a central depository for economic data; (4) it could influence government entities informally, without responsibility for executing programs.

14. *Ibid.,* p. 165, and he points out that some Mexican economists charge that the policies of international agencies encouraged the project-to-project activities of the Mexican government. Cf. Aubrey, "Structure and Balance," p. 537, on the possibility that proper coordination of investment in Mexico before 1954 might have reduced overinvestment as demonstrated by protracted underutilization of capacity.

15. Secretaría de la Presidencia, which also had been the name (although not a ministry) of the office of the presidential secretariat, which had for years managed—among other duties—much of such coordination of development projects as had occurred.

16. Cf. *MV,* Jan. 5, 1959, for celebration by the Ministry of National Patrimony of this centralization.

17. Izaguirre Rojo, "La Nueva Ley de Secretarías," for congressional objection to assigning the "same" functions to the Ministries of the Presidency and of National Patrimony. Cf. Castellanos, "Commentarios a la Ley," on the purported loss by the Finance Ministry of some of its power over contracts and activities.

18. Bustamante, "Discurso el día 5 de mayo," asserting that the intervention of the Ministry of the Presidency is before the investment, and that of the Ministry of National Patrimony commences only after authorization, in order to see that

it is properly used within the general development program; and that the Ministry of Finance has its own clearly delimited sphere of activity.

19. See Chap. V, C, 2, above.

20. Text in Izaguirre Rojo, "La Nueva Ley de Secretarías."

21. *Ibid.*

22. Cf. Castellanos, "Comentarios a la Ley," for early praise of the new arrangement, but the observation that since the Ministry of the Presidency was not given powers of execution, its performance would depend directly on the President of the Republic.

23. E.g., Public Works, Communications and Transport, the Department of Agrarian Affairs.

24. *El Universal,* March 4, 1959, printed a prediction by the public administration expert, Lucio Mendienta y Núñez, that this would be the case.

25. *HA,* Dec. 11, 1961, stated that interministerial commissions had been created for examination of the investments of Pemex, the railways, and the Electricity Commission.

26. PAU, *The Present State of Economic Development Planning in Latin America* (Washington, 1962), p. 15. Cf. OAS, IA-ECOSOC, *Marcha de la Alianza 1961–62,* II, p. 175; *Directorio del Poder Ejecutivo Federal 1961* (Secretaría del Patrimonio Nacional, 1961); Wionczek, "Sustained Growth," p. 166, considers that the organization of the Ministry was defective from the beginning, reflecting confused thinking.

27. *MV,* Sept. 1963, pp. 473–80, for comment on it in the President's annual message.

28. *MV,* July 20, 1959, for the order. Cf. *RESM,* Aug. 1959, pp. 4–5, for comment on the order; *CE,* July, 1959; PAU, *Present State of Economic Development Planning,* p. 16. The content of the investment programs was defined to mean all expenditures tending to augment, conserve, and improve the national capital—and, in detail, to include all construction, additions, and maintenance of public works; exploration, improvement, etc., of natural resources; the same for agriculture and stockraising; acquisition of equipment, vehicles, etc. Among the principles on which the agencies were to found their investment programs were: (1) improvement of economic and social productivity; (2) benefits for a considerable number of the population; (3) completion of works under way, rather than initiation of new projects; (4) cooperation between agencies in investment; (5) minimization of dispersal of investment, in order to complete projects and get them into operation; (6) provide secondary works necessary to make major works serviceable.

Each agency was to: give total investment, considering the trend of recent years, and financial resources; list the investments in order of priority, with justification; append to the program, if appropriate, supplemental investments for use in case new funds should appear. Each agency's program should list: (1) purpose; (2) location; (3) characteristics; (4) whether new work, or under construction; (5) cost of project, and probable date of completion; (6) investment made, in case of work under construction; (7) annual payment on the proposed investment; (8) economic and social benefits to be realized. In addition, if a project required imported goods, their prime characteristics were to be given. Also, the agency was to submit a proposal on financing, specifying the origin and nature of funds, and distinguishing those to come from the budget, those from domestic or foreign credits, and those from decentralized organs or state participation enterprises.

The Ministry of the Presidency was to receive the programs of investment for

1960 not later than August 31, 1959; those for 1961–64 not later than December 31, 1959. (N.B.: the order provided that insofar as possible it was to apply to the investment program of the public sector then being executed for 1959.) The Ministry was to study, seek necessary coordination, and submit to the President a coordinated and ranked program for 1960–64. The President was to authorize the annual investment programs through the Ministry of the Presidency. Desired modifications would be routed through this Ministry. The Ministry of Finance, in agreement with the Ministry of the Presidency, was to draw up the necessary norms for maintaining, during the fiscal year, a proper execution of the investment budget. But supervision of the investment system as a whole was to lie with Finance.

Methods of enforcing the order included: (1) Ministry of National Patrimony to notify the Ministry of the Presidency in writing of agencies either executing or projecting investments not authorized under the order; for this, and to carry out his other duties, the latter minister was ordered to send the former a copy of the program of investment authorized by the President; (2) Ministry of Finance not to permit transfer of funds for an unauthorized investment; (3) permission to seek national or international credits for financing of investment programs must be obtained through the Ministry of the Presidency; (4) national credit agencies (e.g., Nacional Financiera) that deal with international credits will not act for an agency unless the latter's investment has been properly authorized; (5) the Minister of Finance can order the Bank of Mexico to immobilize the funds of agencies deposited with the Bank under law, when such funds are used to finance an investment not approved under this order; (6) the National Bank of Foreign Trade will aid in enforcement. The foregoing on this order is from *MV,* July 20, 1959. Cf. "Revising the Governmental Policy of Public Expenditures in Mexico," *RESM,* August, 1959, pp. 4–5, stating that in recent years government expenditures have contributed toward improvement of the economy by increasing production, and by stabilizing the currency and the economy in general; but that expenditures for public works have been slow and insufficient. The article claimed that the main reasons for issuing the order in question were: (1) to further the economic and social development of the nation for the benefit of the populace; (2) increase the efficiency of public expenditures and investments; and (3) establish definite categories in public investments, so as to complement private investment, or in order to raise the standard of living.

29. *MV,* Nov. 16, 1959.

30. *MV,* Feb. 22, 1960. Cf. *CE,* Sept., 1960, that President López Mateos in his Sept. 1 annual message reported that he was studying the investment program for 1961–64.

31. Cf. Secretaría de Obras Públicas, *Informe de labores 1961–62*, pp. 9, 28, that short-term and long-term investment programs had been sent from Obras Públicas to the Ministry of the Presidency; *HA,* Jan. 15, 1962, for comment on coordination of investment by the Ministry of the Presidency.

32. *CE,* Feb. 1960.

33. Wionczek, "Incomplete Formal Planning," p. 181, for this view.

34. *Ibid.,* p. 167, that the operating provisions of the two agencies were about the same, but that the orders establishing the investment activity of the Ministry of the Presidency included some social and economic objectives (e.g., income redistribution, priority attention to the most backward parts of the nation, and import substitution by local goods) that were not laid down in the original order on the Investment Commission of 1954–58.

35. *Ibid.*, pp. 167–68, that as late as the middle of 1962 the Planning Bureau of the Ministry of the Presidency was very weak, and weaker than the old Investment Commission had been, or than the latter's successor, the Public Investments Bureau. By that date, Wionczek states, the Planning Bureau had a staff of some twenty-five experts, and did some studies, but none of these was made public or offered for discussion outside the Ministry, so it was not possible to comment on them. Wionczek also states that a questionnaire was sent in the spring of 1962 to the Ministry of the Presidency by Jan Tinbergen, and elicited an answer indicating that the Ministry had not really begun integrated national planning.

36. *CE,* June, 1959.

37. *MV,* Aug. 7, 1961. WTIS, "Economic Conditions in Mexico 1961," p. 6, for comment on this order as setting up "for the first time . . . procedures for economic and social planning on a national scale."

38. Cf. Wionczek, "Incomplete Formal Planning," p. 168, on the former order (also reprinted in *TE,* Dec. 1961), as attempting to define the field of action of the Planning Bureau, but failing to provide for centralization of national planning there, merely stipulating that the executive branch "through the Ministries, Departments of State, decentralized agencies, and entities . . . [would] intensify its efforts to . . . prepare national economic and social development plans . . . and outline the means of achieving them"; and on the latter order as recognizing the shortcomings of the Ministry of the Presidency by uniting it with the Ministry of Finance in an interministerial commission to draw up long-range and short-range plans and estimate the financing required. Cf. *ESEM,* Feb. 1963, for comments on both these orders. See *Cincuenta años,* I, pp. 504ff., on the early work of the Ministry of the Presidency in coordinating investments.

39. OAS, IA-ECOSOC, *Marcha de la Alianza 1961/62,* II, p. 175. It also stated that the Planning Bureau was "charged with regional plans and development."

40. *Hoy,* Feb. 2, 1963, called it a "restructuring," including appointment as Chief of the new *Dirección del Plan General del Gasto Público* of Fernando Zamora Millán, long involved in government planning, and well known for his publications on planning and development.

41. PAU, *Organismos de planificación,* p. 63, quoting from the report of a team of experts from the Inter-American Planning Society which visited Mexico at the end of 1961.

42. PAU, *Present State of Economic Development Planning,* p. 16.

43. PAU, *Organismos de Planificación,* p. 62.

44. Cf. *El Universal,* Feb. 3, 1959, for an account of the transmittal by the President to the Minister of Finance of the "economic and social program" for his six-year term and the plan of investment for 1959; and an account of the twenty-one development objectives of the government—e.g., raising the general level of living, increasing national income at a rate greater than population increase, diversification and integration of the economy, stimulation of regional economies, better use of productive resources, better coordination of public and private investment, greater productivity and using foreign credits to achieve it, industrialization, monetary stability, improvement of exports, and adherence to the Constitution and to the Mexican Revolution.

45. OAS, IA-ECOSOC, *Marcha de la Alianza 1961/62,* II, p. 175; PAU, *Present State of Economic Development Planning,* p. 15; *TE,* XXIX, July-Sept., 1962, pp. 479–80, for text of *acuerdo*; *El Universal,* March 2, 1962.

46. E.g., the Ministry of Industry and Commerce might argue for inclusion,

on the grounds that it does industrial planning and has extensive connections with the private sector.

47. OAS, IA-ECOSOC, *Marcha de la Alianza 1961/62,* I, p. 31.

48. OAS Committee of Nine, "Evaluation of the Plan of Immediate Action." Unless otherwise stated, data in the following discussion come from this source.

49. *Ibid.,* p. 92.

50. PAU, *Present State of Economic Development Planning,* p. 16; Flores de la Peña, "Reflexiones sobre el Plan," refusing to call it an economic plan because it lacked "instruments of action that would permit its execution." Flores de la Peña made many other criticisms: The growth rate set was "obviously low"; the concentration of income and retention of privileges of "parasitic sectors of the economy" and of a private initiative that deserves no respect; against the policy of stability, promoted by monetary economists, with high prices, credit controls, high interest rate, insufficient investment, a balanced budget; all of which, he stated, had been proved inadequate in Argentina, Chile, and Uruguay, which followed the line of the International Monetary Fund. He advocated a National Planning Council, outside the government, with representatives of public and private sectors.

51. See Appendix XVII, above, for Investment Plan 1962–64.

52. *ESEM,* July 1964. After formulation of the original Plan, some of the public sector investment programs were extended through 1965.

53. Cf. Wionczek, "Incomplete Formal Planning," p. 174, for comment on this shift in investment emphasis.

54. OAS, IA-ECOSOC, *Marcha de la Alianza 1961/62,* I, p. 31.

55. Cf. also Wionczek, "Incomplete Formal Planning," for skeptical comment on the private investment "coordination" feature of the Plan.

56. Cf. *ESEM,* Feb. 1963, p. 8, for a summary of some of the methods used, including accelerated depreciation.

57. *MV,* Sept. 1963, pp. 473–80.

58. OAS Committee of Nine, "Evaluation of the Plan of Immediate Action," p. 123.

59. Cf. OAS, IA-ECOSOC, *Marcha de la Alianza 1961/62,* II, p. 175; *La Prensa,* Jan. 28, 1963.

VIII. SOME CONCLUSIONS

1. E.g., Mosk, *Industrial Revolution,* p. 307, in 1950 critically observed that the only Mexican plan was to aid private enterprise to expand and to improve its productivity. Many observers repeated this judgment in the apparent belief that it contains some sort of self-evident condemnation.

2. *Cincuenta años,* I, p. 525, for a semiofficial view, published in 1960, that Mexico has an "economía no planificada"; but discussions of various sorts of government planning by a number of authors in the volume indicate that they mean that there is no centralized, comprehensive planning, and that the economy is more nearly unplanned than it is planned—i.e., "essentially unplanned" does not mean "no planning at all."

3. Schaeffer, "National Administration in Mexico," Chap. VII, that there was little "true" planning (to 1949), with coordinated broad goals, detailed programs, integrated supervision of execution; in addition, plans were *ad hoc* undertakings without continuity. Schaeffer remained for a decade the main reliance of students, and they devoted little attention to Schaeffer's caution that he saw signs of change

in the recent work of various agencies. Tucker, *Mexican Government* (1957), pp. 199, 211, found an abundance of planning activity but little of what he termed "true planning" in the sense of coordinated formulation of broad goals, elaboration of detailed programs, and integrated supervision and execution.

4. Glade, "Role of Government Enterprise," pp. 102, 562.

5. Brandenburg, *Making Modern Mexico,* p. 222, that "the relatively phenomenal economic advances of recent years . . . are less a result of 'natural forces' and accident than of state planning in six-year packages.

6. OAS Committee of Nine, "Evaluation of the Plan of Immediate Action," Chap. VIII, *et passim.*

7. Cf. "What is National Planning?" (mimeographed), prepared at the Minnowbrook Seminar, "Action Under Development Plans," Blue Mountain Lake, New York, July, 1964, by a committee of which I was a member. The month-long conference, attended by representatives from seven countries, was jointly sponsored by the Comparative Administration Group (American Society for Public Administration) and the Maxwell Graduate School of Citizenship and Public Affairs, Syracuse University. A few of the propositions developed by the committee are: "planning is a process of intended adaptive rationality in pursuit of goals"; "central planning in a national system may include widespread initiative and participation by individuals and groups, both public and private, outside the central planning institutions of the national government"; "national economic planning consists of coordinated efforts by central institutions to develop some combination of enterprise . . ., spatial . . ., sectoral or subsectoral . . ., cross-sectoral . . ., and aggregate planning . . ."; "national planning . . . varies from country to country and from time to time with respect to (a) the balance between centralization and decentralization, (b) the extent of reliance upon or manipulation of market mechanisms, (c) the degree of generality or detail at specific points, (d) the degree of emphasis upon short-range or long-range considerations, (e) the degree of initiative and autonomy exercised by intermediate bodies and operating units, and (f) the extent of compulsion or pressure, as distinguished from suggestion and persuasion, that may be used by central government institutions"; "although national planning documents are important elements in the planning process, any 'national plan' can provide only partial representation of the significant commitments developed through the planning process"; "in any country, national planning functions are performed by a variety of institutions rather than by a single agency"; "in some societies, informal arrangements and procedures may be the functional equivalents of more highly formalized central planning institutions in other societies."

8. See Chap. VI, above.

9. Glade, "Role of Government Enterprise," pp. 102–03, stated that "the main functions, personnel, resources, and funds essential to the planning process are found within . . . the Bank of Mexico, Nacional Financiera, and . . . other government organs," which exercise a general direction; and in national economic policies; and that the channeling of public investment is "a sort of comprehensive, if loose and somewhat opportunistically administered national development program"; and, he said, if all this was coupled with the more specific industrialization plans of Nacional Financiera, and the plans of other government agencies, "the net result . . . would seem to come fairly close to comprehensive national economic planning in a way which is perhaps more effective than the work of some of the formal planning in agencies in countries like Brazil . . . or Argentina."

10. Cf. Chap. VI, A, above. This is obvious in the control of credit, aid to manufacturing and to export agriculture, and in public investment emphasis on electric power, petroleum, transportation, and irrigation. See also Anderson, "Bankers as Revolutionaries," p. 182, on the consistency in objectives of Mexican policy makers as constituting a sort of planning; WTIS, "Economic Developments in Mexico 1961," that although Mexico does not have formal, comprehensive economic development programming, for the most part national development programs have had a long-range character in education, welfare, health, housing, employment, tourism, agriculture and stock, irrigation, mining, manufacturing, electric power, construction (public works), and transportation, carried on from administration to administration.

11. Cf. Wionczek, "Incomplete Formal Planning," pp. 177–78; Yates, *Desarrollo regional,* pp. 31–33; Chap. IV, above.

12. Chap. VI, above.

13. Cf. Wionczek, "Electric Power," for evidence of this; R. Alfredo Navarrete, "El crecimiento económico de México: Perspectivas y problemas," *Journal of Inter-American Studies,* Oct. 1959, pp. 389–404, that balanced economic growth in Mexico has been due to policies that "considered the interdependence of the principal sectors."

14. Chap. IV, above.

15. *Ibid.*

16. Chap. VII, A, above.

17. Chap. IV, and Chap. VII, B, above.

18. *MV,* March 8, 1965, p. 142, that all ministries and departments of state and decentralized organs and state participation enterprises were to prepare in the next three months their programs of activities for 1965–70, including plans of investment for 1966–70, for transmission to the Ministry of the Presidency.

19. Peña, *Planeación económica regional* (2d ed.), pp. 126ff.; Glade, "Role of Government Enterprise," pp. 97–98, but p. 562, that coordination of the government entities existed in the sense that ultimate administrative control vested directly or indirectly in the executive branch, and in view of the interventionary powers at the disposal of the Federal Government to secure some coordination with national policy in the private sector; Tucker, *Mexican Government,* pp. 211, 213, that there was considerable sector planning, but that integrative and central direction were lacking, and that the time had come for replacement of the project-to-project approach to something more comprehensive; IBRD, *Economic Development of Mexico,* p. 151, had published the project-to-project comment in 1953, in a study done by two IBRD and two Mexican technicians; R. Alfredo Navarrete, "La planeación y la administración financiera del estado," *MV,* Aug. 3, 1964, pp. 458–65, that although "sectoral plans of large scope have been elaborated in some public activities . . . until now in Mexico there has not existed either integral or formal economic planning in its technical sense: that is to say, one or several specialized organs that formulate a national development plan, and an administrative financial mechanism . . . especially for its execution," but he also describes financial coordination by the government; Wionczek, "Incomplete Formal Planning," pp. 178–79, that there has been considerable progress toward acceptance of the need for overall programming and planning, but that it is impeded by the diffusion of political and economic power within and without the government.

20. OAS Committee of Nine, "Evaluation of the Plan of Immediate Action," pp. 19–20, 204–10.

21. See Chap. VII, C, above.

22. *ESEM,* Feb. 1963, pp. 6ff., "Planeación económica en Mexico," notes this lack of inducement to cooperation, pointing out that the goals and detail of government development plans in Mexico are kept so secret that private enterprise can scarcely be expected to share in their execution. The article also points out that "French-style plans" enjoy fine performance because they are in large part drawn up by the private sector, which also executes them.

23. OAS Committee of Nine, "Evaluation of the Plan of Immediate Action," Chap. VIII.

24. This is one of the chief points of Vernon's *Dilemma of Mexico.* Some reviewers have found his pessimism on the matter excessive. But see Shelton, "Banking System," p. 188, on what he judges the anachronism of the "still-powerful suspicion of private profit as an adequate stimulus to productive investment."

25. Cf. Wionczek, "Incomplete Formal Planning," p. 176, for comment on this point; OAS Committee of Nine, "Evaluation of the Plan of Immediate Action," Chap. VIII, on suggestion for a central planning office where public and private sector plans would be coordinated.

26. Cf. Walker, "Nacional Financiera," p. 391, on the role of that institution in a society that does not allocate resources by a central planning mechanism. Efforts to July, 1965, had brought no revolutionary change in the relations between the public and private sectors. There were continued claims of a new system of integration (see *RESM,* April 1965, pp. 3–4, "Economic Coordination as a Definite Goal") while at the same time the new leftist Minister of Industry and Commerce seriously disturbed the business community.

27. Cf. Chap. V, E, above; *New York Times,* Feb. 18, 1962, for advertisement of Mexican Federal Government, stating that "in Mexico, planning consists mainly of the formulation of annual and sexannual investment programs for the public sector . . . which take into account the investment plans and possibilities of private enterprise"; "Iniciativa de la ley federal de planeación," that the projected planning law prohibited discrimination against private enterprises that did not follow the plan, so long as they obeyed the law governing their ordinary activities.

28. Wionczek, "Incomplete Formal Planning," p. 180, states that there are signs in Mexico of increasing acceptance by the private sector of the idea of comprehensive national planning along lines followed recently in France, Japan, and the Netherlands.

29. *Ibid.,* pp. 180–81, and confessing that he may be optimistic; and see n. 22 to this chapter, above. The first six months of the Díaz Ordaz administration (to June 1965) apparently saw little accomplishment in this regard.

30. See Chap. V, A-B, above.

31. See Chap. VI, A, above.

32. See Chap. V, D, above.

33. See Chaps. IV; V, D; VII, B, above.

34. Cf. Blair, "Nacional Financiera," p. 237, on "the diffusion of public development decision-making"; Brandenburg, *Making Modern Mexico,* p. 118, on difficulties with the new planning system because of "disarray in the vast empire of state enterprises."

35. See Chap. C, 2, above.

36. See Chap. V, C, 1, and E, above, and n. 22 to the present chapter; Chap. VIII, B, above; Wionczek, "Incomplete Formal Planning," pp. 180–81, that demo-

cratic planning requires broad participation in its implementation, which requires information and discussion.

37. Schaeffer, "National Administration in Mexico," made this assertion in 1949, and it has been widely repeated on his authority. The sensitivity of the Mexican government to such things as balance-of-payments difficulties or declines in investment often has been cited to the present author as "proof" of the general opportunism of Mexican planning, sometimes even when the respondents were fully aware that it constituted an exaggeration.

38. *Industrial Development,* without mentioning that political problems might be involved. IBRD's *Economic Development of Mexico* (1953) called for a considerable expansion of better integrated planning, but without discussing political problems, which was, of course, quite proper in a technical work by an international agency. The OAS Committee of Nine, "Evaluation of the Plan of Immediate Action," in 1964, together with many suggestions for improvement of Mexican planning, and especially its better integration, did note that it had done useful work. Of course, the Nine's working committee was neither competent nor expected to discuss political problems.

39. Cf. Wionczek, "Incomplete Formal Planning," pp. 180–81; Múñoz Amato, *Introducción a la administración pública,* pp. 122–23; Schten, "Public Administration in Latin America," pp. 9–10.

40. Cline, *Mexico and the United States,* p. 337, put this nicely a decade ago in stating that Mexico has no basic plan because: "Tugs of war are constantly going on within the country and administration to veer the course one way or another. In general this is perhaps the only possible course, in view of Mexico's past. The disadvantages of this 'economic democracy' that reflects changing situations are perhaps less perilous than a fixed 'plan'. . . ."

41. See Chaps. II, A; V, E, above.

42. *Ibid.*

43. Scott, *Mexican Government,* emphasized the conciliatory policies of the PRI; Vernon, *Dilemma of Mexico,* pp. 189ff., pursued the theme to the point of strong doubt regarding the possibility of effective action by the political establishment; but Scott, reviewing the Vernon book (*Hispanic American Historical Review,* May 1964, p. 249), found the latter too pessimistic on this point.

44. See Chap. V, E, above.

45. *Ibid.*

46. *Ibid.*

47. See Chap. V, C, 1, above.

48. See Chap. II, A, above.

49. See Chap. V, C, above.

50. See Chap. V, D, above.

51. Statements on this in Vernon, *Dilemma of Mexico,* p. 188; and in OAS Committee of Nine, "Evaluation Presented to the Government of Mexico," Chap. VIII.

52. Cf. Víctor Urquidi, "Some Misunderstandings on the Alliance for Progress," pp. 223–38 in Maier and Weatherhead (eds.), *Politics of Change,* that "it is easy to mistake the plan for the policies."

53. Peter Bauer and Basil Yamey, *The Economics of Underdeveloped Countries* (University of Chicago Press, 1957), p. 154, for argument in favor of economic systems in which decision-making is widely diffused and coordinated by the market mechanism.

A Note on Sources

Although there are many valuable studies of the Mexican economy, they give little attention to planning. There are no comprehensive studies of the latter subject, or even of planning in given sectors. Nor are there large concentrations of planning materials published by government offices that might be used as the basis for study of the planning system and parts thereof. This study, therefore, was put together from many relatively small bits of information. (Cf. Vernon, *Dilemma of Mexico,* p. ix, that his study of Mexican economic development was "constructed out of thousands of little fragments.") A great deal more of this fragmentary material is known to me than could be incorporated into the present study.

Most of the data used were documentary. About two dozen informants were used in the Mexican federal government, United States agencies in Mexico and in Washington, the Organization of American States and Pan-American Union, and in United Nations offices. The data were sufficient for a fairly extensive reconnaissance of the subject, with considerably wider examination of its dimensions than heretofore attempted. Only the chief categories of sources are discussed here, with reference to some outstanding or representative items. The notes to the text contain bibliographic detail on each item at its first citation (except for those identified in the list of abbreviations), and in many cases considerable discussion of its characteristics and uses.

The following works are excellent on the Mexican economy and government: Schaeffer, "National Administration in Mexico" (dissertation, Univ. of Calif., 1949); Mosk, *Industrial Revolution in Mexico* (1950); Glade, "The Role of Government Enterprise in Mexico" (dissertation, Univ. of Texas, 1955); Tucker, *Mexican Government* (1957); Scott, *Mexican Government* (1959); Cline, *Mexico: Revolution to Evolution* (1962); Glade, "Revolution and Economic Development," and Anderson, "Bankers as Revolutionaries," published together as *The Political Economy of Mexico* (1963); Vernon, *Dilemma of Mexico* (1963); Brandenburg, *Making Modern Mexico* (1964). These studies all have something to say about planning, but none of them makes it a major interest. The Glade dissertation is valuable not only for the great detail on government enterprises, but for his use of a broad definition of planning.

The planning discussions tend to be feeble in the literature on Mexican economic structure and development, politics and government, public administration, and history. Economic development, state intervention in the economy, and various financial subjects are represented by a rather large and often competently executed literature, but it seldom gives more than cursory attention to the planning process. The literature on public administration in Mexico is weak, as the Instituto de la Administración Pública noted less than a decade ago in launching its *Revista.* Scholarly work also is weak on Mexican interest groups, and on information networks and communication systems.

There are three sizable evaluations of Mexican economic development by competent technicians, acting in public or quasi-public roles, that must be consulted by the student of planning. The World Bank's *Economic Development of Mexico* (1953) contained much on the economy and economic trends, but little on how development was planned by the Mexican government. It did recommend more and better integrated planning, but did not try to demonstrate that this was desirable, and scarcely mentioned Mexican planning except by way of praising or criticizing economic growth in areas massively affected by public action. In 1960–62 the four-volume, multiple-author *México: cincuenta años de Revolución* was published in Mexico, with government subsidy, to celebrate achievements in the half-century since the Revolution began. Many of the authors were or had been government officials. Much of the data (especially in I, *La economía,* and III, *La política*) is of considerable ancillary interest to a study of planning, but little bears directly on the planning process. An Ad Hoc Committee of the Organization of American States' Committee of Nine in 1964 completed an "Evaluation Presented to the Government of Mexico on the Plan of Immediate Action for 1962–64" (263 pp.). Although a short chapter (7 pages) was devoted to planning, and comments on the subject occasionally appear elsewhere in the evaluation, very little of the document is devoted to that subject. Recommendations for changes in the planning system are not accompanied by a brief.

Two competent, though brief, essays on Mexican planning are the best studies available on the system as a whole. A chapter in Schaeffer, "National Administration" (1949) was devoted to planning. Scott's excellent *Mexican Government* (1959) found Schaeffer's chapter still the best thing on Mexican planning. Schaeffer, however, scarcely dealt with many aspects of planning under the definition used by the present study, and of course some of it was made obsolescent by the changes in 1958 and thereafter. Wionczek, "Incomplete Formal Planning: Mexico" (1963; 32 pp.), dealt chiefly with planning since 1954, and was excellent as far as it went.

About twenty books by Mexicans purport to deal with planning in general, and some others deal with aspects of planning. Hundreds of articles on planning by Mexicans have been located, and possibly two hundred examined. Diminishing returns became evident early in this process. Most of the books and articles contain only fragmentary data for a study endeavoring to fix the outlines of the major aspects of the subject. This is either because they repeat the usual generalities, or because they tend to assertion without demonstration, or because they adhere to a narrow definition of planning, or because they are highly theoretically and (frequently) deal scarcely at all with Mexican planning practice, or because the data pertain to only a small part of the subject. Many such items are cited in the notes to the text. A few of the better books, and some others that are representative of types, may be mentioned. Bravo, *Planeación industrial en México* (1949); Armas Arias, *Planificación económica regional* (thesis, 1950), with some data on planning in CFE and two regional commissions; Zamora, *Industrialización y planeación regional* (1950), but little on the planning process; Icaza y Conrey, "Principios para el establecimiento de un organismo planificador" (thesis, 1956), mostly theoretical, but with at least a sketch of Mexican planning; Peña, *Introducción a la planeación económica regional* (2d ed., 1960), mostly theory, but some 20 pages on Mexico; Yates, *El desarrollo regional de México* (2d ed., 1962), dealing chiefly with the concentration of Industry; Zamora, *La planeación económica en México* (1962), almost entirely theoretical, without footnotes or bibliography. Two items that belie their titles are: Eckstein Raber, "Planeación económica y agricultura" (thesis, 1957); and Corona Rentería, *La planeación económica* (1959). An example of specialized literature is Moreno, *Los factores demográficos en la planeación económica* (1958), which has value within the limits of its objectives, which do not include discussion of the planning process in Mexico.

Good monographs on Mexican government agencies or on economic sectors in Mexico are not numerous, except on agriculture. This is one of the most severe impediments to examination of the planning system as a whole. Quite a lot of the extensive literature on agriculture was turned over without discovering any deep lodes on the planning process. It is clear that various types of planning have been done for years. It also is clear that many authors have been unable to proceed beyond their dismay that agricultural decision-making and planning are much dispersed. The highly competent monograph of González Santos, *La agricultura* (1957), done for Nacional Financiera, has little to say about planning. Walker, "Nacional Financiera" (dissertation, 1961), has ploughed up much data, but not on planning; Blair, "Nacional Financiera" (1964), is an excellent essay, but not concerned much with planning. Some data on planning by Pemex are in Powell, *Mexican Petroleum Industry* (1956), and more in Bermúdez, *Mexican National Petroleum* (1963 ed.). Villafuerte, *Ferrocarriles* (1959), is an excellent study of railroads, but does not deal with the planning process. Wionczek, "Electric Power" (1964), and Poleman, *Papaloapan* (1964), are accomplished scholarly studies, but they did not set out to investigate planning, so they tell us just enough to indicate tantalizingly that they have discovered data on the subject that did not need to be fully exploited for their purposes. All these competently done sector studies are excellent starting points for research into the sector planning process.

Much of the information on which this study was based was dredged from hundreds of items in Mexican government or private scholarly periodicals. Indispensable for keeping up with relevant developments in the public sector were the following: Nacional Financiera's *El Mercado de Valores* (1940——), which also carries current bibliography on planning and allied subjects; Bank of Mexico's *Examen de la Situación Económica de México* (1925——); and the National Bank of Foreign Commerce's *Comercio Exterior* (1951——). Some other government periodicals were used less systematically: e.g., the *Boletín Oficial de la Secretaría de Hacienda y Crédito Público*; and the relatively new *Patrimonio Nacional,* very useful on the execution of plans. Several dozen private Mexican journals were used, the following proving the most useful: *El Trimestre Ecónomico* (1934——), which not only prints high-quality articles on economics, but also the texts of public documents; *Revista de Economía* (1937——); *Investigación Económica* (1941——); *Revista de la Administración Pública* (1956——). Articles from scholarly journals printed in other countries are cited in the notes.

Government publications other than periodicals are probably the most important category of published source materials on planning. Unfortunately, there is no one place to find out what has been published, nor a single depository from which to make purchases. The texts of laws and executive orders are published in the *Diario Oficial.* The economic and public administration (including planning) content of the *Diario Oficial* is followed by several of the public and private periodicals listed above. The *Directories* of the federal government, now published by the Ministry of National Patrimony, list some planning and economic study and statistical agencies. Many of the speeches of the presidents of Mexico are collected and published, and are valuable in connection with the implementation aspects of planning. The annual (Sept. 1) presidential message to congress is published as an *Informe.* The annual (sometimes) *memorias* or *informes* of the ministries and departments of state and some of the major autonomous agencies sometimes contain important leads to planning activity. Although the data they contain specifically on planning tends to be brief, it does indicate considerable sectoral planning activity that could be pursued agency by agency. Among other agencies, publications of this type were available, for varying years, for the Ministries of National Patrimony (and its predecessor National Properties), Industry and Commerce (and its predecessor Economy), Agriculture and Stock, Education, Public Works, Hydraulic Resources; the Department of Agrarian Affairs, the Federal Electricity Commission, the Papaloapan Commission, Pemex, Nacional Financiera, and Bank of Mexico.

In addition to the annual reports, the ministries and agencies publish numerous items that bear on planning. Only a few examples of items used in this study will be given here. Many others could not be consulted at this time.* The items used in this study include some wartime documents now only of historical interest, such as *Plan de movilización agrícola de la república mexicana* (1945). Others are cited in chapter IV, above. Another type is the Federal Electricity Commission's *Electric Projects for the Republic of Mexico, 1947 to 1952; Report for the International Bank for Reconstruction and Development* (1948). Another, by the Papaloapan Commission, is *Economía de Papaloapan* (1958; 386 pp.), an excellent study, which includes data on the national objectives of the Commission, and on methodology. Of a number of items published by the Dirección General de Estudios Económicos of the Ministry of Economy (Industry and Commerce after 1958), mention is made here only of a series of planning studies for Mexican states, of which the following are known to the present author: *Planificación Económica de la costa de Jalisco* (1956?); *Proyecto de programa de gobierno del Estado de Sonora* (1957; 286 pp.); and two others like this last on Michoacán and on the state of Mexico. The document on Sonora, which I examined, is impressive evidence of the technical resources of this agency. Little effort was made in this study to collect data on municipal planning. Many interesting recent publications by Patrimonio Nacional on the subject have come to my attention; one or two earlier works on the subject are cited in the text, above.

PRI publications are of interest primarily in connection with the activation of national economic plans. In this study, they were used chiefly in connection with events in the 1930's and 1940's: e.g., Luna Arroyo, *¿Qué hará mi país en seis años?* (1935); Bosques, *National Revolutionary Party . . . and the Six-Year Plan* (1937); PRM, *Segundo Plan Sexenel* (1939?); Jara, *Second Six-Year Plan* (1939). Newspapers and popular magazines also are of value chiefly on implementation of plans. The newspaper *El Universal* and the news magazine *Tiempo (Hispano Americano)*, both conservative and pro-government, were used systematically for the years since 1950. Four other Mexico City newspapers and several magazines (including the leftist *Política* and *Siempre*) were used more sparingly.

A number of documents (some in mimeographed form) of use for the subject have been issued by the Organization of American States and the United Nations: e.g., Inter-American Economic and Social Council, *Marcha de la Alianza 1961/62*; Pan-American Union, *Organismos de planificación* (1961), and its *Present State of Economic Development Planning* (1962); Cosío Villegas, "Programmed Economic Development and Political Organization," in UNESCO, *Social Aspects of Economic Development in Latin*

* E.g., the titles of the following publications of the Ministry of Communications and Transportation (formerly Communications and Public Works) make them appear promising, either for their content or as leads to other information: *Estudio de planificación de las telecomunicaciones nacionales e internacionales* (by its Dirección General de Planificación del Programa, 1958); *Estudio de planificación de los caminos* (125 pp., by its Departamento de Planeación, 1959).

America (1963); and, published by the Pan-American Union for the multiple-agency Inter-American Committee for Agricultural Development, *Inventory of Information Basic to the Planning of Agricultural Development in Latin America: Mexico* (1964). Other items put out by international organizations are cited in the notes.

Index